YOUNG
TILL WE DIE

By Dr. Doris Jonas and Dr. David Jonas

MAN-CHILD

YOUNG TILL WE DIE

YOUNG
TILL WE DIE

BY

Dr. Doris Jonas and Dr. David Jonas

Coward, McCann & Geoghegan, Inc.

NEW YORK

SBN: 698-10516-8

Library of Congress Catalog Card Number: 72-94128

PRINTED IN THE UNITED STATES OF AMERICA

Acknowledgment is gratefully extended for the permission to re-
print: *Medical Opinion:* "Five Letters To Harvey," Dr. F. L.
Jones, © March, 1972

CONTENTS

CONTENTS

YOUNG
TILL WE DIE

Part One

HOW IT CAME
TO BE

CHAPTER ONE

The Tyranny of the Cult of Youth

Every weekday morning at a quarter to nine John Newman can be seen emerging from the subway station at Exchange Place, hurrying, preoccupied, and oblivious to the jostling cityscape around him.

He is a tall, broad, well-built man, and he wears conservative, well-tailored clothes. His sixty-four years show in some roundness of his shoulders, but not at all in his vigorous movements or in his heavy-featured but still comparatively unlined face. The New York *Times* and the *Wall Street Journal* that he has been studying at breakfast and on the subway are folded under his arm, and communications from financial services, notes of ideas he has gathered from his reading, and reminders to himself of the clients he must not forget to call are secured together with two or three dollar bills in a money clip readily at hand in his right pocket.

John Newman is an investment adviser and an administrator of several welfare and pension funds. As he enters the monumental Broad Street building that houses his firm's offices, he offers a friendly "Good morning" to the elevator starter and to the secretaries, clerks, messengers, and other account executives who crowd into the elevator with him, but as he reaches his floor, he strides out of it and hurries directly toward his door, not pausing among the bustling and chattering people in the rooms through which he passes. He enters his office, hangs his coat on a hook, and with single-minded attention dials the number of the first of the clients he intends to advise before the opening of the market.

There are four telephones on his desk, and they ring constantly. The voices they connect him with demand his advice, his attention, and his service. During his busy day he follows the news from the business world, from the political world, and from the world of international affairs as it is reported by wire services and ticker tape, and he digests its implications for his clients. When he goes home in the evening, he carries with him company reports, reports of the world's financial markets, and an afternoon newspaper, much of which he reads and absorbs on his way, since most of his evenings are occupied with meetings of the organizations in which he takes an interest or with social obligations.

But next week John Newman will be sixty-five. All this purposeful and totally consuming activity will be, as though at the flip of a switch, suddenly turned off. His firm has a compulsory retirement policy. Next week, on Friday, he will still be a busy, committed man, his time precious to himself and to others, his existence acknowledged and valued by a large number of people. On the following Monday he will wake up in the morning the same man, with the same abilities, his physical condition unchanged and his brain as active as ever, but with no place to go and nothing he has to do.

Next year at a quarter to nine on a Monday morning he will be sitting on the terrace of the house he bought against the time of his retirement, taking a leisurely breakfast and looking forward to a game of cards or a round of golf in the afternoon to help him get through his day.

And what about his wife?

Martha Newman is an intelligent and active woman a few years younger than her husband. She had been a teacher before they were married. When her youngest child became sufficiently independent of her so that she had time on her hands and when the make-work occupations she then found became boring to her, she decided to go back to teaching, which she enjoyed and for which she had a talent. Over the years she has carved out a niche for herself in her academic world and at the same time run her home and done all the entertaining that was a necessary part of her husband's business life. She is an admired and respected person and is at least as busy and as involved in her occupations as he in his. In the course of their years they have had their setbacks and difficulties, but at this stage in their lives they both are what we usually consider successful and prosperous people at the peak of their achievement.

Now, in order to remain with her husband, Martha Newman faces a second retirement.

Perhaps one should call it a third retirement. She gave up her teaching originally when they decided they were ready to have a family. At that time she found that she missed the daily challenge and interest of her profession, but first the prospect and then the reality of rearing her own children offered her a new purpose in life. She made the change willingly, and so she was able to overcome the petty routines and boredoms and annoyances of a purely domestic life that from time to time she found irksome. She is a person who has had a strong sense of obligation and duty bred into her since her own childhood, and that, together with her affection for her family, eventually resulted in her becoming immersed in her new role.

Twenty years later she found herself facing "retirement" from this role too. It came gradually, but finally she was forced to recognize that her children no longer needed her, and that using her time to redecorate her house or to experiment with gourmet cooking did not fill the void that she experienced. Then, however, still in her early forties, she was able to find her way back to her old profession and make a new life for herself. With the wisdom of her maturity and the solid experience of bringing up her own children, she made a rapid adaptation back into a professional life. Moreover, she found great satisfaction in it, even though the problems and frustrations of teaching had increased by leaps and bounds since her earlier experience.

Now here she is once more. She has spent another twenty years of her life building up a career, which must now come to an abrupt end if she wants to stay with her husband. She is in her early sixties. On the one hand, the prospect of relief from the inevitable daily aggravations that are inseparable from the job of teaching today is appealing. But what will she do with herself?

John and Martha Newman have all the equipment of experience and physical and mental vigor to continue leading a full life. They are active and capable people, but they have to face the fact that they can no longer find a useful place in society.

Today we are immersed in a cult of youth. Youthfulness is being foisted upon us. Like a woman wearing a tight girdle, who enjoys the admiration it enables her to evoke but who pays a private price in the discomfort she endures, we feel flattered and self-congratulatory when we present a youthful image, in spite of the occasional twinges of discomfort caused by the mold into which we are cast.

The tides of evolutionary progression reach us via waves of cultural change, frequently preceded by ripples of fad and fashion. When we survey the present scene, our senses give us the impression of a fixed order. Like children who view the world from the safety and stability of their individual playpens and to whom information of it is conveyed only by their senses and not yet by understanding, everything around us seems to have been as it is from time immemorial and likely to remain so for all time to come. Only when our curiosity leads us to inquire about how the variety of nature came to be do we begin to discover the vast changes that have taken place over eons of time, while for countless generations, each in its turn, the world has appeared to be unchanging and eternal.

These changes were achieved by immense accumulations of steps, each so infinitesimal as to have been imperceptible, within the short spans of their lives, to the creatures experiencing them. Today the pace of change seems quickened. Whether it is actually so or whether it only appears to be so to us because of our greater understanding of it is open to interpretation. Despite the evidence of our senses we now know that life has always been and will always be in a state of flux, and that only those creatures survive that accommodate themselves to changing circumstances. Indeed, what we see as the fads and fashions of our times may be the ripples reaching the surface that indicate the presence of an underlying current, or they may be lappings into the future, like the countless trials of evolutionary improvisation, some of which receded again and were lost, but others of which grew into great waves that carried forward the surge of life's design.

Man as a species retains a youthful form. His skin is more delicate and most of his bones are lighter than those of his evolutionary forebears. His teeth are smaller and his nails are thinner than theirs. He continues to grow for a longer period of time. The vestiges of the hairy pelt his forerunners possessed are finer in modern man and less extensive, more like baby hair than like the fully developed total bodily protection and adornment that they grew. His head is larger in proportion to the rest of his body. In all these features and quite a number besides, he more closely resembles the young of other higher primate species than their mature forms. This youthful form has been achieved by a stretching out, a prolongation, of his childhood beyond that of any other model we might take from nature.

At the cultural level there has been a parallel progression. In the lives of earlier agricultural man a child was able to take a semiadult role by the age of six. Boys could and did help their fathers in the field, and girls their mothers with domestic chores. Later, the age of participation in adult activities was delayed until the time of puberty, and still later, educational requirements postponed the taking on of an adult role until late adolescence. Today we find education prolonged until late in the third decade of life, enforcing a condition of childlike dependency on many young men and women up to the age of thirty. It does not make much difference whether the education is supported by parent or state; the condition of dependency is the same.

With this inordinately large segment of the human cycle focused on the concerns and requirements of youth, it follows that youthful attitudes and ideals become fixed in our thoughts and feelings and pull the center of gravity of our lives ever more closely to their earlier phases. The propensities of childhood and youth influence our ideals and the values we hold. The urge to find out, the need to play, the drive to satisfy curiosity, the ability to learn, which are the marks of the young in other species and which in them fall away in maturity, in us are preserved throughout our lives. As research, exploration, experiment, and creativity, expressed in technology, the arts, and sciences, these basic attributes of the child have become the valued avocations of our adults, and those of us who attain the greatest degree of skill in these essentially youthful fields are the most admired of our number. The mature ideals and values—stability, responsibility, the ability to be self-sustaining while fulfilling one's role in an orderly society—are today considered dull virtues, if indeed virtues at all.

Like anything else in nature, of course, such changes do not take place in a straight line or at one fell swoop. We find indications of change in tides that flow and recede, but that

16

finally advance again more powerfully and in more places so that eventually the whole shoreline is covered and altered. In the course of the last two to three thousand years of human history there have been several periods and areas in which cults of youth have flowered, notably in times and places where technological and cultural advances were made and "civilization" achieved peaks. In ancient Greece sculptors and philosophers, statesmen and poets hymned the bloom of youth, and in Elizabethan England Shakespeare sang:

> Age, I do abhor thee,
> Youth, I do adore thee;
> Oh, my love, my love is young!

As the periods of affluence waned, sterner and more mature standards succeeded them, but each new tide made broader and broader inroads.

Right now, in the seventies of this century, we seem to be at the very crest of a movement that has all the appearances of eventually changing the values of all sections of human societies so much that one of them, our senior caste, appears to be in danger of losing its foothold entirely. Youthfulness is at a premium in all sectors of society. All our strivings are toward remaining young. We bend every effort to look young. We clothe ourselves in the fashions of the young. We exercise and diet and pummel our bodies to keep them lean and lithe. Men, as well as women, are encouraged to use cosmetics so that the images we see in our mirrors may reassure us of our everlasting youth. We tell ourselves and each other that we must *think* young. We are indoctrinated by our information media to regard all of life as one long romance—an everlasting spring.

Our aims in life have changed. No longer do we dream of becoming respected seniors, stable and responsible heads of families, dependable leaders of communities. We have taken on the nimbleness of youth. Ceaseless activity has replaced calm contemplation. There was a time when there was a stage of transition in the late middle years in which a person could prepare himself for taking on the status of the esteemed elder. This period has been whittled down more and more, and youthful activity and pace have been continued up to and into the retirement age. The older person, finally making a tentative beginning at slowing down in some of his undertakings in order to accommodate the diminishing physical capacities of his biological state, then feels some sense of guilt in doing so as his family and friends assure him that he is "still young."

In the matter of clothing most older people feel some inclination to follow Polonius' advice, "rich not gaudy," but on all sides they are discouraged from this proclivity. They are persuaded not to look staid, not to indulge in tastes considered old-fashioned. Their skirt lengths are raised or lowered with the latest styles and the trouser legs narrowed or widened regardless of convenience or whether or not they are becoming. The tight trousers and short skirts, designed to enhance the sex appeal of the young, appear incongruous on the elderly, but clothes more suitable to their comfort and status are made so unattractive that they are reluctant to flout the prevailing fashion.

The old ideas of the dignity and wisdom of age are disappearing fast. We impose upon our elderly the duty of acting and appearing young without giving them the privileges accorded those who are indeed young. There are very few positions of social importance left open to the elderly.

Here in America, and perhaps in the highly industrialized countries of western Europe in varying degrees, we seem to be part of the ripple that is lapping at the highest point of the beach. The taste and styles of the youth are being adopted at every age level, and their values are influencing the standards and social aims of all. In other highly industrialized nations, as affluence reaches into the middle and lower economic strata, we see similar trends. Even in Japan, traditionally a country that assigned rank and prestige to its elders, there has been an erosion of this pattern and an increase in the influence of the young. And as less industrialized nations struggle to take their places in the world community, their younger members are leading the way and taking the helm.

In the whole course of Western history until recent times high positions of state were traditionally held by older men, usually with the exception only of kings, queens, and others who inherited their rank. Young leaders in the Western world were so few that their names stand out in our minds—but how many William Pitts were there, or how many Alexander the Greats? One has the impression that until quite recent times a young man would not have met with sufficient acceptance even to offer himself for election to high office, much less have gained the confidence of the electorate. Today there is a trend toward the nomination of younger men in all the echelons of government, and the number of young persons to be found in the ranks of Congress or of parliaments forms an increasingly high proportion. Moreover, even our older lawmakers seek a base for their power and influence by tailoring their appeal to the interest of the very young voter—not rarely even to those of prevoting age. In England and then in America the voting age itself has been lowered, further diluting the voices of the elderly.

In the financial world, in the early years of those of us who are still in our prime, it was unusual for a man to attain a position of high authority until he approached the age of sixty. Today a man is expected to retire by this age, or at least by sixty-five, to make room for younger executives. In those times the "boy geniuses" of Wall Street would not have inspired confidence and would have found very little following. Today people of all ages seem to be willing to pledge and to risk their hard-earned reserves on the advice of such inexperienced operators. The consensus seems to be that such funds will be handled more productively by the youthful, who are considered enterprising and innovative, whereas the elderly are thought of as conservative and out of date rather than as experienced and wise.

In greater or lesser degree such attitudes are seeping into most areas of our social and economic lives. If the results achieved by our ever-younger leaders showed improvement on those of their older predecessors, one might find justification for the shift of emphasis on this basis. Unfortunately, there is nothing apparent in their record until now that would support any idea of their greater efficacy being a cause for the changing mores—not that leadership drawn from the older segment can claim too many laurels!

As it is, inducements and enticements are being held out to gild the lily of early retirement from active life. The whole idea of work as a service to the community is diminished. Work is seen merely as a means to the end of enabling the luxury of an early retirement and a subsequent "life of leisure."

To understand the importance of this change of attitude, one must understand the place of work in a social context. In a species that relies on cooperative work as a means of survival, work becomes more than just this. It becomes a binding force, a strong element in social cohesion.

To see the meaning of work in such a society without having the view of it impeded by such cultural distortions as are singular to man, we might look at the communities of other species where cooperative effort is a factor in their survival. Among the many examples one could choose, the ones that first spring to mind are those of the social insects, where the work performed is of such paramount importance that modifications of bodily form have been evolved to suit each individual to the task it will perform in life. No individual of such a society is without an essential function in it.

None can "retire." The individual that does not perform its function adequately is expendable. Each is allocated to a caste specializing in the performance of a certain task, and this type of social order has had its parallels in some highly successful human communities, notably in the Inca culture of ancient Peru. It is also not without some similarity to the organization of craftsmen into guilds in Europe in medieval times.

Survival based on cooperative work is to be found in other branches of life. Communities of beavers are less rigid in their structure than those of the insects; nevertheless, each animal performs a task that is important to the welfare of the group as a whole, and the work done becomes more than merely a means to the end of constructing a dam or a complex series of canals and weirs. It is an element that binds the members of the group into a cohesive unit.

Other analogies and similarities are to be found. It has recently been noted how strongly the social organization of wolves resembles that of the hunting groups of primitive man, but we probably have to go all the way to man himself before we again find societies based on the cooperative work of individuals to such a degree.

The performance of work is such an integral part of the adaptation of the individual that to deprive him of it is to detach him from his community in a very fundamental way.

We are constrained to wonder how it is that man should have come to regard work as an onerous obligation to be mitigated wherever possible. After all, the making and use of tools were among the factors responsible for our emergence from the groups of our apelike forebears as a separate species. And incidentally, the exercise of the hand and eye in the fabrication and use of those early tools was a major factor in the stimulation of the brains of our forerunners and a source of their increased complexity and capacity for enabling the growth of intelligence and ever greater skills.

Perhaps in this case, too, as has often happened elsewhere in nature with an evolutionary direction that has proved extremely successful, the trend goes beyond the limits of its usefulness. The size and armor of the dinosaurs enabled them to dominate the earth for a hundred million years but ultimately became a source of their elimination. In man the making and use of tools became a means for him in his turn to rule the globe, but man has reached a stage where the tool is made and used almost for its own sake. We derive some pleasure from the construction and use of a sophisticated tool, whether we need it or not.

The idea of work has been downgraded. The ideal is to eliminate work and to employ the tool. In pursuing this trend toward laborsaving tools, women have been robbed of their function in all but the biological area, and a restlessness has been created in half our population that has resulted in widespread changes in our social structure and mores. In depriving our elderly, too, of their part in the work of the community, perhaps it is only a question of time before we are faced with some form of protest from them.

It speaks for the importance of a man's work in life that a bribe for him to leave it must be made very attractive. Pension funds have been established. Why work any longer, they imply, when the means for your needs are assured? There has been a trend toward the establishment of the retirement colony. This is glorified as a kind of promised land where, as a reward for a virtuous and successful life, the older person may spend his declining years basking in a golden age of relief from responsibilities with no purpose other than entertainment and pleasure.

We must admit that this is a more attractive alternative than some others that are open to him. In modern homes space is often at a premium. The less affluent person, who in the past may have spent the last part of his life in the home of one of his children and who may have performed some minor services in return for his keep, is being consigned more and more to less attractive homes for the aged, to hospitals, or to other institutions. It is only the extremely independent older spirit who is able to avoid the blandishments of the promised lands and the pitfalls of the institutions to carve out for himself a satisfying second career after his early retirement.

Most, deprived of any useful purpose for the years that might have remained vigorous and rewarding, while away their time in pursuits that are a young person's idea of pleasureful activity. Facilities for suitably toned-down sports, like shuffleboard courts and swimming pools, are promoted by retirement community developers; games and dances are organized; the company of their peers is offered.

Some, to whom these attractions do not appeal and if they are rich, take themselves off on cruises or lengthy travels. The less wealthy may purchase trailer homes and indulge in the gypsylike wandering that is the dream of many an adolescent. In doing this they detach themselves from the communities in which their lives had content. After the initial excitement such wandering becomes flat—merely a way of passing the time and without meaning, the attainment of each day's destination a mere following on the trail of a pseudopurpose. There is an emptiness upon arrival, and no objective is achieved but the quest for a new destination.

We have traveled to many places to talk to retired people. Now we are in a small town on a large and picturesque lake—albeit the shores are choked with weeds—about half an hour's drive from Guadalajara in Mexico, an area that has attracted a great number of retired people from various parts of the world because of its ideal climate. We make our way toward the marketplace and see an elderly couple getting out of their car, their appearances and voices unmistakably American, and as we walk in their direction, they greet us.

After the usual "You are a long way from home . . ." we introduce ourselves as a couple looking for a place for retirement.

"You've found a great spot here . . . beautiful . . . the weather couldn't be better . . . people are friendly . . . living is cheap. . . ."

We sat down with them to a glass of beer. "What does one do here?" we asked. "How do you spend your time?"

"Well, there's golf. . . . I think there's some fishing, but the weeds are choking the lake. . . . There's a pool nearby, and we see our friends there most days . . ." he trailed off.

She broke in, "We're going to have to cut down on card playing. Bill's been losing his shirt lately. . . ."

Showing some irritation, he interrupted her. "We walk a lot . . . do a bit of gardening. . . ."

A little prompting brought out, "It's a long way from the bustle back home. Gee, it's good not to have to worry about the help, the payroll, the taxes. . . ."

But this was not spoken with much conviction. They seemed to be trying to persuade themselves and each other that they had made the right move. After the couple of hours' conversation that included the above snatches, it was clear to us that they were bored, they probably bickered a good deal, both were drinking more than they were used to and this seemed to worry her, but they both were trying nevertheless to convince each other that they were enjoying themselves.

We talked to a builder who was constructing houses for retired people in woodland around a lake in the Pocono Mountains, two and a half hours' drive from New York City. Most of these were already sold and occupied, but there were five or six properties that were still available. Believing us to be customers, he began to "sell" us the community.

"Never a dull moment here. . . . Plenty of bass in the lake

24

. . . boating . . . swimming. . . . There's something going on every night in the clubhouse. . . ."

We spent the rest of the day walking around the lovely properties, with their tended gardens, the sports facilities, the pathways among the trees, and in the evening we went to the clubhouse.

True enough, wherever we went we found men and women engaged in all kinds of activity. The atmosphere was strongly reminiscent of a children's summer camp, where the bell clangs on every hour to ring the changes from swimming to archery, to tennis, to riding, to arts and crafts. The words of all the people we spoke to were full of enthusiasm—but we had an overwhelming feeling of being on a television show where the emcee goes around asking, "Are you having fun?"

All these men and women seemed to be working very hard at "having fun." Indeed, from the conversations we had, we carried away the impression that they seemed to feel that this was their duty.

On our way back from a visit to an old-age home in up-state New York, we stopped off the road at a lookout point to enjoy the majestic view of the tree-covered mountains extending down to the gorge carved out of them by the Hudson River.

By chance, while we were there, a caravan of three camper trucks pulled up, and their elderly occupants got out and came over to the ledge of rock where we were sitting. One of them, having noticed the license plate on our car, mentioned that he, too, was a doctor and that he had retired from practice a few years ago.

"We've been so busy all our lives we never got around to seeing our own country. . . . We're not the types to play golf all day, so we're doing it now."

We asked where they were headed.

"We don't have a fixed plan. We're on our way south. We

thought we'd stop over if we like a place and, if not, push on."

We asked, "Are you enjoying your retirement?"

"Oh, yes," he replied. "Sometimes I miss my practice, but my wife wanted to get away, and I guess she was right."

His wife added, "Al needed the break."

"We're thinking of doing the same thing," we said, trying to dig a little deeper, "but we wondered whether it wouldn't get boring once the novelty wears off?"

After a side glance at his wife—"You hang on to your practice," he said.

In the final analysis the activities of the cruise ship or the trailer camp are not too different from those of the retirement community. The severing of familial and social ties makes a break in the stream of their lives, and what comes after the break is a palliative that cannot replace the fullness and richness of what went before. The promises of the travel posters and the travel agents' brochures turn out in the long run to be as empty as the developers' golden age communities.

The old are rarely consulted on most of such plans and provisions. These constitute, on the whole, a young person's idea of relaxation, and it is assumed that the old will desire the same. As a matter of fact, the elderly themselves do not give too much thought in advance to what they will do. Throughout their middle years they have endeavored to make financial provision for their retirement but have usually not prepared themselves for their occupation of that time. When we speak to those among our acquaintances who are in their fifties about what they expect to do later on, they invariably answer with such remarks as "We're putting some money aside to buy a place in the country" or "We've got a good pension plan, and we're looking forward to a lot of traveling." On the whole they have gone along with the idea that responsibility-free pleasure is a goal to look forward to, but when they are in such a situation they find that "plea-sure" is not a sustaining diet for all day and every day. Stim-ulation is lacking. Boredom sets in.

What is missing in all these pursuits is a sense of purpose. Whereas for the child play performs an important function in affording practice for the skills it will need in its later life, and for the adolescent sport fosters a competitive spirit and the development of the body, these activities are devoid of purpose in old age. It is the presence of a purpose that ren-ders an occupation stimulating and sustains the interest to pursue it. For creatures in all of nature the very essence of life is that each fulfills a function. In the absence of purpose interest flags and performance becomes perfunctory—a mere whittling away of time, like playing solitaire or patience.

In viewing all this we must ask ourselves some very impor-tant questions. We are going to discuss the presence of an elderly caste among us in a later chapter and show how such a phase of life became established by the processes of natural selection because it filled an adaptive role and served a useful function in the life of our species. As it becomes functionless, will such a caste slowly be eliminated? If what we see consti-tutes a part of an evolutionary process, should it—indeed, can it—be corrected? Before we can answer such basic questions as these, we must examine the role that elderly individuals have played in the overall evolutionary scheme and the con-text in which they have been preserved.

As our medical technology advances and we are increas-ingly able to prolong existence, we find ourselves adding years to our lives without having plans for what to do with them. Is this just another thoughtless disturbance of the bal-ance of nature? As we are now becoming increasingly aware, in other spheres we have been letting our technology run away with us, rather than marshaling it to serve our best interests. Only too late, and after it is done, do we realize the devastation we have caused.

Now that we are gradually beginning to understand the

interlocking nature of all of life, should we not bend our knowledge and all our efforts toward ensuring a cultural niche to replace the lost biological one for that growing proportion of our population that is elderly? This would by no means be an easy task, for to do it organically, it would have to be accomplished in such a way that the preservation of this caste in a healthy and purposeful existence served its own best interest and at the same time did not disrupt the effective functioning of the rest of society.

Does the extension and preservation of youth that we see around us on all sides form a part of some basic trend that would account for it? If it does, can we discover it?

CHAPTER TWO

What Happens to the Elderly in the Rest of Nature

In this book we are dealing with the place of the elderly in our societies, but the term "elderly" is a very relative one. To a child a twenty-year-old is an ancient, whereas a person in the middle fifties may be jokingly referred to as a youngster by an octogenarian. By what criteria can we define our subject?

In the most general terms we think of an old person as one who has retired or is about to retire from active life. But how then can we refer to a person between forty and fifty who retires after twenty years of military or civil service? He may or may not take up another active occupation. Or to the person who has inherited or amassed wealth at an early age and has therefore either not taken an active part in a society's work at all or done so only for a brief time?

Another stereotyped thought about old age is of a person physically weakened, perhaps stooped or ailing, no longer able to fend for himself in a totally independent manner. How then shall we describe the vigorous, physically active septuagenarians? There are those who are our fellow members in the Westchester County Hiking Club. Among them are several men and two women well into their seventies—retired schoolteachers all—who habitually participate in strenuous ten-mile hikes and keep up a brisk pace that several of the younger members find taxing. And then there are those like Supreme Court Justice William O. Douglas, who climbs mountains and whose wife has been quoted as saying that he has more energy than she, who is still in her twenties. Sir Francis Chichester sailed small boats over the oceans when he was in his seventies. And what of an Onassis, a Casals, or the lesser-known ones seventy years old or more who have married young women and who are not too rare in our societies?

To take a more biological criterion as the dividing line between life's prime and old age, it would perhaps be that time when a person ceases to be procreative. Shall we then consider a woman old who experiences premature menopause at the age of forty and a man young if in his sixties he fathers a child? Sexual activity, of itself, is certainly no criterion of age in the human race. There are some who abdicate at an early age and others who continue with undiminished enthusiasm to the last breath.

Obviously none of these criteria affords a very precise yardstick. Nevertheless, we do have a mental image when we speak of an old person. Within somewhat elastic boundaries we think of a person as elderly who has reached a stage at which he has retired from his work, who no longer expects to produce children, and who shows some bodily signs of the wear and tear of life. We ourselves consider that as modern man is slowly approaching a life expectancy of about ninety years, we may arbitrarily divide this span, like Gaul, into three parts: a prolonged youth up to the age of thirty; a prime of life from thirty to sixty; an old age, gradually declining into senescence, between sixty and ninety.

These divisions of life, arbitrary and approximate as they are, can be applied only to the species man and to some of his domesticated animals. They have no relevance when one considers any other species.

We must not presume that it is in the natural order of

things for social groups to contain an elderly caste of post-reproductive individuals. From our own viewpoint within the societies of man it seems that an individual must be born, grow up, reproduce, grow old, and die to live out a natural cycle, but in fact it was not until that comparatively late evolutionary stage when mammals appeared on the scene of life that some came to live past their prime. Most, if not all, other animals and in fact most mammals, too, die during their reproductive stage, bringing it to an end.

In fact, the natural order of things might be said to frown upon the wasteful use of any biological material. Economy of means is the ground rule in all of nature. Life exists to perpetuate life. Each phase of the existence of each individual serves a purpose in the perpetuation of its kind, and when this individual comes to the end of its reproductive usefulness and can serve no further purpose for its own species, it dies, so that its bodily matter may aid in the maintenance of life in other species and so be quickly reabsorbed into the total cycle of nature.

Before we continue with these thoughts, we must acknowledge that there are still very many people, among them some respected scientists, who feel that no useful comparisons can be made between the behavior of man and that of other animals; that the gulf between man and the rest of creation is too wide and too deep for analogies to be found and conclusions suggested by them arrived at.

We must state that our bias is in the opposite direction. We see a unity in all of life. The nature of the living cell that is the basic unit of every organism varies little from creature to creature. True, the differences in the organization of these cells are responsible for the wonderful variety of life's forms, but below this variety is a basic unity: the unity of the boundaries imposed by the range of the possible chemical reactions of the cell as expressed in its responses to stimuli.

This unity is reflected in the functioning of organisms. Moreover, complex responses on a high evolutionary level are elaborations on and direct derivations from those at a lower level. Such a complex endowment as sight finds its ultimate origin in the chemical sensitivity to light apparent in some of the most primitive unicellular life forms. The multitude of marvelous adaptations and specializations of every branch of life all can be traced back through simpler forms until one finds a level of unity. Man's intelligence, along with the cultural flowering that derives from it, is one of these specializations. We can trace its origin in forms similar to those of modern apes and, still further, in forms that, like theirs, stemmed from more primitive primates, other mammals, reptiles, fishes, and so on backward. Man's intelligence and culture did not spring ready-made like Venus from the ocean but were gradually honed from more primitive material, as were the wonderful capacity for flight in birds and the special organs and senses of many creatures that are in categories quite unique to their own species and not capable of duplication in others.

Not strangely, vestiges of many attributes of the earlier forms of our evolutionary heritage remain present in our bodies. Through these we find concrete evidence of our relationships with other living things that go beyond the primitive structure of the cell. There is no element of human endeavor that cannot be traced back to creatures lower on the evolutionary scale for which it also served a function, and for this reason we are convinced that comparisons not only are valid but also provide us with invaluable insights into our own being and behavior.

To return to our theme, perhaps the best examples of the principle of economy of means are to be found in the insect world, where the males of many species die in the act of mating or very soon after, and the females live only long enough to lay their eggs. Let us take a look at some common insects.

Some thirty thousand species of spiders have been studied and named. Some scientists believe that at least as many more remain to be identified. There is no part of the world where spiders do not live. They have been found by climbers on the highest peak of the Himalayas, by fishermen miles out at sea, and by aviators in the upper reaches of the sky. One air-breathing species lives underwater. Some spend their lives housed in silk cocoons. To others a crevice under a stone is home, or the depths of a cave. Some mimic ants and share their burrows. Some change color to match the flowers upon which they wait to trap their food. Some live for twenty years and some only for one. Obviously one cannot speak of spiders in one breath, but a few examples will give the general picture.

Some nursery web spiders live near water. A female may rest on a water lily pad or hide in leaves, holding her egg sac in her jaws. She spins a nursery web into which she places her egg sac. The mother then sits outside the nursery, perhaps at the bottom of the branch on which it is hidden, but with her front feet touching some of the line. After about eight days the baby spiders emerge and begin feeding on the snared fruit flies that they find near them. In all this time, a total of some two weeks, the mother takes neither food nor water, and about three days after the hatching of the spiderlings, she dies, usually with her feet still on the lines leading to the nursery. Her life's task is completed, and she is not allotted an old age to "enjoy the fruits of her labor."

The black widow spider has a bad reputation. She is so named because it is commonly thought that she invariably eats her mate. Actually this is not always true. She eats him only if she happens to be hungry. It has been said that the first rule for survival in the spider world is: If it moves, taste it. The male spider is much smaller than the female and must appear to her to be just as edible as any fly, as indeed he is. Since she is untrained in the principles of ethics, the conclusion seems inevitable. His biological role acted out, as often as not his final service to his species is as a nourishing dinner for his spouse.

A mimetid spider male is inclined to caution. Intent on mating rather than on becoming an evening meal, he conveys his ardor by means of a signaling system. His rhythmic tapping on the strands that support his intended reduces her to a euphoric state, in which she receives him. His survival depends on the speed with which he makes his subsequent getaway.

Clearly, courting and mating are dangerous occupations for male spiders, but hardly less so than is giving birth for many of the females. The presence of the new generation renders both of them superfluous.

The seventeen-year cicada, as implied in its name, remains in the soil in its larval form for seventeen years before emerging, to shed its nymphal skin and seek a mate by loudly advertising its presence in a noisy song, deposit eggs, and then die two or three weeks later. Seventeen years of preparation for the reproductive act, and then, almost immediately, death for the individual while the race goes forward with the new generation.

Among the praying mantises, the very small male clings to the back of his female when engaged in the act of fertilization. The female, her head turned over her shoulder, bites him in the back of his neck, consumes his head, and, as Professor Jean Fabre so eloquently described, "peacefully browses on the remains of her lover! And the masculine remnant, firmly anchored, continues its duty! . . . It would not relax its hold until the abdomen itself, the seat of the organs of procreation, was attacked."

There are many other examples of postmatrimonial cannibalism in the insect world. The golden gardener beetle has the courtesy to wait until the mating season is over but then regards her males as fair game, and the locust Decticus and the green grasshopper, although they show some delicacy and do not attack them as long as they are alive, are all the same not averse to devouring the bodies of their dead mates.

The keeping of the bodily material of the male at the service of his species by his becoming food for his mate when his other functions are no longer needed is not practiced by fishes. But the pattern of death for the parents soon after their reproductive mission is completed is found in many.

As good an example as any is the sockeye salmon, for their value to man as a food has caused them to be studied intensively. As is well known, after spending three or four years grazing on plankton in the Pacific, they return to the fresh running rivers where they were born. More precisely, they find their way back against all kinds of difficulties to the particular gravel beds, often many miles upstream, into which each emerged from its egg some five years previously. Interestingly enough, each sockeye salmon bears patterns on its scales that can readily be seen under a microscope and that identify it with the spawning ground of its origin, much as a man may be identified by the pattern of his fingerprint.

At the time the salmon enter the fresh water they are in peak condition, but from that moment on they cease to feed. Their reentry into the waters of their native rivers also marks the onset of their sexual maturity, and their bodies signal this event by taking on new colors: a general tone of carnelian red except for the head, which becomes green. As the male matures, he also changes his form. His back becomes humped; he grows a black snout and a full mouth of teeth to enable him later to defend his nest. This nest, or redd, is dug by the female. With her tail she digs a hollow about three feet wide and lays part of her eggs in it. She then moves a little upstream and digs another for more of them and continues this process until a total of from 3,500 to 5,000 eggs have been housed and deposited, all within the space of two days. The male passes over the eggs as they are laid and fertilizes them, after which the loosened gravel and sand slip back over them and protect them.

During all this time in the fresh water, a total of about eighteen days, neither the male nor the female has eaten. Their bodies are stripped of all their reserves of fat and have become nothing but vessels for the new generation. With their eggs deposited, fertilized, and protected and the future of their race assured, within a week of spawning both parents —their splendid colors faded and their bodies drained of reserves—then die. The male is usually the first to go. The female digs her fins into the gravel so that her body forms a protective roof over her nest until the last flicker of life.

Of course not all insects or all fishes die at the end of their first breeding season. Nevertheless, so far as we know, none of them lives on to a postreproductive old age, nor would such a phase of life be functional until we come to the level of the mammals in the course of evolutionary development.

While it is impossible to make any statement that allows for no exception when one is speaking of the countless species of all forms of life, nevertheless some generalizations are possible. On the whole, most insects, fishes, amphibians, and reptiles ensure the survival of their kinds by producing eggs in such large numbers that some small percentage of them are bound to survive and be viable. In these circumstances selection is unnecessary for parents that would live to provide care (beyond having laid their eggs in a suitable place) for the newly hatched young. As the processes of evolution refine this prodigality of offspring to less wasteful methods, we find in birds and among mammals species that survive by producing fewer offspring per individual female. This reduction in the number of offspring, however, enforces greater care for those that are produced, and hence a longer life for the parent that must care for them.

There are two ways in which the necessity to protect and care for offspring (that have become more valuable by reason of being fewer) operates to require parents that live longer. At the levels developed earlier on the ladder of life than the mammals, the most vulnerable periods of any creature's life cycle are when it is in the egg stage and the time immediately after it emerges from the egg. In those stages it is an easily available food for a great variety of predators. By retaining the young for the entire fetal phase within the body of the mother, mammals achieved a very great advance in the protection of their young at these most crucial times. Once the mother's life has been prolonged enough for her to afford her body as an ultimate protection to the embryo so that she is present at and takes part in its emergence, other functions justifying her continued existence become immediately apparent: the nurture, continued protection, and training of the extremely helpless newborn.

Among groups of individuals making up any species, their natural variability ensures that among them there are some that have short lives and some that have longer ones. When it is useful to the survival of a group that their individuals have short lives and, so to speak, get out of the way of the new generation, then the short-lived individuals prove to have a selective advantage, and their lines survive. However, when it is of advantage to the survival of a population for individuals to live longer, then the long-lived survive in greater proportion and pass this propensity on to their posterity. This is what happened increasingly among the higher mammals.

The reason for drawing attention to this rather self-evident fact is to point out that longer life in an animal group is not a thing that just happens but is a circumstance that happens only when there is a need for it.

In mammals, then, evolutionary processes achieved forms that lived to be able to reproduce a limited number of young in successive seasons and to take care of them. But even in most mammals there is no need for a further phase, a state of old age, after that of the prime of life.

There are several ways in which a mammal (and incidentally, this also applies to many birds) that is approaching the end of its useful life can be eliminated from the group. Animals may lose their dominant and privileged positions to younger and stronger newcomers. (Good examples of this are the deer, which duel challengers for their rights each season until they finally lose a contest and are replaced by younger males, and the seals, which battle each year for their territories and females and then slip back into the sea to die when they can no longer hold their own.) They may be weakened by injury and lose their physical capacity to forage for food or to hunt. Then either they get edged to the periphery of their groups, where they are more easily picked off by predators, or they succumb to their disabilities. (Female hyenas, which are the hunters of their species, often meet their end this way.) For some the shock of loss of status alone is sufficient to precipitate their death.

The life cycle of an individual animal is by no means an absolute. Both the nature of its life and the time at which it dies are determined by the needs of its group. The process of natural selection does not operate to preserve an individual but to maintain a breeding group as a whole at its highest level of function.

To enlarge on this point and to make it a little clearer, we cannot do better than refer once again to the social insects. In many of them, their worker castes are sterile. There could not be a plainer example of individuals that could not possibly be viable in terms of an evolutionary future were it not for their essential function within their groups. Being sterile, they obviously cannot perpetuate themselves as individuals, but through their work in feeding their queen they ensure her life, and thus a new generation not only of workers but also of all the other individuals that make up their social group. Their posterity is utterly dependent on the welfare of the community as a whole, and this, in turn, depends on their contribution to it.

To take another example that is closer to home, millions of cells are sloughed off by our bodies daily, and these are constantly replaced by new ones in a never-ending cycle so that the body may be kept fit and constantly rejuvenated. In a similar way the death of a whole individual serves a similar function for the community of which he is a part. Individuals are "sloughed off" from the group, as are cells from the body, so that the group may be constantly rejuvenated and improved by new genetic combinations.

By the continuous reshuffling of genes in generation after generation of mating, new variations in individuals are constantly produced. Among these, those that prove the most useful and the most adaptable for the group in the context of its environment slowly come to permeate the whole population, improving its chances for survival as a unit. This in essence is the process of evolution by natural selection. In some cases elements other than simple genetic recombination are involved. Mutations, diseases, and other factors may also play a part, but in the end natural selection of necessity works on all of them and tends constantly to refine the adaptation of the group to its external circumstances.

The process is well illustrated by the well-known observations of a type of moth native to the industrial Midlands of England. This population of moths as it was originally observed contained white, white speckled with gray, mostly gray, and a few quite dark individuals, but the lighter-colored ones predominated. Over the years of recorded observations it was seen that the light moths gradually disappeared almost entirely, while the dark-speckled and very dark ones increased and came to form the majority of the population.

It was pointed out by the naturalist who reported the observations that the smoky residues carried in the air from the spreading nearby towns had slowly darkened the trunks and branches of the trees that were home to these moths. In the early days the dark moths were less well camouflaged by their coloring against the light bark of the trees, and so they were more easily seen and picked off by the birds that fed on them and left few progeny. But as the bark of the trees darkened with the sooty deposits over the years, the few remaining dark moths emerged as the ones better protected by their color, so that the reverse process took place and today it is difficult to find a light moth in that area.

What is important to note here is that the mechanism that is operating serves to preserve the moths as a group. Individuals have no way to preserve themselves as such, but the group does. The varying shades of the wings ensure that there will always be some combination of coloring that will enable *some* of the species to survive and perpetuate the group—even at the sacrifice that there must always also be some few of the wrong color for the current circumstances among them, for it is these which would become the lifeline of the group should its circumstances change again. We might regard these "wrong-colored" few as sacrificial victims, preserved in the inherited potential of the group and performing the invaluable function of ensuring its ability to perpetuate itself in as many varying conditions as possible.

The composition of any living population has been arrived at because each part of it has contributed in some way to the overall reproductive fitness of the group as a whole. In most animal societies, as we have seen, there is no elderly postreproductive caste. Why then in man?

The answer surely lies in the development of the brain as man's chief instrument for survival. The enlargement and increase in complexity of the brain are certainly a biological modification, but they enable a different kind of development from the evolutionary processes that had taken place until that time. We call it cultural evolution. What this actually means is that it was no longer necessary for the body to be adapted to external circumstances, but that now it was possible, through the products of this new feature—the new brain, or neocortex—to adapt external circumstances to the needs of the body. For the first time the retention and accumulation of knowledge by the sheer length of a single lifetime became an asset.

In any complex society there has to be a division of labor, and there are many ways in which this can be achieved. In an ant or a bee society, for example, separate castes have been evolved, each of which is capable of fulfilling a specific necessary function. The reproduction of a bee group is left entirely to the queen and the drones. The sustenance of the group is left entirely to the workers, which do nothing else. Among ants the groups are defended by warriors, whose bodies are modified to make them eminently qualified for this task but available for no other. In man the specialization has been different. One might say that it has been horizontal. Each individual life has been divided into phases in each of which it is particularly suited for a certain role in the life of the community.

To a certain degree a division of labor between individuals exists in man too, but the division is not so absolute. Except for the basic difference between male and female in their reproductive function, human bodies are not otherwise adapted for specific duties. The habitual performance of certain tasks may strengthen or weaken certain muscles and make a person more or less hardy, but these attributes are not carried genetically. On the whole, the performance of the most vital functions of a human group—learning skills; using those skills and reproducing; exercising leadership; and applying and transmitting acquired wisdom—is allocated according to age and participated in by every individual at various times in his life. In the ant, by the time it is fully grown the body is irrevocably modified to perform a single function. In man the bodily changes occur sequentially, in the course of each life, so that at various times the person is suited to the performance of various tasks.

In man the aged contribute to the survival of their group by their becoming the repositories and the passers-on of the group's experience and wisdom. Those tribal groups that preserved their aged thus acquired an advantage over those that did not, and they survived while the others became extinct. There is no element in a living group that has not served its survival at one time or another in the course of its evolution. Moreover, the contrary holds true. When any element that forms a part of the whole or a part of its functioning ceases to have a purpose, natural forces slowly but inexorably eliminate it in much the same way that unused bodily organs or functions gradually become vestigial.

When we point out that there are no elderly (that is, postreproductive) animals in most societies of mammals, that is not to say that they do not have a potential for longer life. All the domestic animals man breeds and protects have the ability to live longer (when they are permitted to do so) than their wild relatives. In these cases the animals are preserved in longer life because man develops some feelings toward them, as he does toward his own family and the friends and associates of his own species. They have become his companions as pets or have served him, and he feels a sentimental inclination to protect them when they show the signs of weakness and the disabilities we associate with old age in man. While this shows that these animals (and perhaps many others) would be able to live longer in certain circumstances, it does not invalidate the contention that they would not live into a senile phase were they in a natural habitat.

It is not in the nature of things, however, for absolutely new forms, or behavior, or social habits to appear suddenly, as if from nowhere. Invariably there are some transitional states to be found that presage the new trend, and this holds true in the case of our present theme. In some of the higher primates it has been observed that a tendency has arisen for some older individuals to survive and to establish a useful place for themselves within the social order of their groups.

A very good example of this is found in the rigidly stratified societies of the baboons. Among them the older dominant males have learned to combine. They use their experience and accumulated knowledge to form an alliance. In this way some elders together are able to resist the challenges of the younger males when they would not be able to do so separately. Such behavior bespeaks the emergence of the beginnings of a higher intelligence, which, incidentally, is sometimes also demonstrated when the troop is in danger.

Normally the dominant males of a baboon community occupy a place in the center of the troop when it is on the move, and the younger males proceed around its edges to protect the group as a whole. However, when a predator was known to be in the vicinity, field naturalists watched a senior animal leave the safety of the center of the troop and scout the surroundings to locate the whereabouts of its enemy. The senior animal was observed in its careful reconnoitering and was subsequently seen leading the troop in a wide circle so that the predator could not get wind of it.

Doubtless this type of behavior, displaying the responsibility as well as the privilege of rank and obviously valuable to the survival of the group, became a factor in the preservation of the older members of baboon societies. The ability to store and make use of the knowledge acquired during their lifetimes gives them a very important function in the life of their groups.

These senior baboons—they have been called senators—are animals that are no longer important to their societies either as procreators or, singly, as defenders, since younger and stronger males are present that could readily perform these functions. Their sole value is the wisdom they have gained by experience, and in them we may see a type of behavior that was a way station on the road taken by man and a factor in the success of those of his groups that utilized the assets of their elderly.

CHAPTER THREE

The Function of the Elderly in the Societies of Man

In some ways the means of evolution and the processes of life seem to be incredibly extravagant and wasteful. Thousands of seeds and hundreds of eggs are produced, where only a few are needed and, indeed, only a few survive. Millions of forms of life exist or have existed; every possible and seemingly impossible shape, behavior, or habitat is exploited.

Yet closer examination reveals this impression of prodigality to be false. The production of vast numbers of seeds or eggs proves to be the most effective way of ensuring a sufficient variety of strains for there always to be some that are adaptive to new circumstances. Those that do not prove viable are recycled into other living forms as food, or fertilize and enrich the soil with their substance and so return the chemicals that composed them to the pool of life's resources. No human mind could devise a utilization of material so total and so economical as life's own.

The same thread of ultimate parsimony is woven into all natural order. No species survives for long when a more efficient one appears on the scene. No individual plant or animal survives if it is less well adapted than others of its kind. An organ that has lost its function gradually becomes vestigial and eventually is eliminated. A social organization of no matter which species, being a living entity, operates in the same way.

In any stable society all its members have to have a function. Functionless members tend to be eliminated, as is any superfluous individual organ, in all of nature. For this reason we do not find an elderly caste in any species until the development of a brain capable of reasoning and of judgment appears on the evolutionary scene and opens the door to a new way of securing the welfare of a breeding group. The presence of the elderly therefore had no survival value to any group until the presence of this type of brain allowed for the storage of information and the utilization of that information in terms of judgment in a situation of danger.

On a lower evolutionary level animals could only contribute to their own survival and therefore to their groups' by purely physical attributes. These included speed in running, strength in fighting, perfection in camouflage. Animals that developed these attributes only inadequately must have been eliminated. In fact, even a relative lack of such adaptations must have been an important factor leading to extinction. Several of the higher primates, including man, could hardly have maintained their existence had they not gradually developed mental powers to compensate for their relative inadequacies, as opposed to their predators, in strength, speed, or camouflage.

Brain power is one of the few biological features that increase and improve with age, albeit to a certain limit. Although we do not yet know for sure exactly where intelligence is localized or how the nerve cells manage to coordinate all the sensory impressions they receive in such a way as to be able to render judgment, we do find that the gradual increase in size of a portion of the brain, the neocortex, and intelligent behavior go hand in hand.

On the whole, it is hardly surprising that so many men and women, including many with contemplative and scientific minds, have thought man to be a unique order, being so special that he must have been separately created and for a special purpose. The particular qualities that are inherent in the enlarged brain have given rise to innovations and departures without parallel in the rest of nature. The ramifications of these are on such an extensive scale that it is difficult to see them as merely a consequence of the enlargement of an existing organ, a change basically not different from the enlargement and lengthening of the giraffe's neck. The giraffe's long neck also evolved because, in its circumstances, the ability it conveyed to reach higher branches had a survival value—and survive the species did, to occupy a niche available to no other. The inordinate development of the neck, though, in achieving its owner's survival accomplished just that and nothing more, whereas the particular organ enlarged in man for the same reason, because of the intrinsic nature of the nerve tissue of which it is constructed, had as a consequence the emergence of what we call culture as a brand-new evolutionary factor.

Simply stated, the new part of the brain is an organ especially developed because it compensates for the lack of certain abilities that would otherwise be necessary for survival. What it actually does is to improve and speed up the capacity to adapt—a capacity that already existed, but by other means, in man's forerunners, as well as in all other forms of life, animal or vegetable. And since this newest part of the brain is in some way involved with a capacity to accumulate knowledge, it seems obvious that in a species that has developed it, older individuals for the first time in the history of life have as much to offer their groups as the young virile members, if not more so.

Among the many things we take for granted about ourselves is that our brain is located in our heads. In fact, the brain could have been situated at any point along the paths of the nervous system. Actually, as the most important part of this system—indeed of the human body altogether—it would appear more likely for it to have developed at some point in the center of the body cavity, where, like the heart, it would have been better protected. Situated in the head, it is in a comparatively exposed and vulnerable location. Of course there is a reason for this. For higher animals the head is one step ahead of the rest of the body into the immediate future. The receptor organs of all the senses except touch are centered there, and touch is not excluded, even though it is more generalized. The first news of the future into which an animal is going is received by the nose, the eyes, and the ears, all closely connected to, if not actually a part of, the brain, and it is for this reason that the brain developed in this part of the body in spite of its being so vulnerable.

However, the brain is not merely the registrar of advance signals from the future. It is also the storage center for the experiences of the past and the supervisor of the activities of all the other organs of the body. The brain picks up the future and relegates it to the past. In registering the impressions of the senses and storing those that are relevant, it turns information into experience. In man this storehouse of experience then becomes the basis for comparisons that permit the selection of the most useful action. The larger the amount of stored information, the greater is the possibility for comparison, and the more likely is the judgment to be the most appropriate.

A child or a young person is constantly busy in building up a ready reference library of experience, and he does this by means of exploration and trial and error. But the amount of experience he can accumulate is limited by the short span of his existence, and when he is perplexed or unsure of the correct action to take, he will find guidance only by "borrowing a book," so to speak, from the brains of his elders. Should he not consult the experience of his elders, the limited amount of his own does not give him so great a variety of possible comparisons. The conclusions he reaches therefore may be arrived at more quickly, but it is not possible for them to have taken into account all possible circumstances, most of which are beyond his ken. It is natural then that his actions are impulsive and oblivious of possible repercussions. Sometimes this works well for him. His experimental tendencies may enable him to hit upon an innovative and brilliant solution. But more often than not, his action proves to have less happy consequences of which he could not possibly have been aware in advance. The older person, having a larger sum of experience against which to make comparisons, of necessity must take longer in selecting a course of action. Therefore his arrival at a decision must be slower, and his deeds less impetuous and probably more conservative.

These simple facts, if one thinks about them in this way, put a physical underpinning below what we all recognize and think of as purely social or cultural phenomena. We take it for granted that, on the whole, the older members of our communities are inclined to be more conservative and the younger more radical, without the awareness that there are biological mechanisms that would account for this. What is more, we must recognize how well this works for us, for in mediating the two extremes we settle on constant and gradual small changes that amount to an equivalent of the adaptations we find elsewhere in nature. Were the conservative older element unchallenged, we should find ourselves fossilized in unchanging societies. Were the radical youthful element unchecked, we should live in a state of turmoil that would inevitably result in extinction. Throughout man's history those changes that have come gradually have proved more successful and useful than those imposed by violent means, just as in evolution great changes have taken place by minute steps.

The knowledge and wisdom of age and the impatience and impetuosity of youth of course represent an average or ideal condition. While a large amount of information accumulated into experience forms the basis of wise decision, other elements are also necessary. The ability to connect relevant items is also a factor. We all know of young people wise

49

beyond their years and old people who are unable to make sage decisions. Yet all in all, experience is the chief foundation of wisdom, and it is on this basis that older people came to have a function in the tribes of man and to be preserved on account of it.

As we have described in the previous chapter, functionless members of living groups tend to be eliminated. Almost universally among the groups of early tribal man, even the revered elder, if and when he was no longer capable of performing his role or if his physical disabilities outweighed his social worth, was put aside. In the folklore of all parts of the world and in many customs that survived in rural areas right into this century, we have abundant evidence that attests to this practice. In rural Norway, in south Germany, and in parts of the Punjab, to this day it is a practice for the father and mother to retire to a kind of dower house on their property when their oldest son is married and able to manage their land. And this symbolic stepping aside is a relic of more drastic earlier practices.

Lest there be any misunderstanding, we should clarify this aspect of our topic here, since at first it appears to be contradictory.

In almost all tribal societies, including those still existing, until recently, when the influence of our Western world began to reach them, a great variety of customs existed that directly or indirectly accomplished the death of their oldest members. These customs were carried out in some groups with the cooperation of the elders themselves and in others without it, and the customs themselves were compassionate in some tribes and in others less so, frequently depending on the external circumstances of the tribe. Nomadic groups, on the whole, and those living in the most vigorous extremes of climate in the arctic or in deserts were simply not able to carry the burden of any nonproductive person and were obliged to dispose of them promptly.

Among some Eskimo tribes it was the practice for an old person who could no longer perform any tasks (an old woman, say, who had lost her teeth and could no longer chew leather to soften it for making boots or an old man who had become decrepit) "voluntarily" to leave the shelter of his family's hut and expose himself to death by freezing on the ice. In a nomadic tribe of central Africa, when old age made a person a burden to his group, at a time when the group moved on it left him behind with a piece of meat and the shell of an ostrich egg filled with water so that he could survive only as long as those meager supplies lasted. The Yakut maltreated and even beat their decrepit or feeble-minded elders, effectively worsening their condition and shortening their days. Stable groups in more benevolent environments were able to, and usually did, ease the senile out of their councils and lives more kindly.

The operative word is "senile." The elders of most groups were honored and respected within them so long as they served a *function* in their lives. Among the Mohave the grandmothers tended the babies and young children, while the mothers worked in the fields. Franz Boas defined this as a system in which the grandmothers ran the "nursery schools" while the mothers had "careers"! In Australia at the turn of the century, according to William I. Thomas, only the old men who had some special ability wielded authority. Of them a hereditary headman, or Alatunja, had the right to call together the elders, who always consulted on any important business, such as the holding of sacred ceremonies and the punishment of individuals who had broken tribal custom. He had charge of the sacred storehouse (often a cleft in some rocks or a special hole in the ground where the group's sacred objects were kept). He determined the time of the Intichiuma ceremony, the object of which was to increase the supply of the animal or plant bearing the particular group's name. The old and distinguished had great influence. But when great age or decrepitude took them beyond the ability to occupy a useful place in it, then each group found its way to excise them, not too differently from the way any living organism eventually rids itself of useless parts or, as we have described in other species, death overtakes any individual whose function is completed.

When we write of the elders of a group, therefore, we are writing of the *functioning* elders. This did not always include *all* the elders. And when senility eroded the abilities even of the functioning, they were sent along the same route as the other nonfunctioning elderly. In some groups they were simply left behind when the tribe moved on. In others it was the duty of a son to kill his aged parent, sometimes after a ritual feast in which the old person participated. The customs were many and varied, but their results were the same. Being elderly, even revered, was not enough. Only as long as they served a function did they retain their places in the life of their groups.

It is tempting to draw a parallel between these and our own practices. We, too, today segregate our elderly in institutions that go by various euphemistic names but that nevertheless remove their inmates from the life of the community. Indeed we go a step further than the primitive groups did, for by insisting upon retirement when function is still possible, we condemn our seniors to this exclusion in many cases before they are ready for it.

In primitive tribes of man, not only those incapacitated by age, but also the lazy, the unskilled, the inadequate members of the group were often ridiculed to an extent that forced them into marginal existence. Usually they were denied the privilege of marriage, and this effectively eliminated their line. This was a continuing process. As disease, birth injuries, accidents, or some genetic combinations produced individuals unable to perform tasks useful to the community, a similar fate befell them generation after generation.

We see some carry-over of this in our own times, when the

general attitude toward "the idle rich" or Shaw's "undeserving poor," the idler or the hobo, is one of a certain degree of contempt. This contempt often, at least in the case of "the idle rich," brings sufficient pressure to force them into leading lives of some sort of service to their communities in spite of the fact that they have no need of material gain. It seems to be borne in upon them, in some ill-defined way, that they must perform some function in order to remain esteemed members of their societies.

It may seem strange that many of the very wealthy find that they have a need to earn the esteem of their fellows. One would think that by very reason of their wealth—their social position assured, their wants satisfied—they would be indifferent to the opinions of the lesser members of their societies. Yet this is not invariably so. Why is it that many scions of rich families feel in some way demeaned if they allow themselves to be referred to as playboys or some equally semicontemptuous term? What we see here is actually an easy-to-recognize example of the deep need for the respect of their fellows that nearly all men have. Without the respect of others it is difficult to feel self-respect, and the need for self-respect has a most important significance in terms of the evolution of our species.

Self-esteem based on respect given by others is the approximate human equivalent of the dominance of some animals within their groups, for their dominance, too, is established and maintained by the recognition of their superiority by other animals. It is almost impossible to overestimate the importance of this factor in the orderly functioning of animal groups. The hierarchy of dominance constitutes the essence of their social order and is the bedrock of the natural means of adaptation to the surroundings, of the preservation of the best stock, and of the very survival of an animal group.

The mechanism is very simple, yet amazingly effective. The word "dominance," which we use to describe this system, is a little misleading. Dominant animals do not normally tyrannize the others of their groups. On the contrary, in many instances they offer leadership and some protection to the rest. However, they have a first right to any privilege that happens to be of value to their particular society. They have a right to the best territory if they belong to a species that customarily stakes out territories. They have a preferred position within a flock, a herd, or a troop. They may mate with preferred females, with more females, or have the right to mate at all, according to the habits of their kind. It is little wonder, then, that contests for dominance between individuals are carried on from the earliest age in most animals, and that the social order is often fairly well established by the time sexual maturity is reached. It is even less surprising when one remembers what happens to the less- and the least-dominant members of animal groups when external circumstances are difficult. In the first place, such animals are normally found around the outer edges of their groups, in which positions they are especially vulnerable to predators and may be picked off far more easily than those occupying a better-protected place. Secondly, when the population is too large for comfort and needs trimming, they are often denied the right to mate. And thirdly and most importantly, when food is in short supply, they are the last to partake of whatever is available and therefore the first to suffer deprivation.

By this simple method many animal groups weed out their less effective members in each generation and preserve those that have marked themselves as superior by their attainment of rank. The attainment of rank is thus not the desire of the stronger to bully the weaker, nor is it a greed to possess or to deny possession to others; rather it is an absolute necessity, often for survival, for life itself. It is little wonder that a drive for rank is so deeply ingrained in all group animals and that man himself, who evolved as a group animal, also has a biologically implanted need for respect and an urge to be the top man on the totem pole.

A fascinating study of an animal dominance hierarchy in action was made recently by G. C. Haber, who spent six years observing the social lives of wolves in the wild in Alaska. He was especially impressed by the many ways in which the social organization of wolves "is almost identical to what anthropologists have pieced together as the social order of early man, or even that of some primitive human hunter-gatherer societies of today."

Haber emphasizes that a pack of wolves is not the "snarling aggregation of fighting beasts" of man's imagination, but a highly organized, well-disciplined group, usually a family unit, "all working together in a remarkably amiable, efficient manner."

One pack, which he followed closely during the entire six years, he describes as "ranked according to the strict convention of a dominance hierarchy . . . each adult knows its position of authority. . . . I have yet to see any case of all-out fighting within an established pack." In the wolves' highly efficient division of labor, the top-ranking adults take on the most important duties. The pack leader (or "alpha" male) is the strongest, fastest, wisest, and most experienced wolf in the pack. "He has the ultimate decision-making power and his authority is unquestioned." He sires the young of the pack, and in critical situations all depend on him and all "regularly acknowledge his authority in a variety of ritualized ceremonies."

The second-ranking ("beta") male is his chief assistant, who directs most of the routine activities of the group. One of the beta male's duties is to attend the whelping female in the early denning period, which he does so devotedly that he could be mistaken for her mate. "But close observation of the pack during the courting and mating period over the past winter indicate this isn't so. So long as the present alpha retains his authority, the top female will remain his and no other male will be permitted to mate with her." The alpha male "delegates" duties to the beta male "much as an efficient human leader would keep a strong right-hand man and reserve for himself only the most important matters."

The top-ranking female is another key individual in the pack. During the winter, while the pack is continuously on the hunt within its territory, she "plays an active, aggressive role in helping to detect and capture prey." During the spring and summer she retires temporarily for domestic duties, but by late May, "when the young first emerge from the den, she begins to turn some of the pup-tending duties over to one or two subordinate male or female adults . . . occasionally she will even leave the pups with a babysitter and lightheartedly trot off with the other adults for a fling on the nightly hunt."

Haber then commented, "The well defined dominance order and disciplined manner in which duties are assigned and carried out, the presence of different generations of the same family living together, the prolonged dependency of the young, the group effort in raising and training them, the co-operative effort of many individuals in the hunting of large prey, and in several other respects wolves, like our own human ancestors, have developed a highly effective means of coping with a wide variety of conditions."

Oddly enough, there is no universal specific standard by which men may reach high status. Their rank is achieved and recognized by sets of values that vary between peoples in both time and place. In this, too, man is not very different from other animals. Among some animals bright plumage may be the focus of competition, among others skill in song, physical strength, red wattles, full manes, or branching antlers. Contests of prowess are sometimes involved, but not always. Sometimes superiority is recognized without being put to the test, or mere threat may be sufficient. No human has to fight all the time to prove his dominance. Everyone in a class of schoolchildren knows who the leaders are, and a bully is seldom among them, just as everyone in a club, a business organization, a team, or any other human group knows who sets the pace. The system probably works in a very similar way among animals. Moreover, among groups of the same species customs may vary slightly in different geographic locations. And so it is with man. In various times and places various skills and attributes have been esteemed, but there is never any doubt in anyone's mind about who are the leading members of any small community or whose opinions and interests are of no consequence, even though none would be able to state with any certainty how he arrived at his estimate.

In point of fact, differences in values occur not only between groups of man but also within groups. Different standards of attainment are expected from children, from the mature, and from the old as different standards apply also to the male and the female. However in past ages, although each stage of life accepted different standards of valued achievement, in each phase one found a stage, especially toward the end of it, where the individual prepared himself or herself to enter the subsequent one. The attainment of successful and virile manhood and mature womanhood was the ultimate aim of all children, and the skills they practiced in their games and education were focused in that direction. Similarly, the status of revered, powerful, and omniscient old age was the aim of the prime-of-life caste. They prepared themselves for this crowning stage of their lives by various means: in some societies by the accumulation of land or other wealth, in others by political power or influence; by success in warfare; by securing deferential followers, or love, or admiration. Old age was a time to enjoy the fruits of these endeavors.

Here we must remind ourselves again that man is one of the few species that preserve individuals into old age at all and the only one that does so to such a degree. This implies that in man there was almost a condition of a preexisting function awaiting individuals to fulfill it. On the one hand, no creature lives beyond its usefulness to a group, but on the other, if the performance of certain functions would enhance the group's capacity to survive, then sooner or later, individuals able to perform them will be evolved.

In man the accumulation and transmission of knowledge were matters of utmost importance to the survival of the group. The new reasoning brain had become the alternative to the built-in automatic reflexes of the old one, and a reasoning brain requires information to enable it to make suitable decisions. As we have said, the greater the store of information, the better the decision is likely to be, all other things being equal. Therefore years conveyed a premium upon those who had lived them not only for their greater number of experiences but also for their longer memories. In the earlier societies of man the old were respected and followed because of their experience and wisdom. They were also the transmitters of knowledge handed down from previous generations, and so they became vessels of the people's traditions. This made automatic their roles as priests, and the priestly role led them to become the ruling (dominant) political caste—if not as priests, then as tribal chiefs or as advisers to tribal chiefs, kings, or successful warriors. Thus they were not only the passers-on of their people's skills, folklore, myth, history, and tradition, but also that segment of the group responsible for seeing that these were upheld and continued. The elderly caste became the citadels of political power, while the mature caste became the warriors, who defended their positions either by arms, strategy, or simple devotion, and their mates, who bore and trained their young to do the same in their turn.

When the noted French anthropologist Lucien Lévy-Bruhl wrote of the old man in a primitive group as "the repository of the sacred traditions and secrets of the tribe that are communicated only to certain heads of families when they have arrived at a definite age," he added, "This old man is encircled by a kind of mystic halo. He is respected and he often enjoys the most exalted privileges. A little linguistic detail throws light on the tribe's feelings. In the language of the Kowrarega (an Australian tribe near Cape York) an old man is called *ke-turkekai*. *Turkekai* means man; *ke* (contracted form of *keinga*) is used as a prefix to denote a superlative degree (for example, *kamale* means warm, and *ke-kamale*, very warm). Consequently *ke-turkekai*, old man, means 'very much of a man': not exactly 'superman,' but a man in the highest degree of the quality of manhood."

And Thomas Petrie, in his *Reminiscences of Early Queensland*, described how at a meeting of the Yarra-Yarra tribe in the province of Victoria, "the natives brought with them an aged head-man named Kul-ler-kul-lup. He was supposed to be more than eighty years old. He was at least six feet in height, fat, and with an upright carriage. His friends— indeed all who saw him—paid respect to him. They embarrassed and encumbered him with their attentions. . . . None presumed to speak but in a low whisper in his presence. . . . Whatever the old man suggested as proper to be done was done; what he disliked was looked upon with disgust by all the men of the assembled tribes. . . .

"The aborigines everywhere and on all occasions pay great respect to old persons. If a number of strangers are going to a camp, the oldest man walks first and the younger men follow. Among the Murray tribes it is considered a very great fault to say anything disrespectful to an old person. . . ."

Not only did the older members of a society set the pace for and guide the destiny of the group as a whole, but also each of them, as individuals, performed the same functions within his own family unit.

So great was the authority of the elder among the Mukjarawaints of Australia that children were considered as belonging to the grandparents, even though the parents took care of them. When D. Seeman reported on this tribe in 1862, he wrote that if a boy was born to a couple and then a girl, the father's parents might take them and perhaps also another couple of children. But if then another child was born, it was up to the grandparents to judge the circumstances and to decide whether it should be allowed to live or not. If not, then either the grandfather killed it or he instructed the father to do so, by the ritual method of striking it against the mother's knee and then knocking it on the head. That such an extreme power was obeyed gives some indication of the extent to which the elder's judgment and authority were trusted and respected.

Although patterns of tribal organization differed considerably among primitive groups of man and it was not always the case that the father was the head of a family, as in our own societies, in most cases the elders of the tribes exerted the same influence in the family units, however constituted, as they did in the tribe as a whole. And then, too, just as family relationships were in many cases organized differently from the way ours are, so also were many occupational roles. Nevertheless, whether the role was filled by a man or a woman, by a relative of the father or a relative of the mother, in all cases seniors were turned to and consulted, and they counseled and guided the younger members of their families.

Males and females in their respective roles passed on knowledge that they had received from their own elders, to which they added the lessons learned in their own lifetimes. In the rest of the animal world, except in some instances in a few other primates (which have been shown to pass on some individually acquired knowledge to each other and to their young), the experience of a species has to be passed on by genetic modifications resulting in deeply embedded responses that we speak of loosely as instincts. Of course the young of nearly all species of higher animals also acquire many of their habits by learning—that is, by observation of the behavior of the older individuals in their groups—but the extent or variety of what most animals are able to learn is to a large extent circumscribed within the boundaries imposed by their genetic inheritance. Modification of behavior in these circumstances occurs, but it is slow. It must await the appearance and selection of particularly well-adapted animals over many generations. Man's ability to pass on to others by verbal means the lessons of his experience speeds up this process considerably and renders his behavior far more amenable to changes when necessary.

The elders were a very important link in the chain of learning and therefore a very important factor in the change-over man achieved. No longer limited in his ability to adapt by his genetic inheritance alone, and with a new type of brain able to accumulate knowledge, the power of speech, and last but by no means least a caste of experienced individuals able to pass on the fruits of these advantages, man now possessed the ability to adapt his behavior, sometimes in far-reaching ways, within the space of a single lifetime.

Each generation did not have to discover anew how to till the soil, to raise food, to distinguish between edible and inedible plants and animals but could build on the experience of its elders. The older persons could also impart their knowledge of medicinal herbs and folk remedies; their skills as nurses and in many cases as healers; their strategies in hunting and in warfare. Above all, they could also teach how to produce tools and use them and could give advice on rearing children.

In the overall picture the most senior members probably rarely taught directly—this would have been a function of the middle generation of parents—but they set the standards by their counsel and advice. In some areas, though, not only advice but also assistance was given the reproductive caste by the elders, especially by older women to their daughters. It is an interesting sidelight that there must have been a long history of this type of assistance in the whole line of primates, for chimpanzee mothers have been observed assisting their daughters with their infants. Moreover, ethologists have reported that some older chimpanzee females hold their clans together by exercising their dominance in favor of their offspring and sisters.

Do we not perhaps see here the first rudiments of the establishment of a class system? In a group where some of the young are favored and protected, accustomed from birth to associate with the dominant of their kind, and do not have to exercise their abilities to attain that dominance in competition with their peers, a self-confidence, or aura, is created that must be very similar to that possessed by the young of the highest rank in man.

Perhaps there is some moral to be drawn from this. Chimpanzees are closely akin to man in a kind of cousin relationship. They, and we much more so, show evidence of a nepotism in this that is actually destructive of good social order if carried too far, since the class structure of the group becomes undermined when rank is obtained by privilege and not by ability.

Be this as it may, the establishment in the group of a habit for the elders to give assistance to their juniors must have been of incalculable survival value in man, for his young are so helpless for so long that they require more attention from their mothers than it is in the power of most to give. The grandmother was then an invaluable aide, assisting in the preparation of food and in the care and education of the children. In fact, the presence of the grandmother to give aid enabled the parents to afford their children the long period of childhood that is necessary in the human young for development and learning. The evolutionary trend to prolonged childhood in man was greatly facilitated by the presence of people able to care for them, for without this intensive care they could hardly have survived. Today grandmother has largely been made obsolete by gadgets. Children no longer hear her tales of the past and traditional stories. The television set has become their oracle. Laborsaving devices have rendered her aid in the kitchen superfluous; traditional recipes and remedies are transmitted via cookbooks, doctors, and pharmacies.

Perhaps we can get an idea of the extent of the change—and loss—if we compare the life of a modern urban grandmother, who at best lives in a small, laborsaving apartment, perhaps with her husband, but often on her own, with that of one of our own grandmothers.

She lived in Ruthenia, in a remote corner of what was then the Austro-Hungarian empire, and except that her life was not threatened by marauding Indians, it was in no important way different from that of a frontier grandmother in the United States—or, for that matter, a rural Englishwoman's at the end of the last century.

For her, a typical day began before sunrise. The hired help had already assembled in the courtyard by then: boys ready to lead the cattle to the pastures; men to work in the sawmill; and girls to milk the cows. She would supervise and assist a maid, who was preparing breakfast for them and packing lunches for each of the boys and men to stow in his belt pouch, for they would not return to the farmhouse before evening.

By the time this had been done grandfather would have joined her, and they would go together, accompanied by an elderly peasant who was their chief assistant, to the barns, where they checked the cattle, one by one, to make sure they were in good condition. This was done while the hired men were eating their breakfast. In spite of the fact that there were between thirty and forty cows, grandmother knew each and every one of them individually as though they were members of her family. While checking the health of the cattle, she would break up the small clusters of young girls, who had just finished milking them and who were giggling, chattering, and flirting with the breakfasting men, and shoo them on to feed the chickens.

These tasks completed, she supervised and helped her daughters, who were preparing breakfast for the immediate family. Her sons, daughters-in-law, and daughters and sons-in-law together with their children came over from their own houses on the property to share a huge farm breakfast every morning.

After breakfast, grandmother and her helpers took some of the morning's milk to the basement, where they prepared it for making clotted cream, sour cream, or cheese, while the surplus was sent to the nearby town. Later in the morning the sound of the thudding pestles as the girls churned the cream into butter made a background rhythm to the cacophony of cackling hens, crowing cockerels, the screeching of the wood-sawing blades, and the honking of the distant geese that pervaded the air of the courtyard.

The butter production under way to her satisfaction, grandmother then walked with one of her daughters over to the more distant part of the farm where the geese were kept. There they were being force-fed, a very delicate task that she herself had taught the young peasant girls to do, and she always watched them very carefully. The geese were very important to her, not only for their fatted livers and their delicate meat that was reserved for holidays and special occasions, but also for their fine neck feathers that from time to time were plucked and preserved for the trousseaux of the girls of the family—to fill the light, warm eiderdowns that were a matter of family pride when they married and had homes of their own.

Among the many other tasks grandmother performed, taught, and supervised in the course of her busy day were baking the everyday bread, and, separately, the fine bread for special occasions, and the cakes; preserving and pickling vegetables; jam making; selecting the mushrooms her young grandchildren brought in from their mornings in the nearby woods; checking the household linen and seeing that it was kept in repair; and preparing the midday and evening meals.

Two hours of the early afternoon were reserved for grandmother's social life. Then she entertained visitors from the town over delicate teacups, bright silver, and fine linen. On the days when she had no visitors, she would sit down with her grandchildren and give them tea and, as a special treat, a very rich cake, called *pfladen*, that was heavy with poppy seed and nuts and raisins. Then she would tell us stories of her own childhood, and we became familiar with the lives and traditions that made up her world.

In short, her days were filled with an endless series of tasks, and in the performance of them she trained her daughters and daughters-in-law, passing on all her own skills to them and, to some extent, also to her grandchildren. Her deep satisfaction and pride in her life were obvious. She would not have wished to change any part of it. It did not enter her mind to think of herself as a slave to her duties. On the contrary, she was the mistress of her domain, and she reveled in it.

Old people thus were passers-on of history through telling tales, and being assistants to the new mature generation, teachers and models for the young, and it is not surprising that they became a focus for the life of the group and a great stabilizing force in it. They held it together as the centers of gravity of the extended families as well as directing it from positions of leadership. When these functions are diminished, respect lessens, and as respect for the elderly waned, families became less cohesive and societies less stable.

Naturally, there is a circular feedback effect in operation here, as in most life processes we observe. In recent times especially, other factors have added their quotas of influence to the loss of the services of our senior caste. Mobility is one of them. The ease with which it is possible to move away and take up life in distant parts of the country or of the world in many cases has removed the grandmother geographically from the area of her most valuable function. Children often grow up now without experiencing the daily sight of their grandparents, and so they become separated from the chain of generations. Respect is difficult to foster by word of mouth rather than by daily example.

In the past when elders not only were valued leaders and advisers but also embodied the traditions, values, and beliefs of their groups, in many societies they became objects of more than respect—of veneration. Anyone who gave offense to an elder would have had a sense of guilt as though he had transgressed against everything that his people held holy, and this feeling was a powerful factor in upholding and perpetuating the established system.

To primitive man death did not make a person cease to belong to his social unit; the living and the dead were as equally a part of it as any other two classes. The habit of consulting the elder in life continued after his death, and the older dead—especially those who were founders of families—tended to become idealized figures, often passing into gods.

Much of man's development passed through stages of ancestor worship. In Samoa it seemed plain that since a commoner was of little account in life his ghost could not be very important, so his spirit was tended and consulted, if at all, only by his immediate family. But the spirit of a great chief was a very powerful ghost and was consulted on all important occasions. In ancient Rome the cult of the Manes was the worship of all the dead of a particular line, en masse. It dovetailed with the idea of the holy nature of the *genius* of a family—that special power that enabled it to continue its existence and that was embodied in the successive heads of

66

the clan. In Ashanti the worship of the ancestral spirits was carried out by the queen-mother at the *adae* ceremony, in the presence of stools, each of which had belonged to a dead queen-mother.

Elements of ancestor worship are to be found in Shintoism in Japan. It existed also among the Greeks and the Vedic Indians. True ancestor worship, as opposed to merely tending the spirit of the dead ancestor, was practiced in all parts of the world (and still is in not a few communities—the Dayak of Borneo, for instance, worship their ancestors as well as other gods and spirits). It is powerful evidence of the indelibly important role of the elders in all early societies of man.

Five centuries before Christ, Confucius gathered and preserved "all the records of antiquity." He called himself "a transmitter, not a maker," and he believed that a good example set by a ruler, or any senior, was enough to ensure model behavior in the follower, or junior. "Not more surely does the grass bend before the wind," he said, "than the masses yield to the will of those above them." Through his precepts, respect for the elder was a stabilizing force in the Orient for more than two thousand years.

CHAPTER FOUR

The Old Are Not the Only Losers

As we wrote the last chapter, we paused for a while to think about what these roles of the elderly had meant to us personally in our own lives.

Our fields of special interest are anthropology and medicine. We have spent much of our time seeking clues in the evolutionary development of man that might throw light on some of the physical and emotional discomforts and difficulties he experiences today. In writing a book of this kind we are motivated by our observation of a social condition that we think should be explained, brought to general attention, and, if possible, remedied.

Normally in any research or scientific endeavor it is a principle that the researcher keeps his own feelings and reactions firmly out of the picture, and he attempts to be as impartial as it is possible for a human being to be. He takes note of the facts he finds and develops his ideas using these facts as his sole building material. But in this work we find ourselves responding on a personal level. Chords of our memories are struck. We are part of the social state, and if a social condition exists, how, we ask ourselves, has it affected us personally?

In reminiscing along these lines we discovered that our own lives had indeed been strongly marked by the elders of our own time and in precisely those areas that have traditionally been the arenas of the senior since the dawn of man.

Social Cohesion

In the life of one of us the family played a role that could hardly be overestimated. Our maternal grandparents had six children, each of whom had married and produced children of his or her own, so that by the time the writer was born she was blessed with the presence of ten maternal uncles and aunts (and a slightly larger number of paternal ones, but it is of the maternal family we now write). In due course, some dozen cousins arrived.

There was no aspect of family life on which the grandparents were not consulted or, if not consulted, then their known wishes or opinions taken into consideration. As they married, each of their children bought homes within a reasonable distance of the parents' so that they could visit each other conveniently. Every Tuesday evening, without fail, all six grown children with their five wives and one husband had dinner with their parents, and every Saturday afternoon they either took or sent their children to join them for tea. On these occasions the parents of in-laws and the brothers and sisters, or nieces and nephews of the grandparents were sometimes included as space and mutual convenience permitted. On all high days and holy days as well, the entire family gathered under the grandparental roof. There was no special event of life, whether birth, confirmation, marriage, or death, to which each was not invited or expected to attend. As a result there was no member of this large extended family who was not on intimate terms with every other member. This is not to say that each person was fond of, or even liked, every other, but whether we liked them or not, we considered them part of our own.

Attendance at the weekly dinners and teas and at the seasonal occasions ensured not only that we all knew to the last detail the domestic events in the lives of all the others but also that everybody knew everybody else's opinion about them. Rather than face criticism from the rest of the family, we all discussed our plans in advance and modified much of our behavior. Contemplated alliances and their potential ramifications were discussed by all in every detail. The prospect of presenting an acknowledged suitor to the rest of the family certainly caused this member of it to think three times before giving encouragement to any one of them.

Life in such a closely knit clan was not an unmitigated pleasure. The compulsory visits and duties were often felt to be burdensome, especially by those related by marriage rather than by blood. The permanent awareness of the opinion of others about steps we wished to take in our own lives could also be onerous. Yet in response to this social pressure, many foolish acts were prevented from occurring. Our demeanor in public was inevitably modified by the knowledge that, no matter where we happened to be in even so great a city as London, there would surely be someone else present who knew a member of our family and that word of our conduct would, equally inevitably, be relayed home and subjected to due consideration. There was no lack of high spirits among the youngest group, but these were bounded by what was understood to be the limit of what would be tolerated.

For a child born into such a family the world was a very stable place. We had no identity problems. We knew very well who we were. We had no doubt about what we would become. The youngest child looked forward to being like the older ones and to enjoying their privileges. The boys knew a great deal about the business of their fathers and expected to continue in their footsteps. The girls expected to marry and to have homes of their own not too different from those of their parents. Boys and girls alike expected to be parents in their turn and eventually grandparents, with authority over new generations.

Like most things in life this stability was perhaps not without some minor disadvantages. The family's unquestioning acceptance of life as it was seems to have generated a similar stability in the domestic staffs it employed. Most of the households included servants who had been with them for dozens of years and who were as aware of their own place and of their rights and duties as was each member of the family. Indeed they were considered, to a certain extent, parts of the family. One could probably describe them as having been associate members.

In our own case, our parents employed a cook in the first year of their marriage who stayed with them for more than forty years, until her death. Both her daughters were members of our household, and her son-in-law was employed by our father. She was a proud cockney and as much the unquestioned ruler of her domain as was our mother in the rest of her home or our father in his office. Her territory consisted of the kitchen-sitting room, the pantry, the scullery, the storage basement, and the top floor of the house, where her and her daughters' bedrooms were. As children we did not enter any of those rooms without her express invitation or permission. When once, on a rainy day, we tired of the nursery and wanted to go to the kitchen to try to make toffee, she firmly told us, "You children keep out of my kitchen. You can make all the mess you like in the nursery." Keep out of her kitchen we did, with the unfortunate result that none of us had the remotest idea of even the rudiments of cookery until we learned the hard way much later on in our own homes. However, good order had been defended. We were kept in our place, and she remained supreme in hers.

This state of affairs persisted until World War II dispersed the younger members of the family over the globe in the course of their military and naval duties and the older ones to various country areas, as the bombing of London destroyed or damaged several of their homes. One grandparent did not survive the war, and the other only briefly. When the scattered units of the family eventually returned to their homes, there was no longer a hub to join the spokes together: no central place at which all could meet on equal terms. Now we waited for an invitation before we visited a brother, an aunt, or a cousin. There were no longer quasi-compulsory gatherings at which the attendance of all was required.

Twenty-four great-grandchildren no longer know who are their parents' cousins, their uncles and aunts, and the relatives by marriage of all of these. Their understanding of a family is limited to the half a dozen persons who make up their immediate parts of it. They may feel glad that they are not circumscribed by the boundaries of duty and convention that governed our lives, but neither do they have their support. They are free to follow which paths they please, but they are deprived of models around whom they can formulate their ideals. They may grow their hair or clothe themselves in exotic styles without fear of criticism, but pressures that might help them avoid pitfalls are also lacking. They swim in a fluid environment into which one cannot plant direction signs. We trod on floors of oak.

It was the presence and the authority of the grandparents that provided this base. Not from a retirement colony, not from a trailer camp, and not from a cruise ship, but from their own home until the end, they provided a focus for the lives of all their offspring, stability to their relationships, a sense of place and purpose for each, and a set of values, firmly upheld, that consciously or unconsciously influenced and guided all of us.

The Transmission of Learning

In the life of a medical student in Vienna between the two world wars, the figures of the professors loomed large. There was an aura about them that was almost godlike. We remember the anatomy professor.

His entry to the lecture hall was heralded by the preliminary arrival of his assistants, themselves in their late middle years. The assistants, with an almost ritual-like devotion to detail, arranged the specimens on a huge table in the center of the amphitheater of students. One of them would pull out a cloth and meticulously dust off the glass containers. Another would lay out the rubber gloves, checking and rechecking whether he had found precisely the correct place to put them. On a tray lay the dissected organ, prepared with a skill that filled the first-year medical students with awe and envy as they compared their own clumsy efforts at anatomical dissection with the perfection they saw displayed by these masterly assistants.

Upon the completion of these rights, which invariably synchronized with the ringing of the bell that announced the commencement of the session, a side door opened, admitting the senior assistant. This solemn, graying dignitary cleared his throat in a symbolic demand for attention and silence (which in any case had already fallen upon the assembled students—even a whisper would have been considered an irreverent violation of the atmosphere), he bowed slightly while holding open the swinging door, and in this moment of solemnity, the great professor walked in.

His physical presence reinforced the sense of his exalted position. His thick white hair set off his scholarly features. His lively eyes half-squintingly surveyed his fiefdom from an angle below his thick overhanging brows, yet above the equally bushy mustache. We felt their beam to be all-seeing, all-knowing. He was massive-looking and very slightly bent. Although not of great height, he gave the impression of being tall.

After several moments of silence he opened his lecture, usually with some extremely pungent remark. "Gentlemen," he would announce, blandly ignoring the presence of his many female students, "no perfection of human engineering can produce a pump like this." He would then proceed to explain the intricacies of the components of the heart. What he conveyed to us was not the information any of us could have gathered from a textbook. It was a revelation that was forever engraved on our minds like the law on the tablets of stone at Sinai. In spite of the fact that we were witness to this ritual day in and day out for a whole semester, it impressed us as forcibly on the last day as it had on the first.

Nor were any of the other professors any less impressive. If our preclinical professors were godlike, our clinical professors—of surgery, internal medicine, psychiatry, and so on—were actual occupants of Olympus in our eyes. We had a feeling of privilege at being in the presence of this circle of exalted men, as a newly ordained priest might feel in the presence of the Pope. The dignity of our preceptors rubbed off on us. From our first student year, at barely twenty years of age, we were addressed as Herr Doktor by everyone, and this radically changed the behavior we might have indulged in without the obligations we felt to be imposed by this form of address.

It should not be thought that this atmosphere was peculiar to the medical school of the University of Vienna. The professors of law at Oxford, of anthropology at London, or of literature at the Sorbonne, just to name a few, created a similar ambience. In these institutions, too, the students were addressed and treated as gentlemen or ladies. The aura given off by the dignity of the professors imparted itself to them and influenced them to identify themselves with and attempt to emulate the personalities of these ideal figures.

Without any knowledge of the presence of an alerting system in the brain (which has only recently been discovered and which, when operative, sharpens perception and makes memories indelible), all these near-modern representatives of the elderly caste had sensed, on the basis of their own experience and the wisdom they derived from it, the necessity for igniting the spark of attention in their students. In the young minds so stimulated and prepared, dry knowledge such as anatomy and law could be easily absorbed, like water soaked up by a sponge.

We cannot help but contrast these personal memories with the experiences of our own children in the United States today, especially since, from what we have learned and seen of many large universities around the world, circumstances appear to be similar or tending in the same direction in them also.

More often than not, the undergraduate student today has no exposure to instruction by a professor in the whole course of his four years of study. His courses are charted by choices from printed lists of required and optional subjects, and he is directly taught only by graduate students not much older than himself. There is no continuity, for as these graduate students complete their own requirements, they move on. The image of the permanent figure of authority is lost. Only the very dedicated student is able to take what he needs from such an arrangement, and even he is often left without inspiration or interest to continue. An esteemed person, whom he might seek to please and by whom he might be rewarded by a word of praise, is absent from his horizon. A model for his aspirations is lacking.

Just as chimpanzees have been known to learn more readily from a dominant senior than from lesser individuals, so the human young need the sight, sound, and example of a respected elder to facilitate their acquisition of knowledge. Not only in man and ape, but also in most other higher mammals and in birds, it is biologically built into the young to learn by observation of their seniors. The presence of a suitable model is a prerequisite of their ability to learn. Today's teaching methods in which younger, nonauthoritarian individuals are substituted for the respected elder negate this biological need.

Today the teacher attempts to pass on knowledge by different means. Usually he is younger, and he makes an effort to fraternize with his students. Even when he is not young, he abdicates the prerogatives of his seniority and attempts to engage the interest of his students on a basis of friendship, which implies equality. As a result, both he and the student have to work harder to give and receive the knowledge that is to be conveyed.

What is more, in the name of progress, teaching machines have been installed not only in universities but also in schools at every level from the kindergarten on. While this may simplify the transmission of knowledge to larger numbers of children, and in the case of the well-motivated child may add to his store, the ultimate result leaves much to be desired. The process of learning is further depersonalized. The knowledge the child has acquired cannot be assembled into context so readily without the presence of the teacher, who, ideally, embodies in his personality the use and place of such learning and who thus becomes an example for his pupil. As a result, the information is not organically integrated. The child or young person knows it but is not made aware of its use and application. Its value is not made apparent to him. He has no emotional connection with it.

In learning there is no true substitute for the spoken word uttered by a person who is esteemed or close. If we turn back to our own experiences, we find that much of what we read in books and found vastly interesting at the time we read it has slipped from our minds or remained only as the vaguest generality. But the knowledge that was related to us by an individual we knew and respected remains with us in all its detail. The precise words, the facial expressions, and the gestures of the person who told it remain associated in our minds with the information we received and fix it in our memories.

The brain of a human being is composed of living tissue

that responds to human interactions. It is not a computer that can automatically take up and categorize information fed into it by another machine, or even by individuals if they have no emotional impact on the learner.

CHAPTER FIVE

How We Recognize the Elderly

It is common practice to take the familiar events and sights of our daily life very much for granted. There are very few among us with sufficient curiosity to ask ourselves why any particular aspect of it is so, how or why it came to be so, or whether it is likely always to remain so. Sometimes we are surprised to find, when by chance we delve a little below surface appearances, that there are very significant reasons for what we regard as commonplaces, or that they fit into a complex larger design and fill out that greater picture, making it comprehensible.

To apply this rather abstract general thought to a concrete example, it is assumed to be a simple matter of fact that we recognize an old person when we see one. Rarely, if ever, do we ask ourselves how we do this; what are the means, the criteria that we use to make the judgment that so and so is an old person. Nor do we often, if ever, ask ourselves why we are able to recognize that old person for what he is. And yet when we think about it, we know that nothing is haphazard in nature: that if a circumstance is present, then there must be an important reason for it.

In fact, the various ways by which we know that a person is old when we see him fall into two categories, the cultural and the biological.

The cultural aspects of recognition have varied in different societies. In Victorian times an older woman marked her status by wearing a bonnet and a shawl, a man with a stiff high collar or some outward sign of substance, like a fob watch on a gold chain, or perhaps by pompous deportment. Among some African tribes, body markings convey the same message. In medieval Europe an older person wore a flowing robe rather than the leg-revealing hose and short doublet of youth. About the only general statement one could make would be that, on the whole, the clothes or ornaments that were considered suitable, or perhaps in some cases the hairstyles, were the chief outward signs of arrival at the dignity of the senior stage.

It might be thought that these cultural distinguishing marks of the elderly person are extremely superficial, and in one sense this is so, since they are largely confined to clothing or to purely cosmetic practices. And yet the fact remains that in most societies and times it has been considered appropriate for older people to wear a different style of dress from the virile segment—which, in turn, dresses differently from the immature population.

While clothing for the reproductive caste is almost universally designed to increase the sexual attractiveness of those who wear it—to enhance the beauty of the female; to emphasize the manliness of the male—that of the older person is stately in effect and seems designed to inspire respect rather than a sexual response. It drapes or hides the body. Except on ceremonial occasions it is sober in color. The expression is superficial, a mere matter of the differences in the color or drapery of fabrics over the body, but the spirit underlying the sought-for impression conveyed by these means is one of a desire to emphasize a differentiation. There is an unspoken but visually dramatized point being made. The older person is making clear by his dress that he has removed himself from the arena of sexual contest. He is no longer to be judged by the same criteria as a young person. Beauty, virility, strength of body to fight or to bear children are no longer the values for which he is to be sought. But he has other qualities to offer: wisdom, leadership, dignity; the presence or absence of these other qualities are the standards by which he should now be judged.

Basically, the biological differences that mark the older person's body are equally superficial. Those characteristics that spring to mind when we examine our mental picture of age, such as a bent back, a halting gait, tremulous hands, failing sight and hearing, loss of teeth, are actually pathological manifestations. They are signs of illnesses that are not unusual in the elderly but that do not have to occur.

The same applies to many of the other conditions that we mentally associate with old age. Forgetfulness is one. But a remarkable thing about the forgetfulness of the elderly is that it usually applies only to their short-term memories. What happened yesterday or the day before, the instruction or the message recently conveyed, and the names of recent acquaintances quickly slip from their minds. They forget where they placed their belongings, which event or tale they have just related. It is almost as though they were conscious that these things were no longer of much concern to them: as if they felt that they would not be around sufficiently long for it to be necessary to concentrate on such things or to register them in their minds.

In strong contrast, their long-term memory usually remains singularly unimpaired. All the sights and sounds, the events and personalities of their own early youth seem to be especially vivid in their recollections. Things long forgotten by their middle-aged children are recalled in precise detail, as though they had only just happened. The intricate details of family alliances and progeny and the genealogy of all its branches remain perfectly clear in their minds.

Can we not see here, in remarkable clarity, the vestiges of the purpose for which the elderly of our species were preserved by evolutionary processes? Recent events, in fact, are not the concern of the elderly. Others are present who can take note of these things and carry them to the future. The quality of their short-term memory is not important to the survival of their groups. It was not for this that natural selection preserved them. It was the long-term memory of the aged that was an advantageous factor in the survival of primitive populations, and that was the most important function by which they were able to serve. This biologically important function is preserved to the last.

There is an analogy to be found when illness strikes. In a sick person the least vital organ or function (apart from the one directly affected) is the first to be impaired. In ascending order of importance one after another succumbs. The most vital, the heart and the brain, are the last to go. And so it is with the memory of our aged. Were we not able to discover by processes of reason the chief function for which they were preserved, this fact alone might indicate it to us. The extraordinary clarity of the long-term memory of older people gives strong physical corroboration to the logical conclusion that their importance to their species lies in their services to it as bearers of knowledge bridging generations.

The loss of short-term memory, of course, is not inevitable. It is as much a sign of degeneration, or illness, as the stooped shoulders, the short breath, the stiff joints, or the tremors of limbs and failing of senses that we mentioned. These things do not have to occur. As a matter of fact, the biological signs of healthy old age are almost as superficial as the cultural ones. To a large extent they are confined to a loss of elasticity of the tissue, which causes it to sag slightly and the skin to wrinkle over it, and to a loss or thinning of the hair of the head, especially in some men, or to a loss of the pigmentation of the hair.

How superficial these visible marks of age are can be readily appraised when we see how easily they can be eradicated.

A comparatively minor tightening of the skin by plastic surgery and a visit to a hairdresser for restoration of hair color or for a toupee are all it takes for the impression of decades to be removed from the appearance of a man or a woman. Many people whose professions require them to retain an appearance of youth, as, for instance, entertainers, give the impression of being ageless by just such easily obtained services or devices. The facility of the transformation makes it abundantly clear that the biological marks of age are indeed almost as superficial as the cultural ones.

This superficiality of the visible signs of age reminds us strikingly of the caste markings of most animals. The special features of the immature of many species separate them from the mature so as to afford ready identification. Partly this is due to growth, but there are other characteristics. The fur of young mammals is usually fluffier, the feathers of nestling birds downier, and the colors or the fur or down are different, usually less bright than in the adult. Among mature animals special colors, markings, or size differentiates the male and the female. This probably is most easily observable in birds, where such markings have proved to be of great value to their groups as a whole even though there seems to be no particular advantage to the individuals.

To show the way these markings or different forms or features in the different classes serve the group as a whole, let us take as an example the black-headed gulls. Some characteristics of their plumage allow recognition of all members of the species, regardless of their age or condition. Besides this, some other features distinguish young birds, while a further set of markings identifies those fully grown but not at a stage of readiness for breeding. The mature adults, in the period of the year when they are ready to mate, are marked by dark-brown feathers like caps over their heads. These marks and features divide the birds into three visually identifiable classes within the group as a whole: the young, the asexual adults, and the mature adults. In their winter migrations all these birds have to be taken into account, and the characteristics that make them recognizable as a species facilitate their ready recognition of each other on their long journey and at their winter nesting places. At breeding times the mature birds do not have to consider any except each other, and they are of the greatest importance to the group as a whole. At other times the young may need and may be given special attention, especially if the group is uncrowded and food plentiful. If the opposite is the case and the group overpopulated, the juveniles and the asexual adults, too, may be treated as expendable. The external markings thus assist the group to regulate itself in the best interest of the whole community, and they therefore aid its evolutionary survival.

Important as they are, however, many of the caste marks found throughout the animal world are indeed superficial. They consist as often as not of a redistribution, or a variation of distribution, of pigment, manifested by bands or patches of color. (Some of the more dramatic features that distinguish male animals have been evolved more as display features for social competition than as caste marks alone.)

This would bring us back to white hair and other signs of age in man. These may perhaps, as V. C. Wynne-Edwards has suggested, also be viewed as caste marks that serve evolutionary purposes. There is no inherent reason why the pigmentation should disappear from the hair of the head in old age. The hair of the eyelashes and eyebrows often remains dark until the end of life. Apparently this form of caste marking served a useful purpose from an evolutionary point of view in man as well as in other animals, and so it was established by processes of natural selection.

It may be more than just a coincidence that the appearance of white hair in certain places, leaving others still dark, frequently coincides with the waning of the reproductive function. What would appear to be a purely arbitrary patch-work surely must reveal the operation of a purposeful mechanism. Among the forerunners of modern man the appearance of an elder, marked perhaps by a bib of white hair on the chest and a white-capped head, would certainly have lent a special air to his presence.

It could well be that a whole head of white hair is a comparatively late development, since the stage of postreproductive old age itself appeared late in our race history. Since nothing appears suddenly on the evolutionary scene, it is perfectly feasible that bands or patches of white hair served as identification for the elderly in such of our forebears as perhaps Cro-Magnon and Neanderthal man. Not infrequently we see even today the so-called *mèche blanche*, or white streak of hair, from the center of the forehead in men and women barely into their forties—that could have been the time of life at which our earlier forebears began to age. Moreover, the whitening of the hair usually does not appear uniformly all over the head but follows a certain pattern. It begins to gray at the temples and then in the center of the forehead, only later becoming white all over.

This may very well be the pattern of an earlier marking. It is not difficult to imagine that Cro-Magnon, Neanderthal, or some other race of early man, reaching their senescent stage, were marked by magnificent streaks of white hair at the temples and in the middle of their heads, the rest of the hair remaining dark. This dark and white striping could have made a striking identifying mark. We ourselves are rather fond of this idea, but of course it is pure speculation. We offer it to the many illustrators who have depicted the early races of man as uniformly dark!

Another feature that is open to interpretation as possibly a caste marking is the more luxuriant growth of hair in specific places in many elders. It is not unusual to see thick hair growth in old men in and around the earlobes and in old women on the face that was not present—or only present to a lesser degree—in their younger years. The hair on the face of elderly women has been associated with a diminished production of the female hormones that are presumed to inhibit it during their fertile years, but that on the ears of men has not received much attention. Pursuing the line of thought that because of natural selection no feature arises and persists unless it serves a purpose, could it not be that perhaps these hirsute adornments also constitute in part a caste marking of the elderly, no matter what the mechanism that promotes them?

It goes without saying that the relationship between the end of the reproductive period and the slowing down of the deposit of pigment or the increased luxuriance of hair in certain areas in some cases is not simple. Many factors are involved, and great variation is present between individuals.

While for the female of our species there is a well-defined end to her reproductive function, this is not so for the male. This would appear to have arisen to prevent an overproduction of offspring, since, in the final analysis, it is the sum of the number of reproductive years of the females that governs the number of offspring produced by a population. Perhaps one can account for the indefinite prolongation of the generative capacity of the human male by the need of the group to have a reserve to compensate for the greater attrition of the male in the pursuits of hunting and warfare. Whatever were the causes that produced the end results we now see, it must have been a matter of importance to the breeding groups of man to make readily identifiable those who lived beyond their optimum reproductive years and slowly came to create the new class.

The fact that this new class came into being (that is, that men and women lived longer) and the fact that they were distinctively marked by evolutionary processes should indicate to us the importance of the presence and functions of the aged to the development of man.

This realization should make us all pause for thought and for much consideration of the trend of the course our modern societies are taking.

CHAPTER SIX

Why Old Age Has Lost Its Value to Society

The Importance of Communication for All Animals,
Especially Group Animals

When we were in Sydney, Australia, we had an experience that beautifully illustrates our theme. We went there in the summer of 1968, primarily to attend a conference connected with the work of the World Health Organization, but also to collect what information we could about the surviving customs of the aborigines before they became totally submerged in the dominant culture and lost.

We were very fortunate to make the acquaintance of Dr. John Cawte while we were there. Dr. Cawte was a professor of child psychiatry, but his special personal interest was in transcultural psychiatry, and he spent all his long vacations and sabbatical time on fieldwork among the tribes of the islands off Darwin, in the north of Australia.

One evening while we enjoyed dinner with Dr. Cawte and his family in their home, filled with artifacts, photographs, and mementos of his field trips, he told us about the seasonal celebrations of an island tribe. These are observed by holding songfests at which the stories and myths of the people are recounted in songs and chants to the accompaniment of music for days on end. He had recorded these celebrations on tape, and we spent the rest of the evening listening to them and looking through the photographs he had taken of the participants so that we had a vivid visual and aural impression of the event.

From childhood on, each new generation of the tribe hears and learns these sagas from its elders, participates in the celebrations when its members come of age, and preserves them in their memories and passes them on to others when they are old. These tribes have no written history. The record of their past is transmitted orally at these festivals, and the feat of memory that enables the singers to continue their narratives for several days is little short of remarkable.

Before man mastered the arts of written communication in its various forms, all knowledge—whether of the past of the tribal groups or the deeds of its heroes, of its customs, its religious and secular traditions, its skills in the ways of sustaining life, its arts, and its superstitions—was passed on in this or very similar ways. The earliest historical documents of most peoples refer to still earlier oral traditions—the Bible is a monument to this.

As a matter of fact, one survival of this oral tradition is still very much alive in the Seder ceremony of the Jewish Passover. On that occasion, which yearly celebrates the escape of the ancient Israelites from their bondage in Egypt, it is the custom for all the members of a household to gather together and for the youngest child present to ask four questions about the occasion. For the rest of the evening the head of the household answers him. He and the senior members of the family recount the story of the Exodus, reciting the events and interspersing the recitation with songs of praise and thanks to God for the salvation of the people. This is followed by a joyous and festive meal in which many symbolic foods play an essential role, and after grace, many traditional folk songs are sung by everyone together. Here, indeed, is a perfect example, still with us, of one generation verbally transmitting the history of a people to the next, year after year and century after century.

And then again, still today in many an Arabian souk in North African countries, we have seen storytellers surrounded by large crowds of intent listeners. They are probably the last representatives of the caste of professional tellers of tales left in the Western world, and their importance lies in the fact that their audiences are largely illiterate. Unable to read novels or tales of folk heroes, the listeners find in the storytellers a major source of interest and entertainment.

The illiterate in our own societies—that is, our preschool children—also relied on parents and grandparents to tell them stories, and these enlarged their view and understanding of the world until the television screen vied for their attention and largely replaced their elders as a source of entertainment and as a peephole into the outer world.

A modern little scene that we all can recognize is of grandparents who go to visit their grandchildren. They want to be with them, to enjoy their chatter, to get to know them, and to be a part of their lives. They look forward to the visit all week, and they bring small gifts for the children with them.

The mother goes into the children's room and tells them, "Grandma and Grandpa are here," expecting them to respond with pleasure. But as often as not, she is rebuffed: "Please wait a minute. I just want to finish seeing this program." When the children's reluctant attention is finally brought to the grandparents, they are excited for a while over the presents, but later, instead of begging them, "Tell me a story," as the elders probably begged their own grandparents in their time, the young ones now find it difficult to wait until they can get back to their television set.

Surely in prehistoric times some elders in some areas must have become aware of the precariousness of maintaining the perpetuation of tribal information only in the memories of their kind, particularly when times of warfare, disease, or

89

drought rendered life a matter of chance. Or perhaps in the course of explaining some special instruction or illustrating some point of a tale, it might have occurred to one or another to draw a diagram in the soil—as we ourselves once had information conveyed to us in the absence of a mutual language on our travels in the province of Jalisco. At that time, lost on a jungle trail, we encountered a grizzled and wizened ancient. He was engaged in opening shellfish, obviously from the shore to which we could not find our way. An Indian, his knowledge of Spanish was slight, but when he understood our query, he quite spontaneously took up a stick and indicated our direction in the dried mud outside his thatched shelter. It struck us then that perhaps such an impulse was the original seed that eventually grew into such sophisticated art forms as the currently much-admired Navajo sand paintings. Perhaps some such practice, or a habit of making a trail mark on the trunks of trees with a sharp rock, may have given rise among primitive men to the idea of making such signs more permanent by engraving them into stone.

By whatever means hieroglyphic writing arose, whether in this or some other way, even when it became codified into a transmittable system it was still at the disposal only of an elite caste of priests, scribes, or learned men by their attainments necessarily drawn from the elders of their groups. Thus not merely the spoken record but also the earliest written records probably were in the hands of the elders and also served their interest and power.

This held true from the times of the earliest tracings on the walls of caves, through those of engravings on blocks of stone and on the walls of tombs or monuments, to those of the discovery of ways to produce papyrus, parchment, and paper that were found to serve as more convenient storage places for the written word.

But even the great writings of the peoples of the ancient Near East, China, and the Indian subcontinent, and of those of Greece and Rome did not eliminate the need for the elderly as remitters of information, for by far the greatest part of these and all other populations was illiterate and unable to make use of those records as sources of knowledge.

Even after the invention of the movable-type printing press toward the end of the Middle Ages, the usefulness of its production was still limited to a very few scholars among each people and to the clergy. Literacy was limited to the ruling classes, and in practice only to a small percentage even of these. Many kings and nobles in all countries depended on their scribes to record their commands and to read to them the communications they received. It was not until the middle of the last century, when the Industrial Revolution and the ensuing technology created a need for a larger number of literate individuals, that education became more general. Universal education became an ideal only in our own century that even now is barely being realized.

It can be seen that throughout the ages, from the earliest beginnings of man right up until our own time, the elderly in our societies held a very important role as upholders and transmitters of culture to the masses. Only in our own times do we find ourselves in the midst of a great change in this facet of our lives.

What, in fact, is the essence of communication?

Communication is more than the simple passing of information from one person to another. Besides this very important ingredient of it, which is the content, there are two others: the method by which the information is conveyed, and the interaction between the giver and the receiver of it.

Wherever group animals exist, communication is a vital necessity. Throughout the animal kingdom information is conveyed by signals of all kinds, utilizing every sense known to man and probably some still unknown by him. As we have said, variations in bodily coloration give vital information in all branches of the animal world. Among invertebrates, fishes, and terrestrial vertebrates of many kinds, such visual signals inform the group of the condition of its individuals as regards the important events of life. Olfactory markings, also extensively used, constitute a more flexible language. Through the giving off of odors and the understanding in their own way of their significance, very many animals are informed of the presence and condition of their fellows and are also warned or invited. Anyone who has a dog as a pet and walks it in the city streets can see how it investigates its surroundings with its nose: how it gathers "news" of the other dogs of its neighborhood by sniffing at the spots where they have left their scent, and how it deposits small amounts of urine on a number of special or favorite places that become, for it, some kind of bulletin boards by which it announces its presence and condition to the rest of the dog population of its area.

Probably still more flexible are the vocal and other sound signals that are also used throughout all the varieties of life excepting only the most primitive. Since we have mentioned the dogs' reception of information by olfactory means and their conveyance of news by chemical ones—which naturally applies to their close relatives, the wolves, as well—we might add here that wolves regularly make their presence known to each other over very great distances by howling (or baying or, as some prefer to call it, singing). Recently a recording of choruses of wolves was made that proved to be very popular. On it one can hear their voices calling, being picked up, and answered and joined by others, while the meanings of their calls are interpreted by the naturalist who recorded them. It might be said that the urine-marked posts are the wolves' equivalent of a local letter that they read with their noses rather than their eyes, while their howling is a kind of bush telegraph: And this brings to mind that the voices of whales —which communicate similarly over great distances—were also recorded and then incorporated into the music of Hovhaness' symphonic work *The Great Whales.*

The communications by sound of all kinds of animals are mostly familiar to us, whether they are the voices of mammals or birds, amphibia or fish, or the special sounds emitted by insects by all kinds of means. But besides these almost universal means of communication there are others more narrowly confined to certain species. These include messages conveyed by tactile means; by ultrasonic impulses; by electrical charges; by the understanding of cues afforded by infrared or ultraviolet or polarized light; by geomagnetic and barometric changes; by changes in concentration of certain gases in the air; and probably by other means not yet discovered or uncoded by man.

In our own line, beginning with ancestral primates and increasingly as man specialized into a separate species, olfactory communication became less important and sight and sound signals became the chief means by which communication was made.

Ability to pass on knowledge is a factor in man's longer life. As man emerged, the type of communication that became important for his special needs differed, if not basically in kind, at least in degree, from the types of communication we have just summarized. All these messages are largely concerned with indicating biological states or condition, with warnings of danger or invitations to breed, and with awareness of direction for locating food or home. Instruction in skills among higher animals is largely obtained by observation and by trial and error and practice in play. In man, for the first time, instruction in skills and values could be given verbally, suggestions offered, and corrections made without the necessity of evolving biologically conditioned and imbedded responses by means of natural selection over many generations. In man, natural selection preserved those groups that were best able to communicate their knowledge

93

and experience verbally. All the forces of natural selection in man have been directed toward the development of his three stages. The first is his prolonged childhood in which the young can learn, increasingly utilizing the capacities of the enlarged brain. The second is the prime of life phase in which mature individuals reproduce, sustain, and defend their kind. The third stage is an old age for the accumulation and transmission of the wisdom of the group.

This brings us back to the nature of the three components of the communication itself.

The Content

The content was largely concerned with the perpetuation of customs, with tales of heroes, and with the passing on of practical information. It is hardly possible to exaggerate the importance of these areas of knowledge to the ability of the group as a whole to survive, and therefore it is not surprising that the evolution of an elderly caste became a special feature of the development of man.

The perpetuation of custom is the main factor in the stability of any group. Within a framework of custom and convention individuals are trained for and accept certain responsibilities in the life of their community; social order is established; the efficient are rewarded and preserved; and the inefficient identified and slowly weeded out. Custom and convention are not purely human practices. Very many animal societies recognize certain conventional forms and practice certain customs. All that is specifically human about these is that among us they largely depend on a verbal or written tradition for their perpetuation.

The tales of heroes told by the elderly in most primitive groups likewise served many invaluable purposes. In the first place they set up criteria—standards by which the young

94

could evaluate their own efforts. The heroes became models for the young. They incorporated the values of the group. They indicated what was or should be possible of achievement. Beyond this they gave the group a sense of continuity. Tales of heroes were the earliest form of history. They acted as a cohesive force, for a common identity with or relationship to such superbeings tied the individuals in a common bond. The identification of each individual with the hero united him with the rest of his group.

Any parent will recognize the importance of this sense of identification with and place in a group or line to a developing human being in the questions most of us are confronted —even pestered—with by our very young children. They cannot be told often enough stories of their own earlier childhood. They want to know what they were like when they were babies. They demand information about what their parents, aunts and uncles, older brothers and sisters were like when they were young like themselves. They find it incredible to learn that their parents and grandparents *ever* were young. They want to know in which way each person they meet is related to them. They never tire of these stories and ask to be told them again and again. Besides this, nursery songs, poems, and tales read to them become part of their lives, treasured in their memories, and, when they grow up, repeated undeviatingly to their own children and grandchildren. These songs and tales create the child's first picture of what happens in the world outside its own experience, enlarge its horizon, enrich its imagination, and are the first steps in its education for life. Such must also have been the case with the tales told by the old in the communities of our earliest ancestors. Is it surprising that accounts of tribal lore were incorporated into religious rites, repeated seasonally, revered, and never tired of?

The third type of ingredient of the content of communication is the passing on of practical information. The value of much of this does not have to be spelled out. The telling of how to fashion and use tools, the passing on of knowledge of the habits of animals that must be hunted, or of herbs and extracts that are useful or poisonous, of methods of raising plants, of ways to obtain shelter, to make clothing, to prepare foodstuffs—all are plainly of inestimable survival value to any group. But there is another kind of practical information that we might not immediately recognize as such. It consists of the accumulated endeavors of generations of man to account for things—to find reasons for what happens.

In the earliest days our forerunners accounted for the vagaries of the world around them by imagining each part of it to be endowed with a spirit, something like their consciousness of their own personal essence. They taught their young of these spirits and of how to keep them benevolent— on their side, so to speak, and not hostile. Such rites of propitiation became formulated into religious beliefs that slowly and in time incorporated the ideals of the group into codes of ethics considered pleasing to the spirits.

These attempts to account for the world around them were the beginnings of science. As understanding increased, horizons expanded. Less was thought to be due to the seemingly arbitrary moods of spirits or gods, and more was comprehended as part of a natural order. Religions became expressions of praise of this order and gratitude for its bounty as well as roads to reward and favor. Slowly trial and error methods, experiment rather than intuitive feeling became the keys to expanding knowledge and understanding, and these, too, were passed on from generation to generation by the elderly.

In this area, too, we see in the insatiable curiosity and questioning about the nature of things and how they work that are familiar to us in every child a reenactment of the earliest beginnings of the means to understanding as it was pursued by our species.

The Method

In the method of communication, as in its content, it goes without saying that there was a continuity from its animal origins. Nothing arises spontaneously and complete, and whatever we now recognize as human speech and gesture certainly came into being as a slow development from earlier signal sounds and movements.

In its earliest form, human communication was direct. It was conveyed from person to person by speech and gesture, later sometimes reinforced by the accompaniment of music, rhythm, and dance. In this it was not too different from some of the methods of communication of other animal species.

The first step away from this pattern was the written symbol, although even this is basically not too different, on a mechanical level, from the marks made by bears or large cats on the trunks of trees to mark territory or to inform others of their presence, and other signals of this kind made by other species. When the written symbol began to express coherent thought, however, the paths diverged. As these symbols became refined into the more economical forms of hieroglyphic writing and then still further into symbols for the sounds of human speech, the necessity arose for a caste to be trained in the production and understanding of them. In fact, one or more persons in each social group would have had to be assigned the tasks of writing and reading and especially trained to perform them. What more natural than that those who were weak, sick, or elderly, and therefore unable to participate in the more urgent business of hunting or warfare or the care of the young and the gathering of food, should be assigned these tasks, and in view of the priestly and storytelling roles of the elderly, who more fitted?

With certain expansions or contractions in the numbers and classes of persons so employed in various societies in different times, these conditions remained more or less in effect until the medieval era, when the invention of the printing press facilitated the extension of literacy. The printing press was the first major change in the method of conveying information since the time of the first symbols in the sand or engravings on the walls of caves. In enabling an increase in the numbers of the literate it also influenced the content of the knowledge conveyed, since this could now be directed to a wider audience. Moreover, the purely mechanical aspects of setting down the word could now be relegated to a young apprentice. So crucial is this development to our theme that we shall come back to it again toward the end of this chapter.

Not until within the memory of many of us living today were any further technical advances in communication made. Now they come upon us thick and fast.

The Interaction: The Value of Personal Presence and Example in Reinforcing Other Kinds of Communication

When any person tells a story to another, much more passes between them than the actual meaning of the words spoken. Gestures and facial expressions, the tone of voice, and significant pauses or the speeding of words all convey nuances. The personality of the speaker leaves an imprint on the mind of the hearer. When a child listens to stories, to the answers to its questions, or to explanations of the ways in which things may be done, as told by its parent, there is a further element present. The child develops some admiration for this omniscient being. He learns the beginnings of respect.

One of us recalls, when her child was small, a rather amusing conversation that took place between her then very young son and her mother, who was visiting him. As the grandmother reported it, she was surprised that he should have known some piece of information that he offered and asked him where he had learned it. "Mummy told me," he said, "Mummy knows a lot of things." After a reflective pause he added, "There's only one person who knows more than Mummy, and that's God. He knows everything!"

Besides the actual information he had gained, this child had absorbed something more. He had learned that an older person had a store of knowledge upon which he could draw, and he respected and stood in some awe of that person. The anecdote affords a simple illustration of the feelings that the younger members of the groups of early man probably had for the seemingly omniscient elders among them.

The personal conveyance of information adds extra dimension to its value. The words alone form the outline of a picture in the hearer's mind. The manner and personality of the teller, his or her authority, the substance of what he chooses to tell—for, after all, every speaker is his own editor —fill in the colors and make the picture whole and real to the listener. What is more, a speaker may be questioned. A point not fully understood may be rephrased and explained. He may be asked to repeat a story, and he may embellish it a little differently in each telling.

The personal quality of the relationship between the teller of a tale, or the bearer of knowledge, and the recipient of it laid a groundwork for that element of respect for the elder that was the cement of the social fabric throughout the history of the development of man, and, as we have noted, the quality of respect is the equivalent in humans of the factor we describe as "dominance" in other animals. It is the instrument by which social order is attained, and its presence is of paramount importance to the stability of any group.

With the advent of the written word something of this extra dimension of communication is removed. The limitations of the written language do not allow the richness of texture possible in the spoken word of the storyteller. The child is the immediate loser, but all of society eventually loses by this change.

No child can model itself entirely on the printed page.

Certainly it can and does draw ideas from it, but unless these ideas can be hung, as it were, upon a living person, they remain unreal. They become the bases of fantasies that do not have the value of flesh-and-blood models. The printed word is only a representation of reality, not life itself. It is a little analogous to the cloth mother that was offered to young chimpanzees in a well-known experiment.

Investigators, wanting to determine the actual degree of the influence of the mother on her young, devised an experiment in which some mother-infant family groups of these apes were left in their natural relationship. Some other young chimps were raised with dummy mothers made of cloth but provided mechanically with an ability to feed them; still others with only a form of wire frame, also equipped with mechanical devices for feeding them. It was found that these last, although sufficiently fed, grew into neurotic adults, totally unable to mingle socially with their own kind. They were withdrawn. They huddled in the corners of their cages, clasping themselves in their arms and rocking back and forth. Later they were either unable to mate at all or, if mated, unable to raise young of their own. They had had no models upon which to base their behavior. The young brought up with the cloth mothers did a little better. The comfort and warmth of the fabric apparently were of some help in more normal emotional development, but still even these did not know how to behave when they were placed with other chimpanzees and were unable to mingle with them in normal social contact. Some of these, which were admitted for only as little as an hour a day into the presence of other young apes but not with elders, were able to make an adjustment to social life later on, but only those raised by their natural mothers attained normal social development.

It is well known that human children, too, in their games imitate the adults they see around them, but perhaps it is not so widely recognized how important a part in their development this imitation plays. We recall some examples that have struck us in our personal experiences.

Once, on a hiking vacation in the mountains of northern Montana, the outfitter for our party had employed a group of wranglers who tended and guided, loaded and unloaded the packhorses that carried the gear to each night's campsite, and who were all members of one family. They were a father and three of his sons, ages seventeen, fourteen, and ten. The ten-year-old had taken the place of an older brother who had had an accident. There was no doubt whatever as to the model each of these boys had taken for his own life. They obeyed their father implicitly and efficiently in his presence, and in his absence performed their duties exactly as if he were there. They took pride in the expert handling of their horses. The youngest was no less efficient than his older brothers. None of them shirked, or even protested, any arduous task. Each seemed bent upon proving himself to be as good a man as his father. And yet in the evenings, when their tasks were completed and they were off duty, they played around as any other young fellows do and were as full of fun. There was nothing unduly serious or prematurely old about any of them. But with the sturdy and capable example of their father in front of them all the time, they had picked up and absorbed his ways and made them their own. In fact, it was amusing to watch how, even in the way they walked and talked, each of them was the "spitting image" of his father. It seemed clear to us that they were going to become responsible members of their community and eventually heads of families of the most desirable type, who would be able in their turn to convey their skills and attitudes by example to their own children.

We had a similar experience in Mexico, where we watched young *charros* of not more than twelve or thirteen imitating every gesture of their fathers and hardly less capable than they in roping calves, putting their horses through intricate paces, and practicing bringing down bulls. The elders did not have to instruct them to do any of these things. The admiration aroused in the young boys by the skills of their seniors was sufficient incentive to goad them to strenuous practice in their attempts to emulate them.

Of course, the propensity of children to model themselves on their parents may sometimes backfire when an example is not so desirable. In the outskirts of Bergen we once saw three small blond Norwegian boys, whose fathers were apparently pipe smokers. They were squatting under a tree and filling clay pipes, of the type given to children for blowing bubbles, with the loose dust they scooped up there. Then they blew through them so that it looked very much like smoke, except that it eventually settled on their faces in grimy masks that almost covered their fair skins and hair. Even though the results of their play were not as desirable as the other examples, the action of these children clearly showed their desire and their natural bent to emulate the living examples they had in their fathers or grandfathers.

We do not wish to overstate our case. The printed word *can* inspire the older child who has already been imbued with the reality of living models. It is the as yet illiterate preschool child who receives the deepest impression from the physical presence of the purveyor of information, but we cannot exclude this factor even in the older child's or young person's ability to learn.

The Prime Culprit

A pebble thrown into a lake sends ripples over its surface long after the pebble has sunk. A person standing on a distant shore may watch a wavelet ride up its banks but cannot tell what impelled it. He sees only an end result. The evidence of what caused it is no longer apparent.

An older person today, feeling himself being displaced by his community—becoming a peripheral animal in its social order—would be hard put to recognize the distant invention of the printing press as the prime culprit for his present discomfort. Not for the first time or for the last has an invention of man, acclaimed as purely beneficial, turned out to have consequences far from beneficial to individuals in times and in areas of activity remote from those that initiated the departure.

The invention of printing from movable type was preceded by printing from blocks. In both styles, the Chinese were the first printers. The earliest known block book was printed by Wang Chieh in the province of Kansu in the year 868. The first printing from movable type was done by Pi Sheng in the years 1041 to 1049.

Popular opinion credits the independent invention of the printing press in Europe in the middle of the fifteenth century to Johann Gutenberg, of Germany, whose Bible is accepted as the first book printed there from movable type, but there is no certainty about the actual originator. Holland, France, and Italy also have claimants to the honor. Like many ideas for which the time is ripe, it seems to have occurred to several men in several places.

The first documents so far as we know were letters of indulgence, and so, in its earliest stage, the printed word remained primarily at the service of the clergy. It is ironical that the church, traditionally led by elders, was the first patron of this new instrument that eventually dislodged the keystone supporting the structure of the power of their caste.

The pioneers were wandering printers, and the work they produced was in Latin. It was England's first printer, William Caxton, who was the first to print in his own language, who translated much of the material he used, and who used a typeface of a design easier to read by the laity than the Gothic or Roman of the Continental printers. Thus it might be said that it was Caxton who cast the first pebble into the pond that eventually brought the resources of the printed word to the masses of people. It took more than four hundred years before the effects of the outermost ripple were felt in our societies. Who knows what the distant and ultimate effects may be of our present trend toward the substitution of work by leisure? The advancing of the age of retirement, the shortening of the workday and the workweek, as well as the shortening of the working life, may have eventual consequences as unforeseen by us as the establishment of retirement colonies for the elderly could have been by the originators of the printing press.

The Information Explosion

The personal interchange of the spoken word had sufficed man's needs for thousands of years before the written symbol supplemented it. Written, carved, or painted records then served him for thousands of years more. The printed word took several hundred years to become well established and available to all and had hardly become so when, in the last century, technical innovations again speeded the pace and altered the character of human communication. The first, if we exclude the famous Rothschild carrier pigeon, were the telephone and the telegraph.

The telephone carried the voice, but the absence of the physical presence of the conversers removed the visual, or nonverbal, cues. The telegraph removed the voice, the sense of an individual's hand to paper, the personality of his handwriting, and introduced a new abbreviated and impersonal form of language. While the absence of personal contact removed the element of intimacy from exchanges of information, nevertheless their convenience, greater speed, and the elimination of the need to travel proved to be so advantageous as to foster their use in an increasingly technological society.

The storyteller, already in a small degree displaced by books, a little later found his role still further reduced by the advent of motion pictures. Radio replaced the town crier more completely than the institution of the daily newspaper had been able to do. Very soon afterward not only the voices but also the memories of the elderly rapidly became more and more superfluous.

With wider education the resources of information stored in the world's great libraries became available to increasing numbers of its citizens. Lesser municipal and local libraries were added to the treasuries of stored information. More recently, electronic and photographic devices have further increased exponentially the hoard of knowledge available without the intermediary of a living memory. The long-term memory of the elderly has ceased to have significant value to the communities in which they live. Photographs, film, records, microfilm, and electronic tape record events as they happen and are stored for future reference. Computers sort out the records and produce the information needed at the touch of a lever. The current mechanization, computerization, and vastly increased capacity for the storage of recorded information, beyond the capacity of a human mind to carry, render it available to anyone who asks for it, depriving the elderly of this ancient function.

It is not merely a question of the immense scale of modern storage and orderly filing of knowledge. In recent times there has also been an increase in its dissemination so unprecedented that it has been called an information explosion. No event of any kind of general interest can take place any longer in any part of the world without the news of it being available via the most sophisticated methods of modern technology and within the space of a few hours in almost every other part of the globe.

105

Nor is it the news alone that is conveyed. Professional analysts of the daily scene fill in background information, discuss the significance of the events, and interpret them in terms that every person can understand. Not only words but also photographs of the occurrences as they happen are transmitted over the airwaves, enabling every person to be an eyewitness of the scene and to judge it for himself. This area—at least the transmission of knowledge, the memory of events, and wisdom gained in the course of accumulating experience—has been entirely withdrawn as a function from the elderly caste.

Well past the stage of transition as we are today in the most technologically advanced societies, we still have some vestiges remaining in our social structure of roles traditionally filled by the older persons among us—although even in these there has been considerable erosion.

It is not coincidence that the areas of modern life that are the last bastions still providing position and influence for the elderly are those that they occupied originally in primitive tribal groups.

In spite of all-pervading cultural changes, there is still no age limit even now for Senators, clergy, doctors, or presidents of universities, although in the United States and especially in England there has recently been discussion about this. In the last category, much younger people than usual have been appointed. Similarly, as we noted that in the body the most important functions appear first and remain operative to the last, so the last remaining social roles of the elderly reflect the first for which they were selected.

The functions now performed by the leaders of church and government were originally combined in the persons of tribal chiefs. The profession of healing was an offshoot of the religious function, and the profession of teaching an offshoot of the role of the seniors in every family unit. The opportunity for elders to take their places in these roles is now waning in reverse order. Teaching, as we have discussed, is succumbing to youth and technology. In the practice of medicine many prefer the services of physicians who are not elderly, feeling that those a little younger may be more up to date in their knowledge.

Still meeting the approval of all is the presence of elders in the Papacy and at the head of most religions, and in the senates of the world. So far no one has suggested that a Pope, a prelate, or a Senator resign on account of his age, although there have lately been challenges to the seniority system in Congressional committees. These are very important roles, certainly no less vital to a group's well-being than leadership in business or other social areas. One would think they would be subject to compulsory retirement on at least the same levels and for the same reasons: to assure the vigor of new blood in the conduct of those offices, and to permit the promotion of younger aspirants for power and influence. But it is not the case. Apparently the human mind is so attuned to the occupancy of these roles by elders that it would appear unseemly for them to be held by younger persons.

But in all other areas of daily life our elders have become, or are rapidly becoming, functionless. Even though they may not actually realize the root causes, they themselves sense this. For this reason, many are themselves removing their caste marks. They engage in exercise to stay bodily fit. They diet. They dye their hair. Without fully realizing what they are doing, in fact, they are attempting to retain the marks of the prime-of-life stage in a kind of self-defense, to prevent themselves from being eliminated from their societies.

The effects of this development branch out into every phase of our lives. We are only now and slowly beginning to perceive how disruptive such consequences have been of old-established patterns and how instrumental they are in enforcing rearrangements of our social organization. We are in the midst of these changes, and they are being felt by all sectors, from the oldest of us, whom they affect the most directly, to the youngest, who is equally affected, if indirectly.

There have been times in the history of the world when populations have been far poorer than they are now. There have been times of famine, of plague, of warfare, and of all kinds of social disruption, but throughout all of these each individual knew his place within his group and the function that attended it. In our modern societies, for the first time, this firm base of each of our lives no longer exists.

Part Two

CONSEQUENCES

CHAPTER SEVEN

Introduction

When we are in the middle of a development that we regard as an achievement of human progress, we are conscious only of its benefits and cannot see its ultimate consequences. Any resident of Mexico City today, for example, busily engaged in the bustling activity of the city, proud of its sevenfold increase in numbers in the past thirty years, its fine new buildings, its beautiful parks, and its improved social services, justifiably regards his surroundings with a good deal of satisfaction. It is only the visitor, less influenced by the progress of its material life and who will probably take a day to visit the ruins of the ancient pyramids of Teotihuacán outside the city, who from that distance will see with some horror the smoggy atmosphere lying like a pall over the once sunny capital and experience the still sunny skies of its environs being blocked out as he returns to it. The city's "progress" is exacting its price in the quality of the air its citizens breathe, in the color of the skies they now see and accept without thinking of it. The price will be higher as lung and respiratory tract diseases increase. But to the individual living his daily life in the city none of these consequences is yet apparent.

When we see these things, which are now clear to us, we must wonder whether some of the difficulties we are experiencing in our own lives are not unforeseen results of the upsetting of the social equilibrium by our own practices, in a

111

similar way that the chain of animal life has been disrupted and the quality of the air and waters of the environment sullied, albeit unintentionally, by our technical "progress."

Even when we are aware that anything we do may have undesired consequences, it is still very hard to visualize what they might ultimately be, particularly when we are a part of an ongoing development or existing condition and see benefits and conveniences in them. Neither Gutenberg nor Caxton, nor any of their contemporaries could possibly have foreseen, when they devised and built their printing presses, that within a few short centuries they would by their efforts have displaced an entire segment of the human population from its social niche.

Unlike the progress of nature, which proceeds so slowly and by such short steps that each millimeter of the way has time to be accommodated by adjustments in all the lives affected by them, the progress of cultural development is so fast that it can only be described as jet-propelled in comparison. At the evolutionary equivalent of supersonic speed we have disturbed the equilibrium of the human life cycle and given no time for satisfactory adjustments to have been evolved along the way. This of necessity must have far-reaching consequences in all areas of human life—in our minds as well as in our bodies and, by extension, in our social life at large. The disruption ultimately affects every one of us, not only those who are the prime victims of it.

A society, after all, is a living organism. When any segment of a society is deprived of its function, it becomes a useless appendage to that organism. Wherever we look in nature, we find that no useless appendage remains for long in the good condition it was in when it performed a necessary function. Useless, it deteriorates or withers away. Sometimes it becomes a source of malfunction to the organism that harbors it.

When we read our daily papers or even look around us at

the local scene, it is apparent that people are beginning to realize that the position of the elderly in our society is a source of malaise. Very few people have yet pinned down in their minds the exact cause of the situation, but they see that the present provisions, if any, for the retirement age group are not satisfactory. Many well-intentioned researches have been undertaken and commissions have been established to determine what can be done to remedy the condition. What has not been done, and what we believe to be most necessary, is to recognize the distant causes as well as the present consequences that are becoming apparent to all. We are convinced that only when our planners recognize those primary causes will they be able to initiate programs that will have some chance of remedying the situation in any fundamental way.

Man appears to have a phenomenal capacity for adaptation. His body can adjust to life on the highest mountain or below sea level, to tropical jungle or to arid desert. For all that or perhaps because of it, we are inclined to sidestep the consideration of his mental adjustment. This may be because of its very great variability from person to person or because of the difficulty in defining exactly what is the essence of the ability to adapt. And then, how reliable is the information we can gather when one person is able to talk freely about what troubles him, whereas another plays down his difficulties and a third exaggerates them? But while it is difficult to give an exact weight to each of the causes, we all are aware that there are noticeable consequences when enforced changes alter a person's way of life.

From these consequences we are then sometimes able to infer the causes that precipitated them, but only by hindsight. At the time no one gives thought, or even wants to give thought, to what could ensue as a result of any change of circumstance. In short, because man is able to adapt physically to almost any environment, it does not follow that he can adjust equally well mentally.

It is not only the elderly who have difficulty in facing a new situation. A young child who is moved from school to school because of his parents' occupations may not voice any feelings of being troubled, but his difficulties may show up in the later development of his personality. Similarly, an older person who is displaced from his accustomed environment may make the move to "a life of leisure" with apparent willingness. Difficulties that arise later are then attributed to the aging process rather than to the uprooting.

Reactions to change in any life, whether young or old, follow certain patterns. The exact consequences for a particular person are only a question of degree. There are some circumstances that must inevitably lead to difficulties for every person, whether previously well adjusted or not.

There are some responses in the elderly that seem to be due only to their age, but that actually arise out of a personal, physical, or character makeup that has been theirs all their lives and that is only intensified in age.

In the first case the difficulties may be preventable. In the second it may be possible only to ameliorate them. In either case we must understand what leads to them if we want to be able to ease them.

Until now we have been discussing the underlying evolutionary causes that led to the present situation. We are now going to take a look at some of the consequences that are with us.

CHAPTER EIGHT

Psychological Consequences

Well-Adjusted Old Age

We are going to talk about the difficulties of the elderly, but to see these clearly, we must first have a picture in our minds of what a contented, well-adjusted older person is like, for only then shall we be able to discern where the differences lie.

The contented older person is very much aware of his importance to his family and his community. He can look back on the achievements of his lifetime with a sense of pride, and he has satisfaction and a feeling of continuity as he sees younger members of his family carrying on his work. His sense of his own secure place in his community is extended and enhanced with every new birth in his family, for he sees his line and everything he holds valuable thus being perpetuated into the future.

Above all, the well-adjusted elder is active. His daily life is filled with occupations that he feels to be purposeful and useful and that are appreciated as being so by members of his family and community. On festive occasions celebrated by his family or acquaintances his manner reflects his satisfaction with his life. Yet for all his strong feelings of closeness and identity with his family he maintains a spirit of independence, and he prefers to attend to his own chores rather than to be aided with them.

In talking to his grandchildren he will tell them of the past. To his own children he will talk of the present. With his contemporaries he will discuss the future, since life is still ahead for him and he has plans for the future that thoughts of his possible demise do not disturb. Many a contented older man, looking out of a window of a home he expects to pass on to future generations of his family, has decided to improve the view from it by planting a tree that he knows he will never see come to full growth, but he enjoys the prospect of it in his mind, as he knows his posterity will see it.

With minor modifications all these statements apply equally to the fulfilled older woman. Like the man she is confident of her importance to her family and society. Where a man may regard the achievement of a sound business, a well-established farm, or a successful professional connection with pride, she will see as her life's work the existence of the healthy, busy, well-functioning family she brought up, and she will view it with pride as her creation. She, too, will see every new birth as some part of her own stake in the future. Like her husband she remains purposefully active. She runs her own home and helps when she is needed by her children or grandchildren. She, too, will delight in passing on her memories to the youngest, her practical knowledge and experience to the older ones, and her thoughts and plans for the future to her friends.

If such a couple sounds too ideal for modern readers, we can only assure them that we were blessed with such grandparents and that in our travels, especially in rural areas, even in the most industrialized countries, we still meet many whose lives to this day fall into the same pattern. Mrs. Esther Hunt Moore, of Hickory, North Carolina, for instance, who was named Mother of the Year in 1970, is such a person. She was an elementary school teacher for forty years, and during her life she has given evidence of her strong spirit in many ways. She was, for example, the first black woman to register to vote in her county. After her children were graduated from college, she undertook postgraduate studies at Columbia University in New York and earned her master's degree at the age of sixty-four. She then went on to teach mentally retarded children. She is now a vigorous seventy-five, still active, and much honored. The ingredients of this satisfactory old age are: a stable relationship with the immediate and extended family, purposeful activity, and a sense of one's own value.

Depression in Old Age

To have such a desirable old age the presence of each of these ingredients is necessary. If even one is removed, the balance is upset, with consequences that may be insidious but that eventually find their way to the surface. If more than one is removed, the consequences become more and more serious.

Let us start with the best possibility, where only one of these ingredients is lacking.

An older couple are in their middle sixties. The man is persuaded by his well-meaning family that he has worked hard enough and that he should take it easy. The woman is asked, "Why should you have the trouble of running such a big house? Why don't you get help?" or "Why don't you move to a small apartment or to serviced rooms?" This customary sort of brainwashing upon retirement is sometimes even supported by their family doctor. "Take it easy," he may advise. "Remember you're not a youngster anymore." A modern myth had arisen that cardiovascular diseases were due to overexertion, but more recently it has been found that the opposite is true. The greatest number of persons afflicted with such illnesses are the desk-bound, not the active, but there remains a general idea in the minds of many that at a certain age one should slow down his activities, no matter how well he feels.

This couple may move to a small apartment a little distance from their original home. Thus they are physically removed, actually dislodged, from their central position—even if voluntarily—at a time when many years of useful functioning could still have been theirs.

In the first flush of the new experience, which is usually accompanied by the slightly envious congratulations of their younger brothers and sisters or older sons and daughters, they take off on a long "second honeymoon." They have a great deal of pleasure making the plans for their journey, perhaps buying new wardrobes and making a round of bon voyage parties, so that their awareness of the change in their status is masked by the excitement of these preparations. At first they find the journey itself stimulating, but after a while they feel they have had enough, and only then do they make the discovery that there is nothing important for them to go home to. When they do return, there is a sense of letdown. Their children's social life has changed its emphasis to the company of their contemporaries. A slight estrangement has taken place that becomes more pronounced as time goes on.

For both the man and the woman the erstwhile feeling of their importance to their family ebbs. In conversations with their contemporaries they begin to talk of their past achievements, or not of themselves at all but of their children. In their eyes now their own lives no longer have present or future merit. Halfhearted attempts to show the mementos of their travels are soon abandoned in the face of the lack of interest of their audiences.

Little by little the question arises as they awaken each morning: What are they going to do with their day? They make some attempts to find useful occupation in community work, but these are often without success: under the pressure of unions, paid workers are given preference. Discouraged, they begin to spend their days in time-filling pastimes, like playing cards. A sense of uselessness takes hold, and this has an all-pervading effect on their attitude and mood. Their outlook on life becomes negative. Nothing really pleases them any longer.

Once this stage is reached, previously cheerful persons become complainers. Attempts by their children to bring them cheer meet with no success and produce frustration on both sides. If their children bring them presents, they are called extravagant, but if they do not, they are chided as being thoughtless. Negative feelings invade their own ideas of themselves. They begin to see themselves as burdens. Why should anyone want to bother with them?

Their change in personality is just as puzzling to themselves as it is to their children. Their first thought is that there must be something physically wrong, and thus begins an endless round of physical checkups. Since most of them are reasonably healthy, even the most trivial deviation from the norm will be seized upon by themselves as well as by their doctors as the gremlin responsible for their general malaise. The most frequently accused culprit is a slightly high blood pressure, but often the "patient" now goes around justifying his change in mood and personality by some such diagnosis as a "weak heart," "delicate stomach," "poor kidneys," "irritable colon," "sluggish digestion," "bad eyes," "hardening of the arteries," or "irregularity," while a host of television and magazine advertisements for remedies support the pseudoreality of these myths. These remedies fail to create any changes in the elderly person, who by now has become quite crotchety, and so a change of climate is advocated.

This may work for a short time. In the absence of a sympathetic ear for their complaints they use devices to take their minds off their troubles. They may take up some activity like swimming or golf, take dancing lessons, or busy themselves with getting together a new circle of acquaintances, but soon enough they relapse into feeling low.

What exactly has happened in such a case? Is such a response peculiar to human beings, or does it follow a basic law that applies to all higher life? In this example we see elderly people either giving up or being persuaded or forced to give up an essential function. To fulfill this function of their earlier years a complex and delicate interweaving of the nervous system, hormones, muscles, and the rest of the body, too, had been established. The sum total of all these processes had fitted the person for his or her function, and this had laid the basis for his sense of well-being. Naturally, from time to time frustrations or disappointments did interfere with this satisfactory state, but such episodes were usually of short duration, and more often than not they gave rise to a sense of challenge, the meeting of which required an intensification of the workings of the individual's resources and so rapidly restored total well-being.

At the stage of retirement all of a person's abilities are still superbly geared to utilizing all his physical and mental capacities, and suddenly, these find no outlet. The reduced activity that may be found is insufficient to drain the available energy. It is like using a high-powered battery that could activate a locomotive to run a toy train.

We as human beings come with certain biological equipment that we have inherited from the distant past. It may be modified in some ways by the environment in which we find ourselves, but essentially it remains the same as it has always been. This equipment *must be used*. It actually demands to be used, for it makes its need to be used felt.

Any organ or organ system exists to perform a function for the economy of the whole body. If, for one reason or another, the function that the organ is designed to fulfill is no longer required, then that organ deteriorates. In other words a bodily organ, serving the body in a specific way, to a certain

120

extent must be served by the body in providing it with work which it must do. Just as the muscles of the body become flabby if not exercised (which is another way of saying that if you want to keep them usable, they have to be used), the same principle applies to the brain. Nonuse or inadequate use of the brain results in a condition of discomfort.

When the human brain is deprived of normal stimulation, at first it turns to its own memory storage and conjures up fantasies to keep itself busy. If this is insufficient, the brain signals a disturbed state, which its owner experiences as boredom. A result of boredom is usually a search for new stimulation. In its milder forms this can be achieved by some fresh activity, but in cases where outside circumstances enforce boredom (such as duty in an isolated military outpost, or a term of imprisonment, not to mention incarceration in an old people's home), then an abnormal state builds up within the brain cells. An approximation that provides a useful image to aid the comprehension of this state is of revving up a motor while it is in neutral. Heat and noise are generated but not movement. But the car was designed for movement and not for being raced in neutral. This condition in the brain leads to different behavior in different persons, but very often it finds release in quarreling over unimportant issues. In some younger persons it occasionally explodes in violence or destructiveness.

This was well demonstrated a few years ago when a detachment of naval personnel was sent to the Antarctic both to undertake scientific exploration and to test their reactions to lengthy confinement without the freedom and distractions of their normal lives. The enlisted men vented their boredom in extremely abusive language. The officers, having to live up to the standards expected of their rank, could not permit themselves this outlet, and as a result of their pent-up boredom they all developed severe headaches. All these men had their work to engage at least a part of their interest, besides the knowledge that their discomfort was only for a limited time, yet clearly this was not enough and their mood was affected. For the elderly neither of these ameliorations applies. For them the outlet is crotchetiness rather than violence and depression rather than headaches.

The brain's constant need for stimuli probably reaches even into our sleep, when the rest imposed by the whole body produces a level of stimulation that is too low for the neocortex, and this may be why the brain dips into its reserve resources during sleep and produces dreams.

It is hardly surprising that, given an opportunity to focus on the self—in terms of a symptom—a bored older person will use the totality of his mental and physical abilities to explore, observe, and concern himself with this symptom. It becomes a new center for his life and the only barrier between him and renewed boredom. In these circumstances it becomes understandable that the "sufferer" will resist all attempts to help him whether by well-meaning relatives, friends, or doctors. By now he has become a bona fide hypochondriac.

That all the symptoms of which he complains are quite superficial and not based on any physical illness becomes obvious when such a person is called on in an emergency. A man may be called back from retirement to fill in when a successor has an accident or is sick; a woman may be called upon to help out in the family when a crisis has arisen. No longer is either of them aware of the pseudoailment. Both pitch in with all their old vigor. As a matter of fact, in these circumstances their total personalities quite often revert to what they had been before.

What has actually happened is that the utilization of all their resources has restored their sense of well-being. Should the emergency pass and their services no longer be needed, their preoccupation with their symptoms will return.

The picture we have sketched in has many variations according to the personalities of the couple, their economic and professional background, their social status, values, and beliefs. Each of these factors modifies the canvas in some degree, but the picture on the whole applies to most, even if some of the details vary.

As discouraging as this may sound, it is still a relatively mild example, for this couple still functions socially. They see friends. They engage in some kind of community work whenever their "ailments" permit, and they have some diversions. No matter how badly the grandmother suffers from her "gallbladder" or "arthritis," when a holiday time comes around and her children and grandchildren visit her, her aches and pains may be duly discussed but they will not prevent her from doing the arduous work involved in entertaining them. And no matter how badly the grandfather is troubled by "rheumatism" or "his stomach," he forgets this when he is able to give business advice to his sons or to discuss the future careers of his grandchildren.

As a rule, a kindly family adjusts itself to accepting a certain amount of capriciousness of this sort as to be expected because of "old age," and this reinforces the prevailing myth that being old means being a little difficult. Unfortunately, this has its repercussions in the way the elderly are treated.

When circumstances deprive the elderly not only of their social importance (as represented by his business or job and her home) but also of the companionship of a mate through death or severe illness, or if they should lose touch with their family (increased mobility is an important and growing factor here), then they experience a profound sense of loss. This pervades all their thinking and reshapes all their ideas about themselves. They judge their own worth by the amount of caring they receive from those around them, and so when they feel there is no close person who really cares for them, a sense of their own worthlessness overtakes them.

This feeling of loss may occur at the death of a mate even

when the marriage was bad or only so-so. To the outsider it seems that the survivor of a bad marriage would feel some relief in being free of the endless bickering, harsh words, and sometimes cruel treatment that are a part of such relationships, and he is surprised to see such a person succumb to deep and genuine grief. But the survivors of such marriages also suffer loss—perhaps not of love, but at any rate of a sparring partner who filled life with excitement and activity. Their hormones were constantly stimulated for attack and defense. Deprivation of this stimulation would have a similar effect on their adrenalin and other hormone production as if one were to take an animal from the wild and put it into a zoo, where all struggle is removed.

It is a little more difficult to understand the grief of the survivor of a couple who lost their feelings for each other quite early in their marriage and slowly developed either a bare tolerance for each other or even a profound but silent contempt. They jogged along because of convention or passivity, each perhaps always hoping to be relieved of the other in some way but never bringing himself to take the step to separate. When one of these mates dies in old age, after a lifetime of barely tolerable living together and a great deal of poorly repressed resentment, one would expect the other to show some relief and is often surprised to see that the opposite is the case. The departed mate had provided a sense of continuity and social standing, and these gave both their lives a structure within which they functioned. Even the feeling of being obliged to carry on in a loveless marriage may have given a kind of pride or strength that enabled each to fulfill other activities. All this suddenly comes to an end. We then become aware that even a loveless marriage can have a stabilizing function in the lives of both partners and that the survivor can have a sense of loss as strong as those others who had better or worse ones.

This sense of loss cannot easily be described in words.

There is a feeling of utter desolation, of the meaninglessness of their own existences. The joylessness of everything that surrounds them has such a paralyzing effect that it is almost a wonder that they are able to carry on from day to day in no matter how limited a way. Well-meant pep talks by relatives, friends, or doctors (along the lines, "You have so much to live for," "You have such fine children," or "Your children love you") have the opposite of the hoped-for effect. The affected persons are keenly aware of all the good intentions and love directed toward them, but they do not have any inner response to it. The abysmal feeling of worthlessness and hopelessness has burned out any semblance of feeling save the pain of self-denigration. Not being able to respond to kindness or the kind intentions shown makes them feel even worse. Then the only feeling they are able to summon to ease the pain a little is that of self-pity.

The Will to Live

We tend to look upon a marriage as a social institution rather than as a dynamic interchange between two human beings. Apart from the possibility that the mutual feelings change, we should also be aware that the married state itself has a different meaning to a couple of various stages in their lives.

Ideally, the first few years are a phase of romantic love, with some periods of friction occasioned by the necessary adjustments two human beings must make to cooperate in living together. In the next period, when they have children, the awakening of parental feeling and the sense of responsibility tighten the bond but put the relationship into a different context. The feeling of love for each other is spread out to include the children. Then, as the children become older and more self-sufficient, the couple tend to look to each other again. They do not lose their love for their children, but it assumes a different complexion. The mutual feeling of dependence between husband and wife grows to a point where it may become what is called a symbiotic relationship, where one cannot live without the other. Sometimes, in exceptionally good relationships of this kind, the couple begin to look like each other, as though they were brother and sister. In such a case when one mate dies, the other often follows within weeks or months. The will to live longer has left him. For one mate to survive the death of the other for long in such a case, he or she would have to have had an extremely strong character to begin with. Only an exceptionally strong sense of self-worth and a dedication to a purpose in life enable the survivors of such unions to call upon their will to live to overcome the grief they experience.

The relinquishing of the will to live is a biological phenomenon. To understand the meaning of the profound emotional changes that take place, we once again have to look at the animal world.

An animal derives a very important ingredient of its life force from its awareness of its place in a social order. It is easy to see that the self-esteem we derive from our standing in our own societies is an equivalent of this. When people lose a mate by death, or for that matter to some extent by divorce, their social standing is changed in many subtle and sometimes not so subtle ways. This is only a minor aspect of their loss, but it is an indicative one. An animal forced to relinquish its place in its social hierarchy, either because of a successful challenge to its dominance by another or because of sickness or other disability, experiences profound bodily changes promoted by its endocrine and nervous systems. It loses all impulse to fight back, not unlike the loss of the will to live in man. Then either it is edged by others or it consigns itself to the periphery of its group. It loses its protected position. It loses its resistance to disease. Parasites that its body accommodated without harm while it retained its dominance now become lethal. In these circumstances it becomes easy prey, or as also often happens, it succumbs to so-called shock death, dying from lack of the will to live even without the intervention of disease or predator.

Now we can understand the meaning of depression in man much better. In this light we can see that these intensely felt, all-pervading responses are not just moods of elderly people being "difficult," whether noncooperative or demanding, but deeply seated responses built in to the process of life itself. They are not peculiar to man. Indeed by their presence they reveal his evolutionary descent from other species and his unity with all of nature.

For casual onlookers it is not difficult to acknowledge this underlying biological response of "giving up" and self-elimination when they see extreme cases in man and recognize their similarity with animal counterparts. But it requires quite a different spirit of understanding in the observer when exposed to an elder who is stubborn, irritating, impossible to please, and generally contrary to identify this behavior as actually a milder form of the same biological process.

Our inclination is to respond with exasperation, to attempt to argue the elderly person out of his mood, or eventually to turn our backs on him. Such responses on our part can obviously only aggravate the situation. Yet these are probably the most prevalent reactions to the stresses of loss, whether of status or of companions. Because of this they are frequently experienced in old age and have come to be associated with it, although no age group is immune to the same symptoms.

Quirks of Character in Old Age

Sometimes it is amusing to see in older people little habits of gesture and speech that have remained with them ever since they were small children. It reminds us that for most people the basic character they developed in their earliest years does not change fundamentally throughout their lives but that it often becomes intensified in old age.

Thus when we see a trait that gives difficulty either to the older person or to those with whom he has contact, we are inclined to ascribe it to old age, whereas in fact it has nothing to do with aging in general but only to this particular person's idiosyncrasies. Earlier in his life the people around him could not help but notice the same irritating peculiarities, but then they were inclined to excuse them on the ground that he may have been tired, overworked, or worried. Much less tolerance is shown for the same traits in an elderly person. It is as though, no longer having an important position in the family structure or in public life, he were no longer entitled to have a temper or a mood.

However there are many factors that may exaggerate personality problems with age. The loss of status and the ensuing lowered self-esteem make the elderly particularly sensitive to any slight, imagined or real. A man may have been sensitive in his earlier years, but in one way or another he was then able to cover this up with an air of not caring or one of arrogance. But when this same man is older, his sensitivity may reach such proportions that, if one of his children should fail to telephone him, he would experience this as a total rejection. His sense of hurt would then drive him to punish that child with silence or with grudging sulkiness. If the culprit should make the awaited telephone call later and try to apologize, it would then take much more than one "I'm sorry" to earn forgiveness.

Often older people of this kind attempt to prolong their rule over the members of their families by instilling a sense of guilt in all of them in this way, although, to do them justice, they are usually not really aware of their motivation. Their favorite phrases, "After all I've done for you . . ." and

"Wait until your children grow up . . ." will sound familiar to many. Of course, other elderly sufferers from supersensitivity may use subtler ploys. "Go on your vacation. Don't worry about me—I can manage somehow," or when their children give a party, "You don't have to invite me—I'll only be in the way." It may seem as if there is some malice in such people, but actually there is none. The pain they experience at any slight is so out of proportion that they cannot handle it, and they forestall it by themselves making the suggestion that would hurt them. To understand the intensity of this kind of pain, one has to go back to one's own childhood and remember how it felt if a parent threatened with some such words as "Oh, you naughty boy. Mummy doesn't love you anymore."

Such a state of affairs can throw a pall over the mood of a whole family. Worse, it is wasteful for the community at large as well as for the family concerned, since the time, thoughts, and energy of so many people are uselessly consumed in trying to deal with the problem—a problem that need not have arisen if some useful function or some sense of personal worth or of the value of his activity had been left to the troubled older person.

Psychological Effects of Disabilities

A variation of this theme is seen in other old people who for organic reasons, such as hardening of the arteries of the brain, lose their short-term memory. If such people happen to be revered, they take this loss with a certain amount of good humor mixed with a touch of exasperation at themselves. If, however, their families only barely tolerate them, then this handicap turns into a mania of persecution. For example, not being able to find a key that was at hand a few moments before becomes the basis for an accusation that someone has stolen it or deliberately hidden it to aggravate them. In time this suspiciousness leads them to hide whatever treasured objects they possess—again forgetting where they were hidden and starting another round of endless accusations. In a few instances where the families show a semblance of understanding, they ignore such accusations, but usually they set off endless arguments and a chain of repercussions.

When hearing fails, a similar set of paranoid symptoms sets in. The modifications are slight. In this instance older men or women, if neglected, attribute this neglect—sometimes correctly—to a loss of respect or a loss of love for them by their families. In their own minds they come to the conclusion that they are disliked, ridiculed, and avoided. They become convinced that unpleasant sentiments about them are being expressed and that only their inability to hear prevents them from verifying what they feel certain of. From this point, it does not take long before they are convinced that they actually hear slighting remarks. It is sad but true that this kind of suspiciousness is apt to be a self-fulfilling prophecy, for this type of family, not too tolerant to begin with, soon comes to hate the very sight of the person who is constantly accusing and berating its members.

If we compare this one with an older person who is afflicted with a loss of hearing but who has the respect and love of his family, we can point up the difference. In the beginning this person will disregard his failing and go on as if nothing were wrong. This may give rise to some misunderstandings, but everyone around him finds these amusing and they are quoted and told as family anecdotes. Although this person will eventually become aware of the loss of hearing, at no time will he attribute malicious gossip about himself to any of his relatives.

The loss of sight has more far-reaching effects because of the increased helplessness it entails. The previously independent person finds it difficult to accept his need for reliance on others. He will try to do things for himself that actually are dangerous for him to attempt and that may lead to serious accidents. A less well-loved person, like the previous examples, will not hesitate to put constant pressure on those close to him. In this case there is a denial of poetic justice, for the loved and independent person is in more danger than the less loved and consequently more dependent one.

Modifying Economic Influences

It would appear that the behavior we have described applies chiefly to the middle and upper-middle economic classes, but human nature, particularly in respect to these deeply embedded evolutionary responses, will on the whole show similar trends, regardless of the economic level.

There are, however, some psychological responses that may well be modified by a person's economic standing. It is impossible to make any general statement in this area, for it is one of floating boundaries and exceptions can be found in each of its fields. Where the difficulties of old age are a result of human relationships, then the response we have described will apply universally. But where retirement from work is a factor, there are several modifying considerations that would involve financial status.

Usually when more competitive effort is required to achieve a position and the mind and the body have been geared over a lifetime to cope with this competition, then the more or less abrupt interruption of the pattern will cause greater dislocation for a person than if he had been engaged in a less competitive field.

While loss of status would seem to affect more severely those who had achieved a higher financial position or one that brought a high degree of respect or influence, any kind of striving at no matter which level may set the scene for a similar sense of letdown when retirement is imposed. A minor union official who, because of his age, was forced out of his post at an election will not feel any differently about it than the head of a corporation in similar circumstances. On the other hand, a person in a comparatively secure position, which he did not have to strive very hard to attain or to hold, no matter what his income may feel his retirement less severely.

Equally, at all levels, there are some who are glad to give up their work. Nevertheless, even for these a vacuum is left that has to be filled satisfactorily if they are to enjoy a serene old age. Economic advantages may help a person fill this void, since he will have more alternatives available to him, but if the selection that a well-pensioned executive makes turns out to be unsuitable to his needs, his emotional responses will have no relation to his bank balance. If anything, he may be more disappointed and experience greater difficulty than a poorer man, for it will appear to him extraordinary that with all the money and possibilities available to him he still is not happy.

On the whole it is fair to state that differences in wealth or social standing make less difference to basic responses than would appear on the surface to be the case.

We have gone into detail about some psychological conditions that arise in old age due to social factors that inevitably lead to symptoms; to factors that arise out of the character of a person but that become more prominent in old age; and to mental conditions that are responses to the normal wear and tear of a long life and that affect some of us. What we have written by no means exhausts the list, but it gives an overall indication of the point that, while in part some of the difficulties of the elderly may be due to wear and tear, we cannot overlook the possibility that these manifestations might be fewer or milder if the social life and status of the elderly were more satisfactory.

A Matter of Interpretation

The loss of a feeling of purpose in life, or a giving up of responsibility, involves a loss of the sense of self. The older person no longer plays the role he sees himself in, and he is at a loss when he attempts to readjust to a new role. He feels a lowering of his status, a feeling that has very strong negative consequences to his well-being and results in a lowering of his self-esteem. This sets up a state of stress that has physical consequences. Any break with his accustomed environment, a difficult hurdle to overcome at any phase of life, then becomes especially hard for him to take in stride.

Before we go on to talk about the physical consequences of this mental state, we should like briefly to clarify some ideas about the meaning of stress.

Because of the human tendency to categorize, it is easier to think in absolutes. This habit often leads us to misleading conclusions. There are varying degrees of stress, and, what is more, stress is a matter of interpretation. One person may put in ten hours of work and at the end of the day feel nothing but gratification at its accomplishment; another will consider a similar day's work onerous and at the end of it feel only exhaustion. A task that in itself is not taxing will, if it is considered unpleasant or tedious, produce mental and physical stress.

To give an obvious example, one housewife will find cleaning and dusting her home so exhausting that she ends her work on the verge of tears and drained of energy; another may perform the identical task and proceed to the next with undiminished vigor. The difference may seem to be in the relative strength and health of the two women, but this is usually not the case. It is a matter of the way in which each of them regards her work. If she regards it as a burden, her feelings will put a brake on her muscular activity. But she knows that if she does not do it she will feel guilty toward her husband and ashamed before her neighbors, so she overcomes her reluctance and forces herself to complete her chores. Because of this she has to expend double the nervous energy and muscular strength that the woman who does not regard the work as a burden has to do.

The difference in their attitudes may be due to one or a combination of several causes. One woman may feel that her work will not be appreciated by an overly critical and carping husband; she may think she cannot do it as well as she would like to see it done; she may have a sense of the futility of the work itself; she may feel that the work is demeaning and that she is capable of a more intellectual occupation. Whatever the reasons, this woman interprets her work as a burden, whereas the woman who was not tired has seen the same work as having a purpose, and she finds pleasure in accomplishing it.

Everything we experience or do in life has an effect on us according to the way we define it to ourselves, and the way we define it will depend on our interpretation of its meaning to us. In this way a set of circumstances will be seen by an older person differently from the way the younger members of his family see it, and his reactions therefore will be very different from what his family expects.

Relieving the elderly head of a business of his responsibilities and freeing him for a life of leisure may be seen by his sons as a loving and fitting filial gesture, but the older man may experience it as a loss of his place in the world. The sons regard the burdens of conducting a business as stressful, perhaps severely so for an elderly person, but to that person his tasks were a source of immense personal gratification and he, like the cheerful housewife, did not feel them to be a burden. Whether or not a task is stressful boils down to the interpretation put on it.

When well-meaning relatives or doctors advise a man or a woman to slow down and take life easier, in some instances they may well be doing a disservice to the person they wish to help. An older man who obviously enjoys his work and who is doing it adequately should not be relieved of it. A vigorous older woman who takes pleasure in running her household, when given a maid by solicitous children, may suddenly, and to them inexplicably, become morose and difficult. Of course if the man is involved in an obviously aggravating and frustrating business or if the woman can no longer perform her household tasks with ease, then the advice to "take it easy" is warranted. It cannot be emphasized strongly enough that what is stressful can be determined only by the people involved. Often we face the paradox that in relieving a person of what appears to be a physical strain, we create in him a state of mental stress. Furthermore, mental stress frequently, indeed usually, brings physical symptoms in its train. In these cases we are then witness to the obverse paradox. A retired person suffering from the symptoms of a stress disease that affects both mind and body, if given work to do, will show measurable and at times even spectacular improvement. The work, which his friends might have thought to be too much for the "invalid" and a strain on him, often turns out to be his salvation.

There are further paradoxes, for nothing is more likely to cause mental stress than not having enough to do. This form of stress, arising out of boredom, is just as taxing as its opposite that stems from excessive demands made on the brain.

Over and above this, our language plays a trick on us in that we use the same word, "stress," for both physical and mental burdens, but there is an important difference between them. Physical effort puts a strain only on the muscles. When they can be exerted no more, they tire and the effort has to stop. The brain does not have such a well-defined fatigue cutoff mechanism. We can feel mentally exhausted, but nothing stops us from continuing to worry and ponder over a problem. It is in this going beyond what our minds can tolerate, whether in the direction of too little or too much activity, that mental stress is created—and there is nothing that can stop it as effectively as tired muscles can prevent the rest of the body from being overtaxed. Physical stress does not cause mental ailments because the body itself sets limits. But mental stress, with its more elastic limits, can and does cause physical ailments.

CHAPTER NINE

Physical Consequences

Because of the subject we are discussing, we must continually remind ourselves that in human behavior as in human anatomy we find continuities from our evolutionary past. The automatic responses of the body to its experiences are deeply embedded inheritances from our remote biological past, and these govern a great deal of our behavior.

In view of this it would seem logical to expect that each human being would respond physically to similar experiences in a similar way, but we see that this is not the case. There are hardly two individuals anywhere who respond in precisely the same way to any given circumstance.

It is here that we have to take into consideration the psychological law we have just been discussing: that any emotional response to an event is determined by the way the person experiencing it interprets its meaning to himself or herself. Therefore infinitely varying blends of all the variables of genetic inheritance, methods of upbringing, social background, ethical values, and personality will determine for each individual *which* of the evolutionary mechanisms that are common to us all will be called into action by his body on any occasion.

For this reason, until very recently physicians resisted the idea of attributing certain malfunctions of the body to mental states. It is only in the last few decades that the principles of psychosomatic medicine have found general acceptance.

A simplified illustration will show how difficult it is to find uniform causes for the presence of what are called psychosomatic ailments:

In a business organization there is a hard-driving and critical chief who does not tolerate any shortcomings. He is short on praise and long on rebuke. He constantly hints that any employee is easily replaceable. To obtain results, he goads rather than encourages. As a result, to give some arbitrary figures, out of one hundred of his employees, five will develop ulcers, another five will suffer chronic indigestion, three show high blood pressure, two have skin problems, six will suffer from persistent headaches, and fifteen have vague psychological symptoms like insomnia, nervous tension, or irritability, while sixty-four will show no untoward symptoms.

Unless a physician examining this group is aware of the personal interpretation that each employee puts on the behavior of the chief, he will be at a loss and will fail to attribute these diverse symptoms to any single cause—particularly in the face of the fact that more than half of the personnel show no ill effects at all.

Today an examining physician may understand that the sixty-four employees who function without impairment do so because, among many factors, their rearing prepared them for coping with trying circumstances and taking difficulties in their stride. The others regard the situation as threatening either to their existence or to their self-esteem, and in them feelings of rage or frustration are engendered.

To use this example to clarify our subject, the fact that we see a great variety or a total absence of physical malfunctions in individuals of the elderly caste as a whole does not exclude the principle that certain psychosocial causes are the triggers that set certain mechanisms into motion. These mechanisms then produce the variety of disabilities that become apparent.

The two most important conditions that threaten the equanimity of the aging in general and lead to most of their special problems are *loss of status* and *loss of purpose*. These are the overall factors for which our societies as a whole are responsible. On a personal level, of course, there are some other factors for which society is not responsible. Foremost of these is grief when a loved companion is lost. Then there are the varying degrees of anxiety about how they will be able to manage possible health and financial problems that could arise.

At all events, irrespective of what the precipitating factors may be, we do often, although not invariably, see certain physical responses in their wake. A physician who has to deal with the illness that arises from them is primarily concerned with curing the trouble. That is his function. From our standpoint, in terms of prevention, it is very important wherever we can to separate the malfunctions that are triggered by social conditions from those that arise from an individual's character or special circumstances.

That physical malfunctions can be triggered by social conditions has been clearly demonstrated many times. One example comes from the Institute for Social Research of the University of Michigan, where Dr. Sidney Cobb examined the impact on the physical and mental health of the workers of the shutting down of a Detroit factory in 1963. He concluded from this study, together with his earlier experiences, "that losing a job exacerbates diseases and even produces new illness." Out of fifty-four men laid off in Detroit he identified eight cases of arthritis, six of severe depression requiring medical help, three of ulcers, five of high blood pressure requiring hospitalization, two of milder high blood pressure, and one of alcoholism as "directly traceable to the plant closedown and its aftermath."

In the last chapter we discussed the effects of loss of status and loss of purpose on the mind. Any distinction between mind and body is of course an artificial one, but it has been customary to look upon mental and physical conditions as separate and so we have followed this pattern. We are now going to consider how physical conditions flow out of mental ones, especially as they affect the elderly.

Loss of Status

Loss of status leads to a feeling of emptiness that is a result of a person's belief that his society has given him up. He therefore feels that what he does has no further value to his group and that he himself has no worth. We have mentioned some of the fundamental physical changes that take place in many animals when they lose their status in their social hierarchies. In man these physical changes are usually less profound because they are overlaid by our cultural evolution, which tends to mitigate the consequences of this type of loss. Nevertheless, the mechanisms that promote the changes in other animals are within us, and not infrequently one or some of them are set into motion.

The feeling of depression that pervades the mind of a person who feels displaced has far-reaching effects on his other bodily processes. A general slowing down of all these processes takes place and is so marked that it becomes apparent even to a nonprofessional observer. A depressed person moves slowly; all his reactions, thinking, responding are slower than usual. Not only does it seem that his body has gone into low gear, but in fact it has done just this. In an animal this is the mechanism that promotes its submission, its acceptance of lower rank, and its possible eventual elimination or self-elimination.

In man this slowing down may go to varying lengths, but the consequences that result from it are not always easy to reconcile with the precipitating social causes. For example, a lowered rate of activity of bodily function may lower resistance to infectious diseases. Lowered resistance of itself is not a very clear-cut concept, although it is recognized that such a condition exists and a great deal of scientific effort has gone into attempting to define it. It is a condition that is responsible not only for increased susceptibility to infectious diseases, but also for the prolongation of the recovery process after operations or accidents. And incidentally, the depressed are far more prone to accidents than others because of the slowness of their reactions as well as of the underlying self-destructive inclination.

Although man retains the mechanisms that carry out nature's design for the demoted animal, the newer conditions of his cultural evolution (that is, the outcropping of his reasoning brain) drive him to resist these forces. Man does not always accept and submit to social downgrading as other animals do. Often he either openly fights it or innerly resents it. Whichever the reaction, an anger is present that ultimately finds its expression in his mind and body.

Usually his most persistent feeling is that he has been *given up* by his society. This may be followed by its own brand of depression, which is in some ways different from that which results from the loss of love (which we shall be describing). In the loss of love the primary reaction is an overwhelming desire not to go on. The individual himself *gives up*. In the loss of status the arrow points in the other direction. The affected person may feel not that he wants to give up but that he has been given up by his society. If this is the case, he *may* be downcast, but he *will* be angry.

This may seem to be a fine point, but it has important consequences if one wishes to help this person. Plainly, one's methods of helping a person who gives up must be different from those that will have meaning for one who feels he has been given up. In practice, of course, it is not always so simple, because occasionally a person may experience a com-

141

bination of these feelings, but one must understand the difference between them just the same.

The consequences of the smoldering anger of the person who feels given up will vary according to his personality, but they fall into certain general areas. Some will be able to vent their feeling in querulous grumbling, others in provoking arguments or in constantly complaining about the unfairness of things as they are. Some will suppress their anger and will be aware of it only as a state of tension, which ultimately gives rise to such symptoms as backaches or headaches. In fact, there is no organ of the body that may not be affected in one way or another by a persistent feeling of anger, but it would take us too far afield to go into all of them in detail.

Loss of Purpose

When an elderly person is deprived of the occupation that had been a focus for his or her interest throughout a lifetime, that person sooner or later becomes oppressed with a feeling of the uselessness of all his present activities. The earlier occupations had given a sense of fulfillment. They were undertaken for a purpose that had endowed life with meaning, and they brought joy. Whatever the reason for the termination of the occupation, whether retirement, illness, or family considerations, any pursuit undertaken later only rarely gives the same feeling of total involvement; this is because the person does not feel that the new occupation has the same importance that the earlier one had. If a technician gives up his job and then spends his time fishing, he may at first enjoy the new occupation, but in the absence of a feeling of purpose eventually it will pall. If he turns to teaching in what used to be his special field or if he turns his avocation into a vocation, perhaps by studying and teaching the habits of fishes, he not only will retain but may increase his feeling of purposefulness, and then the new occupation will never bore him.

Unfortunately, not many people today find such purposeful activity for their later years, and for the majority there is a vacuum in their lives that brings unpleasant consequences. Whatever they start to do sets such thoughts running through their minds as: "It doesn't really matter whether I do this or not," "What is the point of this? It will all be the same in a hundred years," and "Who cares whether my house is clean or my lawn mowed?" With nothing seeming to have any significance, they procrastinate and eventually do nothing. Time becomes endless. Little events, like an expected visit or even a telephone call, take on such importance that days are spent looking forward to them; then, when they occur, the fantasied joy of their expectation is not fulfilled, or if they are postponed to another day, the disappointment is so great that it can hardly be borne.

Insufficient occupation results in perceiving time as slowed down—almost as we see a slow-motion picture—and this has an effect on the rhythms of the body. As with insufficient use of the brain, insufficient use of the rest of the body has equally widespread consequences. These are not unlike those that occur in bedridden patients, although they are less severe. The muscles become flabby, and their weakness affects the weight-bearing joints so that movement becomes increasingly uncomfortable, and this leads to further immobilization. The heart and blood vessels, having less work to perform, adjust to the slower pace, and then even the slightest exertion causes breathlessness. Shallow breathing leads to poor aeration of the lungs and often eventually to congestion. Parallel slackening takes place in all the body's systems: the digestive and urinary tract, the skin, and the neuroendocrine as well.

This description represents an extreme and is rarely encountered. More often the old person who feels no purpose in his life suffers some combination of mild forms of these disabilities. Any one of them separately is then not sufficiently intense to show up in any clinical test, at least at first, and so is disregarded and not seen to be a part of a larger picture. It is only later, after years of increasing idleness, that the full force of the sum of them can be seen and recognized clinically. They are then placed in the category of degenerative diseases, of which they form a large percentage, and are considered an inevitable result of the aging process. Yet once again, if it had been possible to keep the sufferer interested, purposeful, and active in the earlier stages after retirement, in most cases they would not have arisen.

Loss of Love

We now come to conditions that are not inevitable and that only affect some of the elderly. They are not a result of social attitudes and customs but of circumstances of their personal lives.

Love between two people is thought of by most of us as a purely human quality, one of our higher attributes, and one that sometimes inspires acts of devotion and selflessness that we feel reach the heights of humanity. On one level of thinking this is true, but the capacity for the emotion of love, like that for all our emotions, arises from its powerful biological necessity. Like every other physical and behavioral trait it is ours as a result of natural selection and for a reason. The reason for the existence of the power of love in human beings is very simple: Without its presence in every human adult, no human infant would be able to survive. The human infant is helpless for so long that, for our species to survive at all, natural forces must weed out the lines of those unable to give care. The giving and receiving of care, or love, is a matter so essential that it spells life or death for the infant and therefore for the species.

But love, being an emotion, is impossible to measure and hard to appraise. It is not like a medicine, where one can say, "Give two tablespoonfuls three times a day," and the child will prosper. It is more like food. A person can get along on food of a wide range of quantity or quality, and what is exactly the right amount is different in every case. A child can grow up even if his food is not quite sufficient or not of high quality. His physical growth will be affected, and he may suffer from deficiency diseases later in his life, but he will not die. And so it is with love. A certain minimal quantity is essential for survival, but if the portions given are not enough or of poor quality, emotional development will be affected and character disturbances may result when the child is grown, but he will nevertheless grow.

For the human being, love is such an essential part of our being that it has become a continuing need. The dependent love of infancy develops into the tender love of courtship, and then into the protective love of parenthood. For the elderly, if the love they receive from their children is to be nourishing, it must include an ingredient of respect.

Very often this ingredient is missing. Grown children may believe that they are doing everything for their parents that could be expected of them and are then surprised and pained when they see that the older people do not seem to respond. Often this is because the *quality* of the care they bestow upon their parents is similar to that they give their children. They think that if they provide for their material needs and concern themselves with making sure that requirements for their health are met, this is sufficient. In doing this they are bestowing *protective* love on their parents and children alike, but their parents have a further need. Having, over their lifetimes, established their status, they feel that recognition of this status is a necessary part of love for them. For the parents to lose the acknowledgment of this so easily overlooked but vital ingredient is the equivalent of missing an

145

essential vitamin from their diet. A deficiency in love, as in food, has predictable consequences.

When the missing ingredient in the quality of love is respect, the ill effects on both the mind and the body are mild; they easily fuse with and are often mistaken for conditions that we commonly expect in old age. When both the quality and the quantity of love are diminished, it is understandable that the symptoms become more prominent. But when love from another ceases abruptly because of death, then the consequences in the mind and body are extreme and easy to recognize. The milder symptoms of the other stages that ordinarily would escape notice become more apparent in this light and can be seen more clearly for what they are.

The deep grief that plays on the mind of a bereaved person, and that we have spoken of so far as its emotional consequences go, like every other mental distress eventually makes itself manifest in disorders of the body. When it is status that is lost, the residue of anger acts as some stimulant that partly counteracts the body's total response to loss. When purpose is lost, a person slips into a depression through an inertia that overtakes transitory efforts to pull himself out of it; there is usually an internal dialogue going on, as if to convince himself that no effort is worthwhile. But when love is lost, there is no mitigating force to dam the overwhelming tide of despair. There is no anger, no internal dialogue, nothing but the black pit of emptiness. This feeling goes beyond metaphor. The grieving person actually feels the sensation of inner emptiness, and this has a physical basis.

As all the voluntary muscles of the body slacken, so do all the involuntary muscles. When this overall slackening affects the muscles of the walls of the digestive tract, it is experienced as an almost frightening feeling of hollowness, especially in the center of the chest where the food pipe is affected and then in the stomach. A total slowing down of all the life forces occurs, similar to that we described as a re-

146

sponse to loss of purpose but far more intense. Indeed the slowing down proceeds almost to the point of stopping. In a few cases it goes so far as actually to stop the life processes.

Variations of this response, although the attribution of these to depression is more speculative, can be very drastic. Any profoundly felt loss may be a factor either directly or indirectly in some blood diseases and some cancers. The study of case after case of children developing leukemia and of women developing breast cancer after experiencing severely felt loss is slowly building up ground for the belief that there is a connection between the appearance of these conditions and the emotional disturbance.

At this stage of knowledge it is very difficult to make any statement about causes of cancerous growth, since its exact nature is not yet fully comprehended. The best we can do at present is to base our assumptions on circumstantial evidence, and one such piece of evidence is the frequent association of the onset of cancer with a preceding deeply felt loss. There are other conditions that have similar associations. Pernicious anemia, diseases of the endocrine glands, and fulminant degenerative diseases are some of them. Just the same, there is hardly a physician who in the course of his practice has not seen some cases of this nature. At this point we have grounds to question whether at all the increased incidence of cancer and some degenerative diseases in the elderly are due to the aging process or if they are not rather due to the fact that this group is the most likely to experience devastating loss.

One infectious disease that was dramatically associated with depression following loss, in the days before the use of the potent antibiotics that are now at our disposal, was tuberculosis. Literature and folklore were full of stories of heroines dying of "consumption" after the loss of a lover. Moreover, a high incidence of tuberculosis has been recorded whenever families are uprooted in the course of social upheavals like revolutions and wars. That this is not due to deprivation is indicated by the fact that the other families that stay together and remain where they are do not suffer this increase in cases of tuberculosis even if they experience dire hunger and cold. This offers some parallel, although one of higher intensity, to the response by the elderly to the uprooting from their social niche.

In the same context less dramatic but painful and disabling effects—like a wound that heals exasperatingly slowly, broken bones that refuse to knit, or any healing process that is unduly slow—may well be nothing more than other distant manifestations of the transcendental nature of loss.

Valid and self-evident as it is that depression expresses itself in a general slowing down, on the other hand the picture is sometimes made more complex by signs that seem contradictory. Depression may be accompanied by anxiety. When a loss befalls a person who is forced by circumstances to continue functioning whether in the home or at a job, he may become aware of a growing inability to carry on. The fear of the consequences may set up a state of anxiety that accompanies the depression; anxiety tends to speed up some processes, creating contradictory symptoms.

In a typical situation of this kind an older person may complain to his doctor of a rapid heartbeat, nervous tension, or bouts of diarrhea, any of which would indicate a speeding up of the body's activities. After finding nothing physically wrong, the doctor concludes that he is dealing with an overwrought person and prescribes medication to calm him down. In reality, however, this person may be severely depressed, say, about an illness of a wife or husband, and then concern about the possibility of having to live alone, should the mate die, sets up such intense anxiety that this overshadows the signs of depression. In these circumstances medication that slows down (that is, calms) a person whose basic bodily processes have already been slowed by his depression can only aggravate the condition.

Along these lines, the recent discovery of Indian snakeroot as an agent to lower blood pressure has caused a large number of patients to whom it has been administered (particularly the elderly) to be hospitalized for resulting severe depression, for the snakeroot, besides its capacity to lower blood pressure, has a strong tranquilizing effect. This result further confirms that such patients were basically depressed in the first place. High blood pressure was their response to the frictions in their households that were the outcome of their inadequate functioning, which was a part of their depression. The sequence of events in such a case was:

loss → depression → slowing down → irritation of family that attributes the slowness to willfulness → arguments and anger → old person restrains anger in fear of further antagonizing family → high blood pressure → visit to doctor → snakeroot → intensification of slowing down → severe depression.

Less disabling but also troublesome are some other physical symptoms of the slowing down during depression. These include a lower production of saliva, making the mouth dry and leading to a loss of appetite. Since saliva has antibacterial properties, any reduction of it leads to an increase in tooth decay. A simultaneous lowering of secretions in the alimentary tract interferes with the digestion of food. A slowing in the function of the tear gland often leads to irritations of the eye. And last but not least, a similar effect on the sex glands leads to the disappearance of sexual desire.

All these manifestations are very important to understand because they are so frequently considered "natural" consequences of old age rather than simply of depression. But we have only to see a healthy octogenarian with a hearty appetite and undiminished lustiness to realize that any radical diminution of these appetites is not necessarily a concomitant of age. In fact, when the circumstances of life that depress the elderly change and become more favorable (should they find a new companion or a satisfying occupation), the former appetites return.

We are shackled by our language. We have only a one-way word to describe the end result of the aging process: *senility*. But this implies physical deterioration that brings mental deterioration in its wake. We need a word that will carry our thoughts in the opposite direction and indicate the physical deterioration that is a result of mental hurt.

All these physical sequels to the mental disturbances consequent on the changes that are felt in old age and that we have mentioned here are just some indications of the breadth and depth of the problems that may and do arise. Our purpose is not to delineate them in all their details and ramifications, but to draw attention to the intricate and interlocking nature of the various components that cause them.

If we want to reduce the vast waste of the time and energies of an increasingly large proportion of our population— hospital staff, doctors, social workers, and, above all, the patients themselves—we have to come to see that a large part of the problem is social rather than medical.

The heavy load of elderly patients filling hospital beds and doctors' offices at the present time might be substantially reduced if it were more generally realized that when a society shunts aside healthy and potentially productive older people and deprives them of a function in its organization, the consequences to the individuals displaced as well as to the society as a whole go far beyond the immediately visible effects.

150

CHAPTER TEN

Social Consequences

Changing Attitudes Toward Old Age

Habits of day-to-day speech are sure clues to a society's prevailing attitudes and values. What is considered derogatory may be said by a person only about himself; it would be insulting to say it to another. A person may say with impunity, "How stupid I am," but he may not say, "How stupid you are." When we realize that the same applies to any mention of age—that we may say, "I'm beginning to look old," but not, "You're beginning to look old"—it is brought home to us forcefully that to look old is socially unacceptable.

How deeply this is felt can be further illustrated. An older person told, "You look well," would feel flattered, but to tell him, "You look well for your age," would raise his hackles, for the implication is that, after all, he does look old. The comment "How you have aged" can be made only behind his back; if said directly to him, it would be an unforgivable affront.

Not so long ago a man in his twenties or thirties did everything in his power to look a little older than his years so that he would be taken seriously by his associates, qualify for more important or responsible work, and be treated with respect. Today the attitudes are reversed. A man or woman who wants to qualify for interesting work that has prospects for providing a satisfactory career must either be or look young. On the surface it would seem that there are many contributing causes for this. The investment a company makes in training highly qualified personnel, the expense of pension plans or group insurance, and other economic factors are cited as influencing management to hire younger people. All these considerations sound very reasonable and, from an accountant's or an actuary's viewpoint, even convincing, but beneath these more pertinent motivation may be found.

Whenever we are in a transitional period of changing social values and attitudes, it is difficult to crystallize the trend that is unfolding. Our minds are to some extent still influenced by past principles, and we do not yet fully realize that we no longer accept them. It is so recently that our seniors began to lose their original value to society as its guardians of custom and knowledge that it has not yet quite dawned on us that this has happened. There is a growing feeling that old age and everything connected with it are somehow not desirable, even to the point of being distasteful, but still we do not yet spell it out to ourselves in those terms. But the very fact that we feel obliged to seek euphemisms like "golden age" instead of saying plainly "old age" points very clearly to our feelings about it.

These feelings, whether he is aware of them or not, are also present in the person responsible for hiring personnel and influence his choice. Not only will he not say, but he will not even consciously realize, that his selection of staff is influenced by such feelings, and so he will be prone to put a gloss of economic necessity on his decisions.

This applies in all aspects of social life, not only in hiring practices. The image of the elder is of decrepitude; of the young, of vigor. The possibility of vigorous old age with its own brand of mental and personal strengths does not readily come to mind. Political reformers address themselves to youth and shun the elder. They identify conservatism, reaction, and *laissez-faire* with the old, and liberalism, progress, and getting things done with the young. Most politicians have therefore hitched their careers to catering to the demands of the young, and the needs of the old have been neglected. Even the fact that they have special needs was overlooked until very recently.

Given this state of affairs, how does the victim of such circumstances respond to them?

His first and most powerful response arises in his late middle years as he catches glimpses of old age on his own personal horizon. Then, instead of slowly and gracefully easing himself into the new status, he finds himself strongly resisting everything connected with it. It is only a little over a century since George Sand wrote in her *Journal Intime*, "It is quite wrong to think of old age as a downward slope; on the contrary, one climbs higher and higher with the advancing years and that, too, with surprising strides. Brain work comes as easily as physical exertion to the child. One is moving, it is true, toward the end of life, but that end is a goal, and not a reef on which the vessel may be dashed." Yet how many people today in their heart of hearts find it in themselves really to agree with her?

On the contrary, there is a widespread and growing sense of self-consciousness and embarrassment about being old. By every means in their power, the middle-aged strive to prevent themselves from falling over the brink and into the abyss of old age. The effort to retain a youthful shape and appearance, at no matter what cost to comfort or purse, is undertaken as though it were a social duty. On all sides these days we see our older middle-aged with trim figures, clad in clothes in no way different from those of their children, and using cosmetic devices that seem out of place in their postreproductive stage. While it is aesthetically appealing to see vigorous-looking and well-groomed older people, it seems incongruous to see on them the reddened lips and cheeks, enhanced eyes and bosoms, toupees and mod clothes that counterfeit the sexual signals of young adults.

This response against aging is seen in an even more pronounced form when, after retirement, "senior citizens" decide to spend their "golden years" in retirement communities. There, in the company only of one another, they find themselves as segregated and removed from the actualities of life as children in a boarding school.

When age-homogeneous groups are separated from the variegated structure of normal life and live by themselves, their behavior changes. Whether in a boarding school or an army barracks, in a summer camp or a retirement community, a subculture develops. In any of these places the members of the groups behave differently from the way they would in a normally mixed society. The very absence of interactions with other age groups removes powerful modifiers to behavior. Children living in the absence of adults feel no constraint to "be good," and they follow social laws of their own devising. Old people living among themselves seem to feel released from the necessity of being dignified and showing a good example. Each of us in a mixed group is attuned to showing a different type of behavior in different circumstances. We have many fronts, and the front we show depends on the company we find ourselves in. When the number of situations we face is artificially reduced, then the versatility of our behavior patterns is also restricted, and this leads to an impoverishment of personality.

Older people, newly arrived to take up residence in a retirement colony, are sometimes at first taken aback by what they find. It often takes them awhile to make an adjustment to the life there, and they are not always happy about doing so. Unfortunately the financial commitment they have made usually obliges them, once there, to stay on, whether they feel comfortable about it or not.

The positive aspects of these communities are several. They give a sense of security to their members and a feeling of belonging to a group. They relieve them from worrying about being burdens to their children. But the price for these assurances is a sameness of surroundings; a lack of the stimulation of younger people; a shutting out of real life. Having no responsibilities, their lives are reduced to an effort to fill their time with play. Their play, of its nature, is far more purposeless than the play of children, for whether children are in school or on vacation all their activities combine to prepare them for life. Similar game playing by the elderly brings no inner satisfaction in the long run.

The end result of the purposelessness of their pastimes is a kind of boredom in spite of activity. There often follow attempts to stimulate feeling and put emotional content into their lives by mild flirting and by resorting to the mating rituals of their adolescent years. Indeed, the situation they are reduced to by their lives in such communities is very similar to that of the budding adult. The new companionships they find, even the new marriages they not infrequently make, have much in common with teen-age dating. Theirs, too, is love without responsibilities. It does not involve establishing a home and rearing children or providing for a future. The result is the finding of a playmate rather than a mate in the adult sense, and this increases the already present impetus toward the separation of the elderly from their senior rank and the respect that should go with it.

The changed psychological attitudes of the middle group toward the aged are turning the grandparent generation from what used to be a kind of venerated "super-parent" class into a class of dependent, protected, or playful "super-children," and the retirement communities are becoming what might be called the nurseries of second childhood.

Problems of Readjustment

Problems of readjustment actually do not begin in old age but earlier in life when, for a woman, menopause marks the end of her reproductive stage and, for a man, when doubts about his continuing virility begin to assail him.

These are areas that have been discussed at length in recent years, and it has by now been well established and generally understood that, although the ability to bear children comes to an end for the woman, there is no age limit for sexuality in either women or men. However, in spite of this, there is in our societies such an emphasis on maintaining youthfulness that many men and women go on trying to demonstrate youth and vigor for many years after these have passed.

It is not at all an unusual thing to see a woman in her early fifties half-flirting with the young men her marriageable daughter brings home, or the man of the same age vying for the attention of his son's girlfriends. So bent are they on proving to the world at large and to themselves especially that they look as young and attractive as ever that they do not see that they are making themselves slightly pathetic. The long habit of dressing themselves in clothes similar to their sons' and daughters', of treating their children as friends and companions and not as their juniors, of viewing themselves as forever young has blurred the dividing line between the generations in their minds. Added to this, their deep fear of aging and their belief that life holds no rewards or pleasures for the old, but only for the young, make them cling almost desperately to every last glimmer of youth for as long as they possibly can. Their urgent desire to stay young, together with the wishful thinking that is its result, blinds them to the realities of their age.

The first impacts of aging are felt by the woman, since it is just about at the time when she is undergoing the physical changes brought about by the glandular slowing down of menopause that the oldest of her children leave home for marriage, careers, or both. Her busy domestic schedule is reduced and, at the same time, her functional importance. She begins to have time on her hands just at the period of her life when her hormonal output is being reduced with consequences that are felt throughout her body. If her interest is not engaged by external activity, it will be turned inward, and in this particular constellation, she will therefore become more preoccupied with her bodily processes.

Helen must have been attractive as a young woman. Her features are regular, set in an oval face, and her dark hair has a reddish glint. Her pale-olive skin reveals her Mediterranean origin. Even now, when she smiles, she is still pretty, but usually she looks rather older than her actual years.

Helen had a long tale of woe to tell us. For several years she had been experiencing frequent spells of dizziness. She was tired all the time, couldn't sleep well, and became so complaining and irritable that she was making life miserable for herself and for her husband too. She had had numerous checkups, going from one doctor to another as one after another failed to help her. None of them found anything wrong with her, and all of them attributed her difficulties to menopause and had prescribed hormone treatment. The last doctor had suggested that low blood pressure might be a contributing cause of her condition. But nothing helped. It reached a stage when she didn't want to go out alone. She was afraid she might have a dizzy spell in the street, that it would attract attention, and that she would feel embarrassed. It took all the willpower she possessed even to go out to do her marketing in the immediate neighborhood. In the end her family physician, finding no organic cause for her troubles, sent her to a psychiatrist.

It did not take too long to find out that all these symptoms had started soon after an unpleasant telephone call she had had a few years back from her son-in-law. He had asked her in rather a brusque way not to phone her daughter so often—he wanted his wife to make her own decisions, run her own home in her own way, and grow up. Helen was deeply hurt at the time and a little resentful because she had only wished to be helpful to the young couple. But she didn't want to interfere in their marriage and resigned herself to having them for dinner once a week and seeing her daughter only one other day besides.

From then on she began to feel useless. Her husband was busy all day at his office and her daughter no longer needed her. "I'm nothing but a useless piece of furniture these days," she complained.

In her sessions she soon came to understand that the emptiness she felt in her life was dramatically duplicated in her head, a sensation she labeled as "dizzy spells," not having any other words to describe the feeling. The sight of the many people on the streets busily pursuing their active lives emphasized, even exaggerated, her own sense that there was no reason for her existence. She became aware that this was why she had "dizzy spells" in the street but not at home.

It was plain that above all else Helen needed some purpose, some reason for living. She had no skills that would qualify her for a job, and so we suggested that she volunteer for hospital aide duties—but she didn't take the suggestion. She thought she wouldn't have the strength for it.

Since it was necessary to make a drastic change in her life to prevent her from becoming a hopeless invalid, we requested a meeting with her family, and after the situation was explained to them, they were willing to participate in a little strategy. First, her son-in-law apologized, and then he and her daughter together asked her to go to their home two or three mornings a week to keep an eye on their baby and help out with a few domestic chores so that her daughter would be able to help her husband in his small but growing real-estate business. It was amusing to notice that when this proposal was made to her, she didn't stop for a moment to wonder whether she would have the strength to do it but immediately agreed to the suggestion.

Today Helen has completely taken over the weekday care of her grandchild while her daughter is working full time with her husband. What is more, she is considering doing some volunteer work for her church as well. The "dizzy feelings" are forgotten, her manner is cheerful, and she even looks younger. Of course, old habits don't disappear completely, and she complains that the little boy is becoming a "handful," but she doesn't seem to be disturbed by it.

Today many women at Helen's stage of life recognize the need for a continuation of their previous intense activity by some means. Not all of them have such obliging sons-in-law. Many attempt to fill the void with church, charity, and other social involvements. Some find that these occupations help them through this difficult time, but for most they are not nearly as fulfilling as their previous preoccupation with their families. They therefore eagerly await the arrival of grandchildren, hoping to find new involvement and function in helping their daughters with the new generation, only to be rebuffed again as their daughters show an inclination and desire to run their own families in their own way.

The middle-aged woman is then obliged to make the difficult readjustment to condensing her family life and interest into the once-a-week (or however often it is) visit that her children and grandchildren pay her. In some cases this situation contributes to a disturbance in the equilibrium of the senior marriage. The man, who is still busy, comes home in the evenings tired and is met by his wife, who is bored with her day and who wants and needs greater social activity in the evenings. At this point in their lives the man still has the sense of his importance that is imparted to him by his work, while the woman is experiencing the first breach in her feelings of self-worth. The man often fails to comprehend the new needs of his wife, especially since then, at the peak of his earning power, he is probably providing her with more amenities than ever before. Because of this disappointing situation at home he not infrequently turns for company to other women, often those in his employ who are familiar with the work that is his paramount interest. It is not unusual to see the breakup of marriages at this stage as a result of the emotional conflicts that arise out of this situation.

Brian presented us with a near-classic example of this kind of sequence. An acquaintance of ours, he is a conscientious person who takes his work, like everything else he does, very seriously and has great satisfaction in it. He makes a comfortable income and treats his wife generously and with respect, although he has always had some difficulty in showing his affection. The one flaw in his consideration for her is that he had always expected his home to be run as efficiently as his office—a demand that had created a certain amount of friction, especially when their children were young, since it is hardly possible to run a household like a factory. He was particularly annoyed a few months ago when the third cleaning woman in a very short time walked out. "If she's as difficult with them as she is with me these days," he commented, "I'm not surprised."

With righteous indignation he went on, "Nothing seems to please her anymore. She's forever carping, finding fault, and feeling sorry for herself. I work hard, give her everything— What in the world does she want?" He was totally unaware of the cause of her misery and of how he contributed to it. We explained to him that, unpleasant as his situation was, his wife was not just being capricious; that in nature an animal that has completed its function dies; and

160

that his wife's feelings of uselessness had precipitated a similar mechanism. "How would you feel if you had nothing to do all day long?" we asked him. "Suppose your job had come to an end and you had to fill your time shuffling papers while waiting for a new assignment." He understood that because once he had had such an experience, and at that time he had become very irritable and restless.

We suggested that he set aside at least three evenings every week when he would do something interesting with his wife, such as taking her to a play or lecture or paying a visit with her or entertaining a little more. This would help his wife have the feeling once more that she was important to him.

He has followed our suggestion, and there has been a noticeable improvement in their relationship, which, had it gone on as it was, would certainly have ended in a total rift. In this case their mutual alienation might not have led to extramarital affairs or to divorce because Brian is such a conscientious person, but in many others it does.

This is just one more instance of how even a minimal restoration of function (such as being a wifely companion for only a few evenings a week) brings back a sense of being alive and, for this reason, an improved mood.

Difficulties in making a readjustment catch up with the man when the time for his retirement comes. The transition is then harder for him than for the woman, who by then has had several years to make her own adjustment. For the man the transition is abrupt. The first problem that faces him is the necessity of living on a fixed retirement income, which usually means less money at his disposal. Then, having more time at his disposal, he would be able to take more interest in his family and would enjoy doing so—but his retirement often coincides with a stage in the lives of his children when *their* children are leaving home for work or school. Just at this stage in his life their visits become increasingly infrequent, especially since today, with the emphasis on permissive rearing, the grandchildren are inclined to avoid the company of their parents and, even more so, their grandparents'. Until this time the older couple had kept up their home in the hope and belief that from time to time their children or grandchildren might stay with them. Now, with income reduced and no real use for the larger home, they decide to move to a smaller one, and this begins their first real feeling of uprooting.

For many women the onset of menopause brings the feeling that life has come to an end. In recent years a great educational effort has been undertaken, which is still only partly successful, to convince them that this is not so. But in spite of much proof to the contrary, there remains in many a fear of the loss of sexuality and with it their attractiveness. These fears are often followed by depression. Depression at this stage has been attributed to the hormonal change, but this is mistaken. Those women who manage to maintain a sense of involvement and purpose throughout these years rarely, if ever, experience it.

In men a similar fear is frequently expressed in feelings for which the Germans have a very trenchant word, *Torschlusspanik*, and it implies an unreasoning fear that, rendered freely, the show is over. Some men then indulge in the much dramatized "last fling" or the supreme denial of having passed beyond the virile phase. Others become victims of a melancholia not unlike a woman's postmenopausal depression. In men, too, the hormonal factor is often given undue prominence over the social factor when help is sought.

The social consequences of these feelings are to be found in the extraordinary fact that the elderly often seem to acquiesce and even to cooperate in their own elimination from the mainstream of life. It is not unusual for an old person himself to express intolerance for his own kind, and to say such things as "I don't want the company of a lot of old dodderers" and "They are just a group of old fogies."

The strong rejection that the elderly feel against their own caste is so pronounced that even in the consumer market, where there is a discernible division between goods intended for the use of children, adolescents, and young adults, no separate sector catering to the requirements of the old has crystallized. A Columbia University professor who made a study of buyer behavior said, "Many older people don't want to be reminded that they are old, and they often tend to react against advertising and marketing programs that separate them from the masses."

One of the world's largest manufacturers of baby foods, in the course of its market research, discovered that many elderly people were using its products. To open a new market, it decided to put out a line of "senior foods." It found no buyers. The elderly kept on buying the baby foods, only claiming when asked that it was for their grandchildren.

The owners of two elaborate restaurants built especially for the elderly in connection with retirement communities near Tampa, Florida, and in Riverside, California, had a similar experience. The old people would not patronize them.

The president of a large shoe manufacturing concern, which sells some of its products to the elderly, states, "We find that there is no such thing as an old woman anymore. . . . A few years ago there was a much sharper demarcation between what grandmother wore and what mother wore." Similar observations were made by women's wear manufacturers, some of whom have recently ceased producing styles for "mature tastes." Their conclusion was that people no longer want "older-looking clothes."

Perhaps we can realize how far the rejection of old age has gone when we consider these examples of the old rejecting themselves. Having been deprived of self-esteem, they, like all minorities in the same situation, begin to dislike themselves and try to avoid identification with what has become a despised group.

Prejudice against any form of aging is so strong that its influence carries back into comparatively early stages of life. The first gray hair or the first wrinkle in the face conjures up gloomy thoughts and forebodings whenever it appears. By the time they are only halfway through life both men and women often experience a mild panic in their anxiety about what they feel to be a door closing on their youthful and useful stages.

Right now, at the time of writing, there is the beginning of a groundswell questioning the very basis of the whole concept of retirement. So far, the attempts of governmental agencies and those who are responsible for formulating policies to improve the lot of the elderly have been concentrating on improving the conditions that now exist. Attention has been focused on larger social security benefits and improved medical care, but these do no more than intensify the basic problem. They promote, not decrease, dependency, and they do nothing to help the elder fill his time constructively. It is ironic that those members of such panels who themselves are elderly, whether they are physicians, sociologists, or politicians, advocate such things—and forget that the reason for their own well-being and physical fitness is precisely that they themselves are active and purposeful.

Here and there, however, there are lone voices in the wilderness that call for more biological and more meaningful solutions, and these remind us that old age can be a time for ripening rather than for decay. We can only hope that their voices will be heard.

The Effect on the Young

When any part of an organism is malfunctioning or nonfunctioning, the affected part, even if it is not a vitally important one, does not suffer its ill effects in isolation.

To give an example of the possible extent of the effects of even a minor malfunction, an ingrown toenail, causing pain, forces a person to limp. In doing so he uses his muscles in an unaccustomed way, and the pressure on the weight-bearing joints is altered. What started out as a rather insignificant injury to the flesh of the toe may thus end up as a pain in the lower back. Should the toe become infected, then the consequences may be even more widespread.

And so it is with any upsetting of an established social equilibrium. The displacement of the elderly results in the breakup of traditional family patterns. Children who in the recent past saw that their parents had parents thus became aware of the relationships between generations, and this gave a sense of continuity to their lives. Healthy, functioning old age could then be a reality to them, for they had a model. More than that, strong personal bonds could be established across the generations. For children who are reared in the presence of, or even partly by, their grandparents, it is possible, as they grow up, to have old age in view as an integral part of life and not as a poorly understood kind of existential nothingness as is now the case for so many of our young.

On the principle of "for want of a nail . . ." until the battle was lost, so social disruptions apparently affecting only the older members at one end of the family eventually catch up with even the youngest.

Nuclear groups living in the absence of their extended families are not as firmly rooted as those that feel themselves to be part of a larger whole. The ability to be free to sever roots almost at a moment's notice and to go anywhere at any time is advantageous to a technologically oriented economy, but it has profoundly disruptive effects on the total social organization in the long run.

The young children of such small mobile family groups have no opportunity to develop a sense of belonging to any place or to any line, and therefore it is not possible for them to develop an identity with and loyalty to either. With identity and loyalty go a sense of responsibility and duty. If the responsibility, duty, and loyalty are directed only to such a small group as the nuclear family, then responsibility to the larger community must be lost to sight, and this must then become an ingredient in the disruption of the larger society in the same way that the absence of the nail was a factor in the loss of the battle.

In this process a circular feedback is set up, for unattached, rootless young people are more inclined to migrate again in their turn. A society then becomes one of windblown tumbleweed rather than firmly rooted shrubberies.

It does not take much imagination to see that this circle can also operate in reverse. By reestablishing our elders as functioning members of society we may help in recementing family bonds and thus effect a stabilizing influence on the lives of our children. This could only be an advantageous factor in the restoration of good order in our societies at large.

Part Three

WHAT WE CAN DO ABOUT IT

CHAPTER ELEVEN

Introduction

> I find everything detestable that merely informs me,
> without increasing my power of action or stimulating
> me directly. —GOETHE

In this part of our book we want to give some concrete suggestions for courses of action that could be undertaken to help older people lead their lives in full to the end.

At this particular time there seems to be emerging among a growing number of us a realization that the lives of vast numbers of older people are unsatisfactory to them and unhappy, and it seems to us that there is a readiness to try out new solutions to their difficulties.

Not a few sociologists have attempted to define the problem. Among them, Wilbert Moore emphasized role ambiguity. In 1951 he wrote:

> Perhaps the fundamental problem of the aged in industrial societies is that they have no definite place in the social structure. That is, there are no regular, institutionally sanctioned responsibilities for their care and social participation which square with both traditional values and the requirements of an industrial system.

and in 1960 W. E. Burgess made the same point when he spoke of the "roleless role" of the retired:

In short, the retired older man and his wife are imprisoned in a roleless role. They have no vital function to perform. . . . This roleless role is thrust upon the older person at retirement and to a greater or lesser degree he has accepted it or become resigned to it.

Currently sociologists are again trying to clarify the true meaning of retirement and all its implications. They have formulated a theory of disengagement that has provoked considerable discussion and controversy. In this theory retirement is thought of as a direct outcome of disengagement in later life, leading to loss of role, to withdrawal from society, and to a narrowing of function. Looked at in this way, it is a "phasing out" from life.

Preceding the disengagement theory was the activity theory, which took into account the extending of the lifespan. Those who promoted the activity theory were more optimistic. They minimized or denied the necessity for any slowing down in old age. They regarded retirement as an "unfortunate event."

It is our belief that the concept and the very word "retirement" are counterproductive to the welfare of the elderly. We should like to find acceptance of a term that would imply simply a transition to a third phase of life in the same way that the graduation ceremonies in some United States schools and colleges are called a commencement ceremony. We do not refer to a "retirement" from school. The young person has completed one phase of his life—his education—but he is commencing another—his mature period. We believe that upon completion of the mature period a person should be able to look forward to entering a third phase in which certain new roles would be open to him and that his society would come to have certain expectations of him. We call our concept the Third Phase Theory. In accepting this view the "roleless role" would be eliminated and a stage of life entered in which the role of the elderly will be defined and established as a new force in societies.

So far, the only schemes organized on a large scale are those that deal with material needs. By this we are referring to government-organized plans like the social security system in the United States, the national old-age pension and health insurance schemes in Britain, and similar state-sponsored plans. But it is becoming clear to an increasing number of concerned people that to provide the basic material necessities, while a first essential, is not enough. The schemes that are in operation ensure that old people do not starve. But human beings need more than to be provided with food and shelter. They can be starved in other ways.

We have discussed how the historical process, especially within the last hundred years, has resulted in a cutting off of the old from the lives of their communities and of how this has caused a great deal of unnecessary unhappiness, besides contributing to an unrealized degree to an increase of chronic diseases, crowding our hospitals, draining social assistance facilities, and burdening the social structure.

The chapters that follow contain several suggestions of lines of action, and the spirit of these suggestions is to give to older people the sense and the possibility of remaining active participants in their communities. Underlying the proposals is an attempt to take into consideration the true psychological needs of the elderly, based on the biology of the human species.

The principle that has guided action until now has been the idea that at the end of a working life people should be "rewarded" with a period of leisure in which they could enjoy their declining years—an attitude that has been *caricatured* in the United States by the commercially promoted idea of "fun" in the "golden age."

What is emerging, more clearly all the time, is that a satisfactory life in old age can be achieved only by a feeling of *usefulness*. What we have thought of as "fun" turns out to be a misreading of the activities of children and young people. Their "fun," that is, play, is basically preparation for the activities of life. That they so clearly derive pleasure from their practice of skills is an indication that this practice—"play"—serves biological ends and is therefore rewarding. "Play" serves no biological purpose for elders. By this we do not mean to eliminate recreational exercise. No matter which way one looks at adult recreation, true recreation involves a lot of work, whether by the body in active sport or by the mind in reading or other stimulation. We have to separate recreation from leisure. Anybody who participates in a game of tennis exercises the mass of muscles that demand use but are not usually used by urban man and exerts as much or more physical energy as a hardworking lumberjack. That it is a voluntary activity makes it pleasurable. Leisure, on the contrary, is nonwork and, especially, nonpurpose. These two concepts are not clearly separable, partly because in many areas they overlap and partly because leisure at its extreme is just as unacceptable as backbreaking work. Leisure, unrelieved by meaningful activity, is boredom. This, in a nutshell, is the new problem.

The dawning of a change in attitudes toward this problem is dramatically highlighted as we write. Today on page 45 of the New York *Times* is an advertisement, taking up more than a third of the page, for two retirement villages being developed by the same enterprise. The text of the advertisement runs:

YOU CAN LIVE IN YOUR OWN CONDOMINIUM HOME, AND SHARE IN A LUXURY WORLD OF RECREATION. EVERYTHING'S RIGHT AT HAND. RESORT-SIZE SWIMMING POOL WITH SUN-PATIO. NINE-HOLE PITCH-AND-PUTT GOLF COURSE. BOATING. FISHING. SHUFFLEBOARD. HORSESHOES. AND ALWAYS SOMETHING GOING ON AT THE COM-

MUNITY CENTER. MOVIES, CARDS, POOL TABLES. SEWING AND
WOODWORKING SHOPS. STUDIOS FOR CERAMICS. CLUBS. ON THE
GROUNDS, A STAFF TO TAKE CARE OF EXTERIOR MAINTENANCE. A
GATEKEEPER AND PATROLS FOR ROUND-THE-CLOCK SECURITY. IN-
SIDE YOUR CONDOMINIUM IT'S YOUR OWN QUIET, PRIVATE WORLD.
BRAND-NEW, UNDEMANDING, WITH ELECTRIC APPLIANCES, AREA
THERMOSTATS, AIR CONDITIONING.

Turning over to the back of this page, on page 46 we find
an article headed ONE FEAR FOR WOMEN IN 60s—TO WAKE UP
WITH NOTHING TO DO. This article starts with the words "She
yearns for letters and phone calls from her children; she
knows that it is more important to spend time with her husband than to wax the kitchen floor; she passes the white-
haired women on the benches in Central Park and can't believe she's one of them; she fears widowhood. She is the
woman in her 60s. In recent interviews with a number of
women aged 60–69, they discussed what life is like at their
age. There was unanimous agreement that their happiness is
measured according to the amount of meaningful activity in
their lives. Those who were most active seemed to feel least
aware of their age and relatively free from the emotional
complications that are associated with aging—ennui, aimless-
ness, estrangement from youthful society. . . ." One of the
women interviewed, Lavinia Russ, an author, was quoted as
saying, "One of the worst things that can happen to a woman
of our age is to wake up in the morning with nothing to do."
Another, Rebecca Soyer, the wife of the noted artist, who, by
chance, is a neighbor in the building where we live, is
quoted by the reporter as having "beaten the retirement
malaise by immersing herself in Head Start* and remedial
reading projects."

Dr. Lillian Gilbreth was an ardent advocate of this atti-

* Head Start is a preschool program designed to bring children of disadvantaged families up to the levels of achievement of other children starting
school in the first grade.

173

tude. She was an industrial engineer and management consultant, an efficiency expert, and a pioneer in time-motion studies, who died recently, still active at ninety-three, having been made famous by one of her daughters in the book *Cheaper by the Dozen*. Three years previously, when she was over ninety, she traveled and lectured in the Soviet Union, Denmark, Britain, and Spain, and later, when she was back in the United States, her speaking schedule often called for five lectures a week. When she was interviewed after one of these lectures, she said, "Age needn't determine what one is able to do. It's really a matter of marshaling your resources, using time sensibly and well. I have taught that, and have lived by that principle."

Dr. Gilbreth of course was an exceptional person. Nevertheless, to avoid that deadly boredom that is the outcome of inactivity—whether we call it leisure, retirement, or taking it easy—our societies have to make it possible for *all* older people to be able to use their time and energies in ways that can be fulfilling to them.

In some of the general areas we shall suggest, tentative starts have already been made. In some, fairly well-established programs already exist. Others are suggestions based on the evolutionary past and the present psychology of the elderly, but they have yet to be tried in actual practice. They may or may not prove to be feasible. Some may seem inconsequential in scope, yet they too are prompted by considerations of what are the fundamental needs of the elderly so that we can help them put their efforts into those spheres that they were evolved to function in. It may not seem to be a very profound suggestion to ask an old lady to read to a child, but in doing this she is fulfilling an aspect of her destiny and therefore she receives a satisfaction far beyond what so simple an act would seem to justify.

Again, some of the suggestions we shall make may appear to be naïve in the light of present political and social realities.

But the growing pressure from the large and increasing minority of older people among us may well transform what appears at present to be a naïve suggestion into a practical necessity. It is certainly not outside the bounds of reality to envisage that, before long, the elderly will again become a political power by force of their numbers, as they once were in the societies of emerging man by reason of their special attributes.

It is not our intention to provide a "how to do it" manual. Our desire is to focus some thinking along lines that we believe could prove fruitful and beneficial. We have a feeling that the time is ripe. Right now more and more people are questioning the prevailing assumptions. There is an awakening to psychological realities. In our discussions with professional and lay persons who have had firsthand experience with elderly men and women, we find lately an almost unanimous agreement on the value of useful activity in old age. Basic to our thought is the belief that "to provide" should be reserved for childhood. Adults, and especially older adults, need the opportunity to perform.

CHAPTER TWELVE

The Need for a Widely Based Research Council

Not by physical force, not by bodily swiftness and
agility are great things accomplished, but by delibera-
tion, authority, and judgment; qualities of which old
age is not deprived, but with which it is, as a general
thing, even more abundantly provided. —CICERO

A few universities have set up research projects that have
attempted to define the actual state and the actual needs of
the elderly population.

Among them, the University of Oregon-Portland State
University instituted both long-term and short-term training
programs in an effort to determine suitable methods of preparation for retirement. Similar investigations have been
undertaken by the Institute of Gerontology of the University
of Michigan-Wayne State University. Ypsilanti State Hospital, also in Michigan, offers courses on better treatment
and restoration of aged persons "hitherto destined to round
out their lives in drab mental hospital environments." The
same hospital also carried out other work relating to retirement, especially the part that churches could play in aiding
the aging. Their purpose was to find a basis for training teachers in this field. At George Washington University the Department of Health Care has completed texts for two courses
in social gerontology.

Research that is of great interest to insurance companies was conducted by the University of Denver, where it was found that the evidence refutes the stereotype of the older driver as being unsafe. On the contrary, the study revealed that in some states older drivers have fewer accidents per driver and better driving records than drivers of all other ages.

In 1969 the Administration on Aging provided funds for the National Gerontological Society to establish a committee on research and development goals in social gerontology. The objectives were to survey existing research; to recommend subjects it considered worthy of the support of public and private funding; and, more specifically, to make recommendations in the areas of (1) work, leisure, and education, (2) living arrangements for older people, (3) social services for older people, and (4) the economics of aging.

Commissioner John B. Martin, Jr., of the Administration on Aging, estimated before a Senate committee that "personnel required for programs devoted solely to serving older people will increase from approximately 330,000 today to at least one million by the early nineteen-seventies; that within the next two or three years there will be a need for five hundred or more additional persons to serve in State and Federal planning, coordination, and evaluation agencies; eight hundred more senior center directors; from eight to thirteen thousand management personnel for retirement housing projects; and from twenty-three to thirty-one thousand additional trained workers for recreation programs for older people." His concluding recommendation was: "The need for personnel with specialized knowledge in the field of aging is reaching emergency proportions. An immediate all-out effort on the part of Government and educational institutions is essential if the situation is to be improved. Implementation of the recommendations contained in *The Demand for Personnel and Training in the Field of Aging*

177

should be the very minimum action taken to meet the need for trained personnel in programs serving the elderly. Omnibus legislation for this purpose should be introduced at the earliest feasible date."

As can be seen, many starts have been made. But these, among several others, especially by universities (the Cornell University Study of Occupational Retirement, for example, or the work of the Institute for the Studies of Leisure at the University of South Florida) as well as by the government, all are pilot projects with limited funding, and their impact has not been widely felt by the public. We ourselves, occupied as we are with this subject, were not aware of many of them until we made intensive inquiries and resorted to the material of reference libraries. The average man in the street (if he is not destitute and therefore a client of social agencies that might direct him) is not aware of the existing facilities or those in the making that might help him solve some of his problems. This also applies to many of the public and private enterprises to which we shall be referring in the following chapters. We believe that all these efforts are too widely dispersed and that their impact could be more effective if they were coordinated and centrally directed.

And then there is another point. In an affluent society, when a segment of it suffers deprivation, a clamor will arise to alleviate the hardship. The thinking in such attempts is largely along the lines: If a person has no shelter, let us provide one; if he is penniless, let us make him an allowance; if he is sick, let us provide him with medical care.

Until very recently it was considered the obligation of each family to look after all its own members, including their elders, in case they were sick or disabled. Among the less wealthy the building up of their families was undertaken by the seniors with the view in mind that in their old age, and particularly in case of infirmity, their welfare would thus be assured. In fact the efforts they invested in their families

178

were their premiums for their social security. This provided for an orderly transition from one stage to the next, and problems in old age were simply a part of the life of the family as a unit. The elderly were not a separate problem to government agencies. If they were poor, they were part of the whole problem of poverty in the society.

The problem today is much more complex, not only because the number of older people has increased, but also because there is no longer a caste of elders clearly divided into the well-to-do and the poor. There are many subdivisions, and these keep increasing. All of this requires careful study, on the one hand to delineate the problems as they exist for all the elderly, and on the other for the special classes of old people within the group as a whole.

To give an example of the changing picture, today in the United States fewer than 10 percent of adult children make any monetary provisions for parents who do not live with them. On the contrary, money is more likely to flow in the other direction. Middle-aged parents are accustomed to giving money to their children, and this habit often continues into their old age. Middle-class parents are ambitious for their children, and they help them if they can; if they cannot, they are still reluctant to take money from them, feeling that this would interfere with their meeting their own needs.

It is not without significance that the older person has a reluctance to become dependent on his grown children. His feeling that he would lose some part of their respect for him if he did so is probably the last vestige of his sense of status. We think, in this regard, that the attitude of the eighty-two-year-old mother of one of us was not untypical. In her lifetime, right up to the last week of her life, she took the greatest delight in entertaining us with meals and in preparing special delicacies for us, but she adamantly refused to accept even the smallest gift.

But if giving cash is not a common practice, living together is. Of all old people who have living children, more than one-third live with one of them. This is not invariably to help the elder. Sometimes the older person is helping the younger. Other families live together because they always have. Isolated and uncared-for old people may be less numerous than has been thought. Perhaps because they are concentrated among the applicants for public assistance, welfare officials may overestimate the proportion of the needy or lonely old. A survey made about seven years ago revealed that there are more old people living with their children today than the total number of old people who were alive forty years earlier. At the same time we find retirement colonies proliferating, if for no other reason than because there are more elderly people, and this simple fact explains the present wider variety of problems. For useful policies to be formulated at government levels, a great deal of in-depth information still awaits collection.

We should bear in mind that in earlier times the life expectancy of the poor was low in comparison with that of the richer classes. The existence of a caste of elders was thus largely restricted to the elite classes. By reason of their standing there was, therefore, no great problem. From them came the wise old men, the rich old men, and the influential old men of social groups. Nor should we overlook the fact that many wise, rich, and influential old women were among their number.

Since the advent of rapid technological advances and the many cultural and social developments that resulted from them, the situation has changed. Improved working conditions, nutrition, and health care have extended a longer life expectancy also to the poor, who now form a new variant of the senior caste. Even here there is a further subdivision between the working poor and the indigent poor. Among the indigent poor the elderly have never known respect or possessed standing, any more than any others in this category. All of them are and have always been wards of society. The greater number of old from this source add their weight to the percentage of elderly in the general population, but their problems are different and have to be dealt with in a distinctly different way.

The elders among the working poor in rural communities contributed their share by helping to grow food and by taking over domestic chores. They therefore always had and still have a useful function in the economy and lives of their families to an extent that their families could hardly manage without them. For this reason they have never lost the respect of their juniors, and they remain to this day models of a desirable social order. They serve to emphasize one of our main theses: that wealth of itself is not a factor in a contented old age. The rural poor, in most instances, retain their self-respect in old age better than many among the urban rich.

It is among the urban working lower-income groups and reaching into the middle-income group that the new problem exists. Money brought in by their wage earners governs the lives of these families. Food has to be bought, it cannot be grown. Space is limited, and additional space is costly. Any non-wage-earning member of the family, whether a child or an old person, is a burden upon its resources. Labor laws and customs, governed by humanitarian considerations, have shortened the working life from both ends. Child labor laws and earlier retirement goals have appeared on the scene and like all well-intentioned social reforms have a desirable ideal in view. Longer schooling and earlier relief from the "burden" of work sound like purely humanitarian motivations, but in truth, economic pressures formed a large part of the motivation that brought these measures into being. The only way for wage earners to maintain a high level of wages was by reducing competition for their jobs in the face of the reduced need for man-hours brought about by mechanization. As another example of unforeseen—and in this case not so distant—effects, the wage earner brought upon himself the burden of supporting these two displaced groups. Like a physician who prescribed penicillin for a disease, which he cured, and then found that he had to cure the effects of the penicillin, well-intentioned and even successful measures frequently bring in their wake undesirable consequences.

In this area the need is seen for a specialist whose sole study is the "ecology" of human relationships. This expert is the social psychologist, who is not distracted by sentimental or political considerations. He must eschew short-range expediency, his goal is the benefit of the society as a whole. If that goal is achieved, every segment of the society in the long run is better off. He must always keep in mind that the improvement of conditions for any one segment at the expense of any other eventually works to the detriment of both. Often he must espouse unpopular views, since long-range goals rarely satisfy immediate demands. On the contrary, the satisfaction of immediate demands often makes fundamental improvement of conditions impossible and leads to patched-up and jerry-built social structures.

The elderly have become a part of the pool of incapacitated or otherwise nonproductive citizens who have to be cared for by the state. As can be seen from the projects mentioned at the beginning of this chapter, and many others like them, official thinking is still along these lines. They have been lumped together with dependent children, the unemployed, and the disabled and have become a statistic for which certain monetary allocations have been reserved. In this way the elderly have become the concern of the statistician and the sociologist. Specialists in these two fields have looked upon the elderly in their own terms, which have essentially been to deal with the satisfaction of their physical needs within the possibilities of the budgetary allocations of the government. Their fundamental psychobiological needs have not been considered, perhaps understandably, since these cannot be included in statistics.

Only in recent times is it beginning to become apparent that these measures are not enough. A *team* of specialists is necessary, headed by a social psychiatrist or a biopsychological sociologist, who would coordinate the efforts of a gerontologist, a gerontologically oriented psychiatrist, an economist, a lawyer, a labor leader, and an historian, together with the sociologist and statistician, and at least some of these specialists should be women. The coordination of knowledge from all these fields is required in order to recommend sound programs.

Their function should be broadly based research into all aspects of old age (encompassing psychological as well as material needs) that can be utilized as a basis for advisory and counseling services. Their findings should be at the service of government at all levels to ensure the proper planning of programs. They should also be in a position to brief private industry on how it can serve the elderly segment more effectively. There is hardly a consumer industry that could not benefit from the advisory services of such a group.

We might add in passing that the news media could render no better service to the elderly public at large than to give wide publicity to their findings. In the New York *Times*, for example, there is a daily listing of activities and events of special interest to, and suitable for, children. A routine daily listing of services and opportunities for the elderly along the same lines would be of great value. The elderly, after all, outnumber young children in our population, and so it must be also in the interest of the newspapers to publish information that is useful to them.

The broadly based research councils we have proposed could also take it upon themselves to form, or instigate the formation of, subsidiaries to deal with direct counseling of the aged, and these subsidiaries would have many functions, including:

> *psychological counseling*, specializing in all the areas for which the elderly have the greatest need;
> *economic advice* in its various aspects (after loss of job; retirement income; new enterprises; investments, with the special requirements of the elderly in view), for the economic needs of the elderly have a different perspective from the needs of the middle group;
> *a directory* of nonprofit social services open for recruits, and any other counseling services for which a need became apparent.

These advisory councils could be government-sponsored or privately sustained. They could have an extremely important role in acting as a research arm for a government Department of the Aged.

All their endeavors would be directed toward finding ways and providing means for the able elderly to regain a necessary function in the working order of their societies without displacing or disturbing other segments of the population. Only in this way will it be possible to restore the well-being of our older fellow citizens in any meaningful sense, for there is no other path to restore them to the esteem of their groups and thereby to reinstate their own feelings of self-worth.

CHAPTER THIRTEEN

The Need for an Educational Campaign

What is a great life? A thought of youth realized by
ripe age.   —ALFRED DE VIGNY

Seeds of a widespread movement to stir the elderly into
action on the scale of the women's liberation or the black
civil rights campaigns are being found in many places and
are already taking root and sprouting in some.

At the General Assembly session of the United Presby-
terian Church in Denver in 1972, Margaret Kuhn gave elo-
quent expression to the aroused feelings of a large number of
older people. She said, "Age-ism is just as pervasive in our
society as sexism," and she spoke scornfully of the "paternal-
ism of homes for the aged" and the stereotyped idea of the
old as "fuddy duddies clinging to the past." She found that
old people at the present time "are very responsive to being
radicalized," and she added, "They form an explosive, positive new force in Church and society." She went on to de-
plore "the immoral waste of precious human resources that
results from mandatory retirement rules that automatically
scrap-pile people just like old automobiles."

To get action on what she feels so urgently should be
done, Margaret Kuhn has founded a movement called significantly the Gray Panthers, designed to follow the aggressive

tactics used by the Black Panthers. Here is a nondenominational movement of small proportion. So far she has only two hundred members, but they have already begun to lobby in Washington and elsewhere.

When interviewed during the session, she made many colorful remarks that echo much of what we have written. She declared, "I wouldn't play shuffleboard if you paid me $100." What she called the "asinine activities of those damned golden age clubs" are anathema to her. Margaret Kuhn is a handsome woman who would not feel flattered if told that she looks younger than her sixty-seven years, and she asserted that social action is one of two involvements that alone are necessary for the mental health of the elderly. The other is sex. "Sex is a beautiful thing until rigor mortis sets in," she said. "Our society is lewd when it chuckles about 'dirty old men' or 'old women' who angle for attention. That is another kind of age-ism."

The Gray Panthers led by Miss Kuhn is but one of the sprouting seeds in the field of old-age activism. Another is in Manhattan, where a group of about five hundred women from all over the country and from Canada met at Marymount Manhattan College under the sponsorship of a group called OWL (Older Women's Liberation). The theme of this conference was that these women find themselves rejected by the younger members of the women's movement as well as by America's youth-worshiping society as a whole. They felt that they had special needs above and beyond those of the women's liberation movement in general; that "wrinkles, gray hair, and menopause do not automatically relegate a woman to the scrap heap." Barbara Seaman summed up the atmosphere of the meeting when she said, "Men in middle age are regarded as at the height of their life and careers, while the middle-aged female is retired and put on the shelf —both as a sex object and as a person."

Characteristically, one of the speakers, Mrs. Landesman,

stated, "I am a happily married housewife, and the reason I'm here is because my role in life has been pretty much confined to motherhood. But now my children are grown and I'm no longer a mother, and I'm worried because I'm not trained to be anything else."

A seventy-three-year-old woman spoke on behalf of the Jeannette Rankin Brigade, which she helped found, and said she came to "assert that age does not mean anything in spite of the fact that we call ourselves older women."

All these groups and others like them are small, and they are widely separated. Nevertheless, they give evidence of the feelings harbored by a large number of older men and women. In a later chapter we will mention others who have organized themselves into committees for political action.

When the need for any large social change arises, it always finds expression at first through a few of the more vocal and aroused members of the groups affected, and usually, in the beginning, they are not taken very seriously. The great majority of the sufferers of any social injustice is usually inclined to go along with its society's standards and accept them, even when it is their victim. It is this majority that has to be aroused before effective changes can be made.

It is an interesting sidelight that throughout history the greatest social revolutions have occurred not at the moments when oppressed groups were totally subjugated, but at periods when the dominant groups themselves realized their injustices and began to relieve them. Historically, this is the turning point. Protest movements then mushroom, spread, and often develop into revolutions.

This stage has now been reached as far as the elderly are concerned. The dominant middle-aged group not only has recognized the need to alleviate the lot of its elders, but has begun to make tentative steps in this direction. Therefore, by all historical precedent, this is the strategic moment to engage in the type of teaching and propaganda that has become known as consciousness raising among the great masses of the elderly.

The first step is to attempt to restore a sense of pride in being what they are. Just as other oppressed minorities tried to hide their religion, skin color, or nationality under a mask of conformity out of a sense of the disadvantage or shame these brought, but learned that they could achieve their ends only when they came out boldly, acknowledging their own essence, so some of our elders are attempting to teach their peers that a mask of youth neither helps nor becomes them. It seems odd that it is necessary to state anew how vital it is to uphold a person's self-respect. All of us, after all, are aware of how painful it is when we ourselves feel that we are being demeaned. On the other hand, if all is well, we take our self-respect for granted and do not give it a second thought. We have to keep in mind that it is essential to that part of our well-being that stems from being accepted members of a group—any group whatever.

The elderly, through a circumstance of technical development, have lost their function in our societies and, with the function, the respect and esteem that are every human being's needs. Since the "elderly" includes all of us—for unless we die an early death, it is a phase of life that every last one of us at some time is going to be in—in sheer self-defense we must do something concrete to remedy the situation. This is not a sphere in which we can take a "Let George do it" attitude, nor can we take the view that there are plenty of do-gooders around to help those in need and that they will do what is necessary. This is not only a personal necessity for every single one of us, but also a public necessity. It is important to a nation as a whole that this significant segment of its population be reintegrated into its socioeconomic life.

This would seem to be so obvious a task for every responsible agency to undertake that we must wonder how it is possible that it has not already been done.

The real difficulty seems to be that as yet the problem has not been defined in any fundamental way. The awareness of the presence of a severely deprived group calls forth a response that would help its individuals as though they were invalids or needy. But what we have to understand is that in this area it is not only the impoverished older people who are severely deprived, but *all* older people, rich and poor and middle groups alike. They are deprived on an emotional level that affects every aspect of their well-being, whether psychological, physical, or social.

Before any useful steps can be taken, a large-scale campaign has to be undertaken so that not only government agencies but all of us, those who are already in the older category as well as those who have yet to enter it, may come to understand what the real necessities are.

This campaign should stress that old age of itself is not incapacitating; that, on the contrary, to deprive a person of purposeful activity *is* incapacitating; that the longer a person is usefully employed, the longer he or she is likely to stay fit and feel well; that the respect of his fellows is an absolute essential to a person's mental and therefore physical health; that a person retains the respect of his fellows only as long as he has a function and is needed. As soon as he or she is dependent and no longer needed, he loses respect. It is therefore society's business to see to it that the possibility for useful function is available to its elderly members.

To get these ideas accepted, an effort would have to be made on a scale similar to the public relations campaigns that are undertaken by any organization for civic or medical purposes. Good examples are the campaigns to impress the public with the dangers of smoking and with the signs indicating a need for a checkup for the possible early treatment of cancer.

In this case a campaign could be initiated by any gerontological association, and it should be supported by the government to assure a wide impact. It should use every avenue available to reach the public, including books, lectures, advertising, articles in newspapers and magazines, discussions on television and radio, and dramatizations. Added interest might be aroused by including information about the remarkable careers of some old people in all walks of life.

Other aspects of the campaign would have to be directed to older people themselves. First, they must be made aware of what is at the root of their problems, and then they must be encouraged to revise their own views of old age. This could be done in the way that any deprived or abused groups that have developed low self-esteem as a result of their treatment by others have been helped in renewing their pride in themselves. The importance of their role in their society should be emphasized and recognized by everyone—not least the elderly themselves. They should be encouraged to consider themselves as holding a separate status, not to be confused with those in their prime or with the youth, and their status should be associated with dignity. The old must be brought to realize that to receive respect, self-respect is a prerequisite.

American blacks have found that the black studies programs, informing them of their own history, their contribution to the world's culture, arts, music, and their part in the development of their country, have been invaluable in restoring their pride in themselves. The American Indians have also embarked on teaching their young of their own cultural past and have found this a potent method of restoring pride. The old of all colors and classes could be greatly helped by being taught the essential role they have played in the evolutionary development of man and the part they still could play in the stabilizing of human societies.

Such a campaign directed at the elderly and designed to increase their understanding of the role of their kind in the past and of their potential value to human societies would have a very useful by-product. The "Black Is Beautiful" campaign was an aid in restoring pride to the black community in the United States, but it also had the effect of drawing attention of the rest of the population to the values and worth of their black neighbors and, to a greater extent than before, accepting them. In the same way a program to raise the pride of the elderly could not help but come to the attention of those not yet old. Informing them of the resource they have in their old people would help them learn to treat them according to their needs, and it would also help them prepare for their own later years.

Modern marketing methods have utilized the techniques of the "campaign" to introduce new products or ideas. The concept of the campaign, as its name implies, is borrowed from theories of warfare. A general staff devises plans to effect a victory over opposing forces by every means that will minimize its own losses and expenditures and maximize the possibility of the speedy attainment of its purpose. This is the guiding principle also of every public relations campaign. The public toward whom the campaign is directed is in fact the enemy. Either it has no knowledge of the product or idea that is being promoted, or it has resisted it.

Of course, the banner of the campaign has to fly over a sound product or a socially acceptable idea. Inferior products or fraudulent ideas cannot long survive the rigors of a campaign and any rising negative response of the public. In effect, they would lose. Then again, if the product or idea is valuable but the methods of promoting it inadequate, it will meet defeat in this case too. An essential of any campaign is its timing. Often invaluable ideas are presented ahead of their time, when the public is not yet ready to receive them or when circumstances make it impractical to set them into motion. Then, too, they will fail. However if the idea is sound, it will be presented again and again and will eventu-

191

ally find its way into the consciousness of the public when the time for it is ripe.

We feel that the time for the promotion of such ideas as we have discussed is now. All through the Western world there has recently been an intensification of concern about the lot of the elder. In the Communist world the problem has not been so marked. Needing all their hands to build up their economies, their elderly were inevitably drawn into the social and economic lives of their countries, but as their efforts met with success and they are becoming more industrialized and urbanized, they also are beginning to institute retirement policies in some areas. It is an irony that the problems of the elderly become more acute as their societies become more affluent.

Like every campaign, this one must be made on many fronts. A most important consideration, which should be uppermost in the mind of every person connected with such a project, is that at all costs its dignity must be maintained. Dignity is precisely the most essential element to restore to the older person. It is easy to foresee that such a campaign, unless very carefully handled, could leave the way open to material for comedy. In the past the old have been the subjects of comedy and satire, and this is the last thing we would wish to open the way for. This would especially apply to programs undertaken by the media that also deal in entertainment, such as television, radio, the theater and cinema. All these media could provide excellent forums for the dissemination of knowledge of old age and its values and problems as long as the tone of the material made it clear that the subject is of vast importance to everyone.

The best way to assure that suitable and valid material is available to all who can use it advantageously is to initiate steps for the establishment of departments in universities that would deal with problems of old age not purely as medical problems or purely as socioeconomic ones, but as an as-

192

pect of the total life of man. Such departments could be funded by the government, by foundations, labor unions, or the consumer industries that would ultimately benefit by the opening up of a new sector for their wares.

These new faculties should not be associated with medical schools but should be a part of the general programs offered by universities to all students. They should be led by men and women with special qualifications in the fields of psychology, anthropology, and sociology. Ideally, they should be subdivisions of departments of biopsychological sociology. Special health problems would remain the domain of the gerontologists in the medical schools.

Special courses, visiting lecturers, and special publications could be encouraged by the provision of special funds for these purposes. Such courses would contribute not only to the students' comprehension of the role of the elderly, but also to their understanding of the evolutionary development and biological functioning of societies as a whole.

CHAPTER FOURTEEN

Psychological Preparations for the Middle Group

To be seventy years young is sometimes far more
cheerful and hopeful than to be forty years old.
—OLIVER WENDELL HOLMES

The early Greeks had a symbol for eternity that they
called the *ouroboros*. It was an image of a snake as a circle,
biting its own tail. Unless one looked very closely, one could
not see where was the beginning and where was the end.

Contemplative minds, seeking the causes of effects and the
effects of causes, have formulated such symbols in several
parts of the world and in widely separated times, using the
images of their own cultures. The ancient Chinese symbol-
ized the same idea with a dragon encircling the globe, and
Shakespeare spoke of the child as father to the man.

Modern minds, with their scientific bent, refer to all life as
a process. No living being is an entity, finite, of itself. What
it is today is the result of what it was yesterday and flows into
what it will be tomorrow. Moreover, the flow is not in one
direction alone. The interlocking and overlapping of untold
numbers of circles of other existences modify it or have a
part in forming it. What any of us is today is the sum of our
experiences and being on all our previous days and, even
further, of the previous existences and experiences of our
forebears through all of time.

This is not a purely philosophical concept. It has vastly important practical implications. If we are the sum of all our yesterdays and of all the yesterdays of our ancestors, then what we shall be tomorrow and the day after can be largely determined, or at the very least modified, by what we are and do today.

We have only to flip the pages of a family photograph album to see how the baby becomes the young person and the young person a man or woman, without being able to discern the later form in the earlier one unless with the benefit of hindsight. No simple exercise can show us better that there is no time in our lives when any of us is an absolute. And just as in our middle years we are the result of our past and are in the process of becoming our future, so is our old age not an absolute. It can be modified by our present.

In our middle years we are in a position of strength. We have chosen our paths and are well on the way to accomplishing our goals. We have established our positions in life and have a good idea of our abilities and the possibilities they offer. The positive advantages of middle age endow us when we are in it with a feeling of confidence and permanence, and it is for this reason that it is just in these middle years that we are least likely to look ahead with thoughts or plans for our old age. The strong feelings we have about ourselves as entities, of what and who we are and where we belong, prevent us from identifying with our elders. Yet this is just the time to be looking ahead with plans for shaping our personal future, for planned or unplanned, the future will soon be the present, and it is far better to meet it prepared from a position of strength than for it to fall upon us unexpectedly, like tiles loosened by a strong wind from the roof of a building we may chance to be walking by.

The first thought that customarily comes to mind in a middle-aged man or woman, if by chance either should think of his own old age, is that he should stay in good health. He will then be careful with his diet, avoiding fatty or choles-terol-rich foods, watch his weight, be careful about getting sufficient exercise, and will go to his doctor for regular checkups. In summary, the thought of growing old is associated with the fear of losing good health.

Many people, anxious to take every reasonable precaution, visit their doctors in much the same way as they take their cars to the mechanic for a ten-thousand-mile or a twenty-thousand-mile checkup—tighten a few bolts, readjust the carburetor, tune up the engine, and the car is good for another ten thousand miles! In our gadget-oriented Western societies it is easy to have an image of our bodies not unlike the motors of cars, and a visit to a doctor is then considered to ensure that our own internal mechanisms will work without giving trouble for the next six months or year.

With this kind of outlook we are misled by our faith in the shiny, elaborate, impressive machinery with which many doctors' offices today are equipped. We take a machine's verdicts as final and are inclined to overlook the fact that a machine can only analyze the data it is fed. But the human body is not a machine. Its processes may be determined by such nonabsolutes as whether or not we slept well, ate too much or felt hungry on a particular day, and, above all, our mood. A man undergoing a checkup on a day he has closed a satisfactory business deal will surely cause a machine to register a different verdict from the one he would receive from it if he went on a day when he was tense and worried about the outcome of his negotiations.

Doctors, being part of the same cultural spirit, cannot help but be subject to similar influences. And so, when a sickness occurs shortly after a satisfactory checkup, the doctor, as well as the patient, is often surprised and at a loss to account for it.

This kind of mechanical approach invades our attitudes

196

toward all things human. Responsible officials and concerned laymen alike have attempted to relieve the distresses of elderly men and women by making efforts to supply them with larger pensions, better housing, or more available medical care. While all these are certainly desirable and conducive to comfort, they do not begin to solve or even recognize the most significant elements of the older person's needs. These are his mind, his emotions, and his moods. Since we have so far not discovered a gadget that can measure and classify these, we find no place for them, and therefore we all too often discount their importance in judging a person's health.

A doctor practicing in Santa Fe, New Mexico, tells this story:

"A certain volatile building contractor has been sporadically in and out of my office for several years. When he is excited, which he usually is, his blood pressure is astronomical, but his heart size on X ray is normal, and so is his cardiograph. On forced hyperventilation his astronomic pressure drops to normal in a few seconds.

"He had the usual minimal work-up for hypertension, with checks on kidney function and investigation of various forms of adrenal overactivity. He was then put on a mild blood-pressure sedative, which afterward he usually failed to take, and was asked to come back for periodic recheck, which he also failed to do.

"Not long ago I saw him again and he told me he'd been talking with a friend of his who advised him to report to a certain clinic for 'a good checkup.' Five clinic doctors put him through the same tests, then subjected him to a radioactive scan of his kidneys, injected dye into his aorta, and made X rays while the dye passed through the renal circulation—a test not without hazard. He was then told they thought he'd be all right, and he was put on essentially the same medication he was on already. He was enchanted by it

197

all, and told me, with shining eyes, it had cost $1,500 but fortunately he had insurance coverage. When I told him I'd given him the same reliable information for much less, he was offended, not at them but at me. I haven't seen him since."

Another doctor, who is connected with the Geisinger Medical Center in Danville, Pennsylvania, echoed this theme when he published in a medical journal a distillation of his own impressions in the following tragicomic series of letters:

June 16

DEAR HARVEY,

Alice is in a dither. Shall she pack the striped or polka-dot bikini? I myself settled on hiphugging surf-riders and a pair of bongos. Old friend, your invitation was irresistible! Do you really think Spray Beach can cope with three swinging septuagenarians in January?

We just returned from my 50th reunion at Kenmore, a pleasant affair made even more delightful by my shooting a 90 in the golf tournament, and our discovery that excellent martinis are still mixed at the Hamp.

Retirement has been much better than I anticipated. I still keep up connections with old friends by doing consultative work at the office two mornings a week. Perry lives nearby, and has two teenage ballplayers who like to shag grandpop's flies. Alice and I get out to a good restaurant once a week or so—you know my weakness for cheesecake!

A nagging backache (from a solid 5 iron shot last week?) has convinced me to have a checkup. I suppose we should do the same for our bodies we do for our cars. So I am going to the Atwater-Marshall Clinic for one of those thorough physicals which are in vogue. They call it "health maintenance"—preventive (or is it preventative?) medicine.

I'll let you know how it goes.

WINSTON

Lion Hotel   September 21

DEAR HARVEY,

A note on hotel stationery isn't much, but I want to brief you on my day at the Atwater-Marshall Clinic. Such efficiency, and everyone I saw was polite and friendly. They don't miss a thing here, I'm sure.

At 8 o'clock this morning, I filled out a long questionnaire covering everything from measles to bed-wetting. In quick order I had blood taken; drank some sugar water; had a chest X-ray, cardiogram, and breathing tests; had blood taken again. About 11 o'clock I saw my doctor (Kenmore '58!) who went over my forms and asked some more questions. I felt a bit embarrassed, since the best I could come up with was the appendectomy I had in the service, and a bout with the hives 25 years ago.

My backache disappeared two months ago, but I felt obliged to mention it too. After a thorough exam, my doctor ordered more studies. "No stone unturned about that back pain, etc." So I am scheduled for tests tomorrow morning: IVP, spinal series, sigmoidoscopy, and barium enema. I see him tomorrow afternoon for the final report, which I anticipate will be good. In truth, I have never felt better.

Alice surprised me tonight with a lovely meerschaum for my collection, and a pound of John Cotton. At least I can have a good pipe in the morning, even if I do have to miss breakfast.

WINSTON

November 18

DEAR HARVEY,

These past two months have seen a great change in my life. I never thought much about my health before, but since my trip to the Clinic I seem to be devoting almost full time to it. Most of the tests were normal, but a few have revealed unsuspected problems that demand preventive measures.

First of all, I am a diabetic. My blood sugar tests were mildly but definitely abnormal, and the same was true of my cholesterol and uric acid. My cardiogram showed a few premature contractions and some changes that the doctor regarded as "nonspecific," but which might indicate coronary artery disease. The X-rays of my colon showed diverticulosis. A therapeutic dietician instructed Alice and me in a special diet—diabetic, low fat, low cholesterol, low residue. Good-bye to nights out for dinner, and to cheesecake. In fact, it has been good-bye to almost everything I enjoyed eating. No highball before supper. And the deepest cut of all, the doctor said I have to give up my pipe.

I am taking several drugs now: quinidine to stop the premature contractions, something to lower uric acid, a capsule to control my cholesterol. I test my urine for sugar every morning, go to our doctor for a blood sugar every month. So far I am doing well, he tells me. But somehow I don't feel the same.

The doctor told me to "take it easy," so I felt it best to give up my mornings at the office, reluctantly have confined my golf to a few turns on the putting green. Alice and I still look forward to visiting you this winter, though I'm afraid I won't be a very sprightly guest.

Do you have a good internist in Spray Beach?

WINSTON

December 28

DEAR HARVEY,

I am indeed sorry that Alice and I will be unable to come to Spray Beach next month. May we have a rain check? I have been fatigued and irritable—I guess I miss that old tranquilizing pipe—and have grown thin. Really, I would cut a rather poor figure on the strand. I sleep poorly, but hate to get up. I don't mind the pills, I've grown accustomed to them; and the diet isn't too hard to follow. Actually, I don't much care if I eat or not. My doctor can't find anything wrong, and I am following to the letter all the instructions of the Clinic.

Harvey, it's astonishing how everything can go to pieces

all at once when you're 70. I can hardly believe I felt so well last summer.

Winston

March 8

Dear Harvey,

Win passed away on Wednesday. He was admitted to Cedars Hospital a week before with a case of flu which turned into pneumonia. At first they gave him an excellent chance to recover, but he just didn't seem to care. I don't believe he wanted to live.

Our doctor told me that before Win died his cardiogram, blood sugar, cholesterol, and uric acid were all normal.

Alice

The truth of the matter is that for most people, if they have reached their middle years in reasonably good health, the likelihood is that as long as they maintain their habits they will remain reasonably healthy. There is certainly no harm, and indeed some benefit, in regular medical checkups. The only disadvantage to them is that they are often regarded as a kind of insurance guaranteeing continued good health.

The middle-aged person in good health who wishes to prolong it into old age must realize that his current satisfactory state is not due to the mechanical working of his body organs alone, but to the sum total of his life-style. If he feels well, it is because he is active, interested in his occupations, planning for the future rather than dwelling on the past, feeling concern and taking responsibility for others, as well as because his body is functioning as it should. And if he wishes to continue to feel well in his later years, he must find a way to preserve this activity and interest.

Unfortunately, this supremely important element of general health is not sufficiently understood and appreciated. Those who are in their middle years would do well to ponder on this. Whenever they have contact with their elders, they should see this as an element they should do everything in their power to uphold if it is present or to restore if it is not. They should not focus all their attention on the performance and comfort of the body alone.

By far the most important reasons for a change for the worse in health of people as they age are the emotional effects of drastic social changes in their lives. As we have stated, these often have physical consequences.

The single most important thing a person in the middle years can do to ensure a satisfactory old age is to get his mind "tuned in" and, so far as possible, accustomed in advance to any changes that will have to be made, so that he can be prepared for them. It is a strange fact that most prudent men and women, while they are still healthy and employed, arrange for insurance against sickness and unemployment. They arrange for the distribution of their property after death while they are still alive. Many, if they are able, build up a reserve of funds to take care of their monetary needs in their later years. But it is a very rare person who makes plans in advance for the use of the time that will be available to him after retirement, and there is no substitute for purposeful activity and involvement for the maintenance of good health at any age.

Each woman as she reaches her middle forties and each man in his middle fifties should be very much aware that decisive changes in their lives are not too far ahead of them, and that one of the chief elements of the change will be that they will have a great deal of free time to dispose of. They should also realize that unless they find a good use for it, this free time will cause them to experience changes of mood, a deepening sense of uselessness, and, ultimately, apathy and its psychological and physical aftermaths.

First and foremost, then, the most important thing to do at this time, while still fully occupied, is to give consideration to discovering which occupations would fill life with interest and challenge later on. It does not make a great deal of difference what the exact nature of the chosen occupation is. What is vital is that it is undertaken in a way that gives the doer a feeling that its outcome has some value. While it is helpful if the task chosen has some social significance (because it is just the loss of a functional place in society that is being compensated), there are no absolutes here. The activity does not have to be an earthshaking one. If a man or woman is interested in gardening and if, besides growing flowers and food for his personal use or pleasure, he also devotes some time to crossbreeding and producing a new strain of a vegetable or flower that would be useful or pleasing to others, this activity would certainly bring its own satisfactions.

If it is possible to set aside any time during the still busy years, it would be rewarding to make a start in the occupation one has in mind to take up later. Then one can find out whether it brings the satisfaction anticipated, and if it does not fill the bill, there is still time to seek another.

If no occupation immediately comes to mind as something one would really like to do, it would be worthwhile to give up a little current leisure in order to read or to attend lectures so as to broaden one's view; in the process perhaps this would open a door to a new source of interest or involvement that could be taken up when the time for retirement arrives. In the following chapters we shall make some suggestions about a wide range of activities for which there is an unfilled need for recruits and in which the elderly could easily participate.

If a satisfactory occupation can be found and started so that it will present no difficulty to expand and continue it after retirement, the mental well-being it will engender will go far to halt the physical accompaniments of the depressions that so often arise in retirement. The search for such an occupation should have at least as much priority in the middle years as the more customary medical checkups.

Nowadays we give our adolescents special courses in school in sexual matters to prepare them for their adult life. It would be just as important to prepare those in their late middle years for the transition they too are going to make into a new stage. This preparation would be largely of a psychological type, and the paramount importance of maintaining self-esteem the chief emphasis. The part played by the loss of self-esteem, as we explained in Part II, has to be fully understood, and also the fact that self-esteem can be maintained only when a person has the feeling that his life is important and that what he is doing is useful and necessary.

At this point we are assuming that the campaign we suggested in the last chapter has aroused enough interest to create an audience for such courses. We readily concede that the average person in his early fifties will at first not be too eager to participate in instruction of this kind, since he will feel it to be tantamount to admitting that he is getting old. However, those prepared by the campaign to regard old age in a positive rather than a negative light may form a nucleus around which others may gather later.

The contents of the course could, in part, elaborate on the matters we have discussed in the first two sections of this book: the original importance of the elderly in the societies of man; the importance of having a function in the life of a society; the importance of his status in the life of an individual; the direct and indirect consequences of the loss of any of these; the various expressions of depression in the elderly, both the overt and the camouflaged; the importance of recognizing some of the quirks of old age as camouflaged depression; the importance of mental stimulation at least as great, if not more so, as the need for physical activity.

The deeper understanding of what can happen to a person's feelings about himself in the case of disability, loss, or retirement from useful function would serve two purposes. It would enable those still in their prime to help their elders in ways that would sustain them and not foster depression. At the same time it would help them prepare for avoiding some pitfalls in their own later years. This type of instruction could have a further useful offshoot in that the understanding thus gained would help dispel the contempt, impatience, and condescension that are sometimes felt toward the elderly.

These courses could be sponsored by a mental health organization either on a community basis or through corporations as a public service. The cooperation of women's clubs, fraternities, and church and political organizations in providing facilities and audiences could be enlisted.

Our belief in the need for this type of preparation is clearly shared by Commissioner John B. Martin, Jr. While giving evidence before a Congressional subcommittee, he made the following plea:

> In the Administration on Aging we are convinced that it is just as logical to prepare for the later stages of life as it is for the earlier stages. We agree with the view of the subcommittee expressed in 1967 that participation in programs of this kind is essential. We think, Mr. Chairman, that this is the time for a much expanded effort in this area. I suggest that the time has come to promote the widespread expansion of retirement preparation with the announced objective of making it available in the foreseeable future to all middle aged and older people who can be encouraged to take advantage of it. In our opinion there are a number of models that have been developed and tested sufficiently to warrant their being publicized and being made available for immediate use.
>
> I particularly want to stress this point. I have been surprised and discouraged to find on my return to Federal

service that probably not more than one third of the departments and agencies in the Federal Government have offered or are offering organized opportunities for retirement preparation to their employees. It seems to me, Mr. Chairman, that the Federal Government, which is the nation's largest single employer, is admirably equipped for assuming leadership in this area and that it should do so. Failure to assist its own employees to anticipate and prepare for their retirement years is also a failure to set an example for others.

It might be objected that such an educational program would entail a large expenditure of time, money, thought, and other resources of individual talent and involvement that could have been engaged in other fields. But what will the situation be like if we allow it to continue along the lines it has already taken? With the trend in our time toward longer life at one end of man's span and a lower birth rate at the other, it is common knowledge that the proportion of the elderly in the total population is steadily increasing. This population will become a chronic drain on the economic and manpower resources of the community in any case and, at that, without offering any benefits in return. In fact, between these two alternatives, we actually have no choice, for to continue with the basic philosophy we have now (which is one of putting a finger into the hole in the dike rather than of stemming the flood at the source) will in the long run be as costly, if not costlier, in all resources as pursuing the more basic course we are suggesting.

Even if we disregard a purely humanitarian consideration to ease the psychological plight of the elderly and rectify some of the social inequities and if we stress solely economic factors, we shall discover our advantage to be on the side of taking the more radical method.

The advantages can be readily summarized. In retaining or drawing back a large number of the elderly in the mainstream of economic life, there is no doubt that we shall decrease the incidence of the so-called illnesses of old age. Even beyond the immediate relief of the pressure on hospital space and staff, the beneficial ramifications of these two factors alone would be so far reaching as to defy a statistical evaluation. For the middle-aged participants in these educational programs, their contribution toward pulling such a large sector back into the activities of the community not only would reap a harvest as a salvage operation for the emotional health of their parents, and eventually their own, but also would provide economic rewards. If instead of being forced into a parasitic existence at the edges of their societies our seniors were restored to active participation in them, a great drain on the tax-paying middle group would also be relieved.

As Senator Jennings Randolph of West Virginia stated before a Congressional committee on February 6, 1970, "Underutilization of the older worker is probably costing our nation billions of dollars in terms of lost production and services and added expenses for unemployment compensation and public assistance. More importantly, the impact on these individuals in terms of frustration, despair, and the loss of the sense of dignity and status is incalculable."

CHAPTER FIFTEEN

So Much to Be Done

Have you ever been out for a late afternoon walk, in the closing part of the afternoon, and suddenly looked up to realize that the leaves have practically all gone? And the sun has set and the day gone before you knew it—and with that a cold wind blows across the landscape? That's retirement. . . . Have nothing to do with it.   —STEPHEN LEACOCK

Up to and including the present time the United States government has concerned itself in the problems of aging only with finding employment opportunities for elderly persons (defined as fifty-five or older) who are retired or unemployed (for fifteen weeks or more) and who have "no reasonable expectation of other employment or training, and reside near the job site." This is characteristic of the general emphasis on only the material needs of old age that we have mentioned several times. With the single exception of the Retired Senior Volunteer Program (RSVP), which we shall discuss later, no provisions are made for better-off elders, much less for the well-to-do. On this basis it is apparently assumed that they have no needs.

In the last few years the Department of Labor has supplied funds to the National Council of Senior Citizens for their Senior AIDES programs. AIDES is an acronym for Alert, Industrious, Dedicated, Energetic Service. Among their projects are several in the fields of health and social welfare.

The plans are funded only for limited periods. While this one was in operation, however, it was remarkably successful. For instance, in Huntington, West Virginia, an assessment was made of the work habits of the elderly participants in the project, and it was found that they have a deep sense of responsibility; are especially reliable and have a definite desire to work; require less supervision; are willing to work extra hours and without pay; and are very punctual.

Some seventy-two physically handicapped old people were among the enrollees, and their performance was outstanding. It was reported that they required very little attention and clearly demonstrated their abilities to perform vital tasks. A legless former schoolteacher worked as a recruiter, sometimes even going from door to door in his wheelchair. An elderly lady with arthritically deformed hands nevertheless performed clerical duties in maintaining records.

Another project was conducted by the National Council on Aging from August, 1967, to November, 1968, in twelve communities. It was called FIND (Friendless, Isolated, Needy and Disabled), and it was undertaken under the aegis of the Office of Economic Opportunity to "understand better and to document the characteristics and needs of the elderly." It suggested action to "(1) locate the elderly poor and identify their needs, (2) involve the elderly poor in community action programs, and (3) strive for new services for major unmet needs."

A further program, Late Start, is sponsored by the National Retired Teachers Association and the American Association of Retired Persons. This one is designed to provide a new start toward independence for disadvantaged older persons, and its goals are to develop latent skills and interests with opportunities for helping others either as paid employees, volunteers, or just as informed friends, and to raise the level of involvement in the community.

To show how far a little ingenuity will go toward finding

solutions for problems when there is the will to do so, we might take the example of Project WORK (Wanted: Older Residents with Know-how) in Long Beach, California. Despite a high rate of unemployment in that area, WORK succeeded in placing more than fifty elderly applicants in productive jobs.

Such pilot plans, through which private groups as well as the government are testing the possibilities of employing the needy old, could well be the inspiration for other projects for the occupation of those who do not need public monetary assistance but who *do* need purposeful activity to put their time to good use.

There is a great deal of important work that is not being done and that people over sixty-five could do very well. More than that, no other age group in the population could do it as effectively as they.

Much of this work is of a cultural nature. Cultural pursuits in a rapidly growing society are apt to be overlooked. They are thought of as luxuries, as mere ornaments to life, and they do not receive the priorities they deserve. First consideration is given to the filling of material needs, and cultural and other needs that serve the long-range quality rather than the immediate wealth of a community are commonly left to voluntary organizations or to the consciences of civic-minded individuals. There is no sustained and coordinated planning, and the results therefore cannot achieve their full possible impact. In long-established societies cultural endeavors are often directed toward the entertainment of the privileged. They are usually not thought of as a necessary part of the social existence of all the people.

But there is a deep-seated need for cultural cohesion. We see an expression of this under our own eyes. The young today are devoting much of their best energies to finding a system of values and a context for their lives, and they are doing it by themselves, since their parents have neglected this vital area and let it go by default. There was a time

210

when religious training and the observation of religious rites filled this need, but today the majority of our young people do not receive religious instruction and neither they nor their parents find strength in the precepts of organized religions. This has left a void that literally begs to be filled.

The parent generation, of necessity, is involved in the pursuit of material needs. This cannot be otherwise, for it is its function. The bearers of culture and tradition, by their evolutionarily determined role, are the elderly caste—the grandparent generation. When this generation is cut off from its family base by early retirement and the consequent alteration of life-style, the young have no focus on which to shape their own identity.

This need is so deeply felt that we find our young seeking an identity in the company of their peers in floating groups not anchored to any stable community. They reject the materialism of their parents exactly because it is devoid of cultural content. Earlier parent generations, equally preoccupied with the material welfare of their families, had at least the observation of their religions to mitigate one-sided pragmatism. This was greatly facilitated by the presence of the grandparent generation, who were the upholders of religions as well as the arbiters of secular traditions. The adolescent generation, now largely cut off from this source of stability, is adrift and searching for a direction. They seek it in new forms, whether in the arts or in messianic politics. Especially in music their participation is almost indistinguishable from the religious involvement of earlier generations. They find in their choral groups, their ballad singing and guitar playing a companionship and unity that has a spiritual quality. But without the presence of elders and with the natural progression of their years as they move out of their adolescence, these groups fall apart. They are constantly coalescing, breaking away, and recoalescing like patches of algae on the surface of a pond.

It is into this void that we must call back our grandparent

generation. Youth's differences are with their parents, not with their grandparents. When they tell each other and the world, "Don't trust anyone over thirty," they have no thought that anyone exists on this earth over the age of sixty-five. To them such elders are either an alien race or lumped together in their minds with the middle-aged.

Because of the absence of a bridge between them, so far no friction has arisen between the young and the grandparent generations. Perhaps we can go so far as to assert that even had there been one, there would have been no friction, for from the earliest times there has been an affinity between the very old and the very young.

In suggesting to the elderly—indeed, in reminding them of their task—that they turn their attention to the cultural needs of the young, we are offering them not only an activity that can put content and interest into their own lives, but one that in the process will enable them to act as catalysts to draw the young back to their communities. They would once again have an opportunity to be the anchors of their societies.

In writing these words we can hear, with our mind's ear, a strenuous objection that this idea is not practical on today's scene; that the vast majority of adolescents are actively engaged in cutting links with older generations and gaining their independence.

In the first place, it is the biological business of adolescents to gain their independence. This has been true since the dawn of history—indeed it is not even confined to the world of man but is a part of the life-cycles of many species. However, the basic contest is between the young and the parent generation. The young often find a soft spot in their hearts for their grandparents, if they have contact with their grandparents at all. As a matter of fact, an adolescent recently said to us, "You know, teen-agers and grandparents have a common enemy—parents!"

212

We have personal knowledge of a group of older people, at the Stephen Wise Free Synagogue in New York, that functions very well in providing facilities for a group of high-school-age young people to take part in cultural and civic activities, and we feel sure that there are many others like it, especially in other church groups. We think it would be worthwhile to try to extend the effort to the general community level, among the larger numbers who are not church-affiliated.

There is no question that many cultural activities already exist, especially in the large urban centers, but these are mainly directed to the middle generation and actively involved even an extremely small percentage of this. By far the larger numbers are only passively involved as occasional audiences. Since there are so few people actually occupied in these fields and mainly on a voluntary basis, those elders who entered into these activities would not displace, but supplement existing efforts.

Besides this, we feel that cultural activities of older people should have a different slant. They should concentrate on providing opportunity for the young to become involved in group activities within the framework of their communities and not be forced to seek a solution for their needs outside it, rather than in extending existing facilities for the middle and senior groups, although this too could be done.

This whole field would provide a prime new territory for staking out possible second careers for our retired population, especially among the better-educated groups. For some a certain amount of supplementary training might be necessary, but many are already well equipped.

Sometimes when we talk about jobs that we think would be desirable to undertake, we find agreement but also a comment such as, "That's all very well, but how do we go about getting it started?"

It is not a difficult task to organize any type of action once one has made a firm decision to do it. Usually it does not take more than a few telephone calls to friends or acquaintances to find one or two who would be willing to work on a worthwhile project, and each of these can just as easily find one or two more. The initiator then has a committee with whom he or she can work to define goals and to determine practical ways of achieving them. From time to time some of the original workers fall out, but others may be invited to join in their places. Indeed, a worthwhile undertaking usually needs only minimal active recruiting, for once it is in operation, its very presence attracts volunteers, and in this way it is kept viable.

Group Activities for Adolescents

As we grow older, our needs change, but there is no stage of life in which the elderly could not play a helpful role. The part that elders can play in enriching the life of the young child is rather special, and we shall come back to it in a later chapter. For the adolescent the great need is to have a feeling of "belonging"—of having a place in a group he identifies with, where he is known and his presence valued. There are few ways to satisfy this need that equal participation in cultural activities based on the home community.

Since the dawn of history, dance, music, and drama have been closely interwoven with man's strivings to find meaning in his life; they were the forms in which he expressed his religions, and his most important occasions from earliest times have been celebrated in rituals composed of these elements. Plainly dance, music, and drama are as deeply rooted in man as the symbolic representation of his impressions and feelings in speech itself. Man as a species has been described by some as the "symbol-making animal," and in the arts he has found his ultimate symbols.

One does not have to be especially gifted in any of these fields to use them as forms of expression. Every society, from

214

the most "primitive" to the most "civilized," takes pleasure in the special talents of some of its individuals, but this does not alter the fact that everyone, gifted and ungifted alike, has a need to use them. From very early childhood each of us expresses himself in movements and sounds that are the elements of dance, song, and drama. When a child jumps up and down in glee, he is using the elements of drama, for he is expressing his feeling of joy in action and sounds that convey it.

Through these very basic forms of expression man has found his surest way to bind individuals into groups and groups into larger communities. They offer the most natural and obvious place to start in any effort to recement human communities.

Choral groups; dramatic societies; musical groups, including all the styles from ethnic or folk music through the classical and to the latest forms; informal associations for country and folk dancing—all could play a very great role in integrating the young with their communities. These groups do not form themselves. They have to be encouraged and organized. Meeting places must be found, administrative work done, teachers and leaders obtained. This is the type of work that is being done, with very good results, by the Stephen Wise group we have just referred to.

Besides these basic activities many other smaller circles of young people with special interests could be encouraged. While people of any age with special interests usually find ways to enjoy them, it would still be a useful service to channel these into the life of the community, and there are many ways in which the elderly could become involved in the establishment and running of special interest groups.

In all this work and by their very presence and participation, the elderly could serve their fellows in such an important way that it would provide its own rewards, regardless of whether the work was paid or voluntary.

Although the work in itself would be rewarding in every

way, appreciation of it in the form of such honors as plaques and certificates would add even more incentive. As every organizer of groups of workers for charitable causes knows, any form of recognition is as much a spur for voluntary effort as it is for any other kind of endeavor. Testimonial lunches or dinners are often given for outstanding workers for good causes, where the attainment of the goal in which they are interested might be thought to be reward enough. During World War II the United States government issued badges and certificates of merit to volunteers who manned bond-selling booths successfully. Prizes of no great monetary value, such as inscribed books and the listing of their names on honor rolls, also provide great incentive to workers in many fields. Any or all of these methods could be used to reward the elderly for their participation in such communally valuable undertakings as we have suggested, even if some of them are paid, for, in according honor to the worker, the value of the work itself in sustaining his self-esteem (and thereby his emotional and general health) would be multiplied.

Cultural Enrichment of the General Population

A field that would provide a natural occupation for the elderly is the founding and supporting of local historical societies. This does not have to be confined to financial and administrative support but could include participation in searching out documents, recording local lore, collecting biographical material about distinguished local citizens, and preserving historic sites.

This activity could spread further into the revival of local customs and perhaps the reactivation of local crafts. Such activities frequently lead to serendipitous discoveries—perhaps to finding people who are interested in some ancient and forgotten craft and who could be helped in resuscitating it. Many people today find great pleasure in restoring or reproducing old musical instruments, or making models of historical ships or trains for local libraries or museums, all of which requires meticulous research as well as skill. The elderly could bring such people together by locating them and getting them in contact with each other and could perhaps assist in the research.

Any of these activities would enrich the life of a community, and they all require many kinds of skills that elderly people could provide: skills in organization, research, inspiring general interest, as well as the simpler routine jobs connected with keeping them going once started.

In the same general spirit there is much that could be done to beautify towns. Even without large projects, like the establishment of parks, that require considerable public funds, many smaller projects could be undertaken, the sum of which could be even more telling. A drive for window boxes planted with flowers along the main streets; the planting of flower beds in the town centers; the planting of trees and shrubs; participation in the cleaning up of local grassy or wooded areas and their maintenance—all these would provide satisfying occupation for the elderly and help restore them to their communities at the same time. Such enterprises have the additional advantage of being continuing occupations, for flowers, trees, and shrubs, once planted, must be cared for and replaced from time to time.

A very good demonstration of what can be done in this direction has been given by the National Farmers Union, which set up the Green Thumb program and operated it under a grant from the Department of Labor as part of its Mainstream project.

This particular program was for the elderly poor. It permitted them to earn up to $1,500 a year by working three days a week. During 1970 more than 2,400 of them improved or built more than 350 roadside parks in rural America; planted more than 1,000,000 trees, flowers, and shrubs;

cleaned out lakes; built picnic places and campgrounds; and helped restore and develop historic sites. Concretely, this program provided employment opportunities for more than 2,000 low-income elderly people in rural districts and, together with a sister project, has helped remove more than 10,000 from the poverty category. The degree of self-respect and consequent well-being it restored at the same time cannot be measured. At the 1970 hearing by the special subcommittee on aging of the Senate Labor and Public Welfare Committee an eighty-eight-year-old male witness testified: "Those two boys left me, and the name of the first one was Arthur and the second one was Ritus. You put them together, and it meant arthritis was in my arms. At my age, I believe that Green Thumb is the reason I am living today. If it hadn't been for Green Thumb, I believe I would have faded away."

At the same hearing one Senior AIDE, who had found new meaning in retirement after obtaining work at a local marine museum, testified: ". . . I knew when I got up in the morning it was going to be a repetition of the day before. It was not very pleasant to know it was the same thing all over again. But since being down to the museum all that has changed. I know when I get up in the morning that I have some place to go to."

Everyone who has been engaged in looking into these programs has expressed enthusiasm for them. When Kirschner Associates presented its evaluation of the work done by the Green Thumbers, it included the following assessments:

Their work was of high quality.

The participants were overwhelmingly enthusiastic about their jobs.

They enjoyed working outdoors and with others in a team effort.

The program more than doubled the incomes of the participants.

Many workers reported that their work helped improve their health as well as their outlook on life.

Unfortunately, the continuation of such valuable work applied to poorer people depends on continuing grants. But there is no reason why those who enjoy pensions or some other private means should not undertake similar work on a voluntary or expenses-reimbursed basis, for the sake of the personal satisfaction involved, as we have suggested.

Another area of service that has a place for as many recruits as can be found is the improvement of life for those old people who are disabled and not able to help themselves or to leave their homes. Who are more qualified to understand their needs than the healthier and more fortunate elderly? They could establish meeting places where the disabled and therefore lonely old could be brought together to spend their days in company and with some diversions or occupations; they could arrange transportation for them so that they could take advantage of such amenities; they could plan occasional outings. This list could be extended. It is subject only to the goodwill and imagination of the organizers.

Some concrete examples are before us. In Worcester, Massachusetts, a group of elderly volunteers set up the Doll-Making Workshop to provide pleasure for underprivileged children. They showed a new sense of purpose when they changed the direction of their efforts to preparing materials to help the mentally retarded of their community. And in Maryland older volunteers are providing in-home services for homebound elders. They shop for food, obtain prescriptions, prepare meals, do the laundry and straighten up the house. "Their presence in the home is often a final pipeline to the community for the old people they assist. In emergencies they remain with the aged individual, giving comfort and reassurance that someone cares, until other arrangements for care can be made."

There is also a place for the elderly in the artistic life of a community that is not confined to providing facilities for the young. There is a need for the enrichment of the middle generation's life in many communities that are distant from large urban centers. In these, older people could aid in the formation of drama societies, orchestras, and lecture programs by seeking out and encouraging talent; by obtaining the services of directors, conductors, and lecturers; by staffing halls where groups could meet; by helping in the necessary clerical work; and even by participating if they are able to and would enjoy doing so.

One could also envisage a corps of older people who would act as library aides. Where there is no local library, they might help found one, occupying themselves with the collection of books and other material. Where libraries exist, they might help them extend their services by staffing them after hours, enabling their use by the segment of the community that is not able to go to them between nine and five. This activity might also be tied in with local history and subjects of special local interest. Some library shelves could be devoted to these and be maintained by a group of elders, who could also search out material for them. Such an occupation is tailor-made for older citizens whose interest in the traditions of a place and its personalities and past is strong.

Another field that comes to mind as a useful occupation for the more energetic elders is cooperation with antipollution efforts. They could aid in the organizing and collection of recyclable materials. Most housewives would cooperate in separating glass bottles, clean paper, tin cans and other metals from their garbage if they knew these would be collected regularly and serve a useful purpose. Older people could also band together to check and report on polluting chimneys, sullied waters, littered streets and lots, and follow up to make sure that these sore spots were being dealt with effectively.

In line with the cultural endeavors we are suggesting in this chapter, the elderly could help improve the lot of the hospital patient. In this instance we are not thinking of paraprofessional help to nurses and doctors, which we will discuss in another chapter. The services we have in mind here are the personal ones that the medical and nursing staff is not called upon to do. The elderly could circulate books and magazines to the patients, mail their letters, and perform small commissions for them. Their mere presence as interested and friendly daily visitors making a round of the wards would bring a great deal of pleasure to many long-term patients. A group of volunteers performs precisely these services at Mount Sinai Hospital in New York, and their work is greatly appreciated.

Not only hospital patients, but also elderly people living alone in their own homes would derive untold comfort and help from this kind of interest. Here and there members of some senior citizens councils and also some church-sponsored groups of elders have instituted programs called Dial-a-Friend. They prepare lists of housebound older people whom they telephone at regular intervals to check on the state of their health and welfare and help them in getting assistance when necessary. Such mutual-help programs are also beginning to make their appearance in some housing developments where there are a number of older tenants.

If in some smaller communities it is felt that none of these occupations would be sufficient to offer steady activity to their able elders, it should be possible to organize them into a volunteer pool, whose members could be called upon as a need arises, in much the same way as temporary office help is sometimes organized. Many new fields of activity that could not be envisioned or planned for in advance would surely become apparent. The very existence of such a pool would suggest new uses for its services, and for its members the meetings themselves that would be called from time to time for the discussion of possible projects would help form bonds of companionship and mutual interest.

The categories of possible occupations in the cultural lives of their communities that we have discussed here are by no means exhaustive. We also realize that some may be more practicable in some areas or countries than in others. Our aims are simply to indicate some directions and to remind our readers that so much could be attained by a constructive view of the elderly citizen—a view that recognizes the fact that the community needs him as much as he needs the community.

The actual enterprises undertaken must be subject to local needs and local possibilities, but everyone stands to benefit if a more imaginative attitude is taken in meeting the psychological needs of the elderly than has been the case until now.

CHAPTER SIXTEEN

Servicing: Filling the Gap

To grow old means to begin a new occupation.
—GOETHE

In 1970, in the United States Senate, a bill (S-3604) was introduced to authorize the Secretary of Labor to establish a community senior service program for low-income individuals aged fifty-five and over who would render needed services that would not otherwise be provided.

Included in this bill was a recommendation for effective ways of training and retraining older persons. "Employment opportunities for mature workers cannot be increased exclusively by measures designed to eliminate discrimination based on age," was the reason given.

That effective training can retain the elderly worker in service and at the same time produce important financial dividends through the upgrading of skills was demonstrated by the plumbing and pipe-fitting industry and the Port of New York Authority. Also the work of Meredith Belbin in England showed that certain training techniques are clearly superior to others for mature workers.

Women have not been overlooked in the experimental projects that have been funded through work originating in Congressional committees. As part of the National Farmers Union's Green Thumb scheme another program, called

Green Light, was initiated for elderly women of low-income groups. The women enrolled in this plan provided community service as aides for teachers, nurses, librarians, and in the school lunch program and the food stamp program. An ambitious pilot project was undertaken in eastern Kentucky to repair the substandard homes of elderly poor people. It trained older persons as construction workers for this endeavor to improve the houses owned by blind and otherwise disabled recipients of public assistance as well as by the elderly. In the first nine months after they began in September, 1968, 230 homes were repaired.

A particularly instructive model is offered by the city of Martins Ferry, Ohio. That city has developed, operated, and backed a business that offers services and income opportunities to its older citizens. This project demonstrates that a small city can significantly increase such opportunities at reasonable cost and that their availability in a community goes a long way toward replacing boredom and despair with new interests for a retired person, whose services and handiwork benefit the community.

By odd coincidence, when we were preparing material for this book, we outlined a very similar if more extensive program. In discussing it with interested people we met the objection that the idea was not feasible because of restrictive labor practices, but in the light of Martins Ferry's experience (which we learned of later), we think it may be useful to give our own idea here.

In the era of affluence in which an increasing number of people live, especially in the Western world, our daily convenience is more and more at the mercy of that growing armada of gadgets and appliances that have replaced manual help and dexterity. We have become used to so many of them that we feel handicapped when, as inevitably happens to any mechanism from time to time, they fail to perform as they should or break down because a part is worn out.

When our manual skills were our only means of helping ourselves, if we found we could not accomplish a task in one way, we tried another and could adapt our methods to achieving our goals. But automatic devices know only one method, and if any small cog in their wheels is loose, the result is a total standstill with no alternative means. In many instances we cannot even revert to manual methods. In a household that has become used to the service of a washing machine, there is no longer the space or facility to wash clothes any other way; there are no tubs large enough, no space for drying. We can no longer go out and chop wood if our heating system breaks down.

The manufacturers of most appliances offer factory servicing for their wares, but these services are necessarily limited to the first few months or years of the gadget's life, and after that we are on our own. Even if we wish to avail ourselves of the manufacturer's service, it is often too inconvenient to do so. A housewife in Kalamazoo whose electric toaster or radio breaks down will think twice before she sends it to the manufacturer, whose plant may be in Kansas or Cleveland, as would a Liverpool housewife before shipping hers to London or Leeds. The inconvenience and cost of sending it is sufficiently great to incline her to go out and buy another rather than go to the trouble of having hers repaired. This may be good for the manufacturer, although even this is questionable, but it is bad for our personal economy, our general ecology, and our conservation of resources.

In our more urbanized communities we have come to be extremely dependent on the smooth working of our mechanical aides. The number of devices that can need repair in most households today is astonishingly large. If we stop to count our own, we find ourselves surprised.

When we buy a gadget or an appliance, it is usually accompanied by a piece of paper that guarantees its service and gives the name and address of the manufacturer. Over the years such pieces of paper are usually lost, especially since none of us expects to have to use their information within the periods of the guarantees, and after that time their usefulness is somewhat academic. The manufacturer has sold his business, or it is operating at another address or under a new name; his servicing agent has changed, or changed his place of work or telephone number, or is too far away for convenience. In short, when we need this type of service, we find ourselves dependent on a local repairman, of whom we know neither his name, his address, nor how to find him.

We might wonder why it is that such services—shall we call them Mr. Fixit shops?—do not exist in every neighborhood when the need for them is so clear and comparatively urgent. It seems that, because of its nature, work of this type is conducted by one-man enterprises without sizable capital at their disposal, and for this reason they are poorly organized. The people engaged in such services often have the skills but not the business experience necessary to keep their shops running as profitable concerns. They often close down after brief periods or after several years of struggling with problems of obtaining adequate help and financing or of coping with the paper work connected with running a business, reporting for taxes, and the like.

Of course these conditions apply most acutely in countries where the scale of wages and the cost of rent are high, since a repairman's time and his place of work are the chief components of his charges. But while the difficulty and cost of obtaining repair services are probably the greatest in the United States, the direction is the same in other Western countries. As wages and rents rise, fewer such services survive. Besides this, advanced technologies breed inventive designers who frequently change models, further decreasing the incentive to get the older ones repaired.

In the previous chapter we suggested a number of fields of activity open to the more affluent elderly or to those with a higher educational background. For those elderly persons whose interests and abilities when they were younger were not scholastic and who have spent their lives engaged in manual work, whether in factories or independent crafts, there is a wide-open place for their energies after compulsory retirement in filling this need that is close to the personal comfort of every one of us and becoming increasingly so.

Since one-man repair shops in large urban centers are becoming more and more difficult to sustain on a profitable basis, if we do not wish to be reduced to being obliged to throw away any gadget that develops a minor malfunction, we must attempt to reinstitute such services in some way. This is not merely a question of personal or even national economy, but of global necessity. We are beginning to realize the untold harm to our environment of wasteful economies based on planned obsolescence. It is not only desirable, but imperative, to conserve our resources by every possible means, and the reduction of waste by maintaining our equipment is an elementary one. The establishment of large servicing centers would go a long way toward achieving this.

This is plainly a task that involves organization and planning on a large scale. It could be undertaken by a government agency, but we believe it would be more effective if carried out by private industry. Because of the nature of servicing needs, it might even be advantageous for a group of larger industrial firms to cooperate in setting up a joint committee. There would be several inducements to make such a scheme attractive to them. First, it would be better than any advertising campaign to improve their public image; second, it would improve their customer relations because of the availability of servicing; and third, the operation could eventually be self-sustaining and might even produce a profit.

Such a committee could set up a parent agency that would offer financing and know-how to regional centers which it would license, along the lines of franchising enterprises. If successful, these could branch further into local centers. The prime objective of the regional centers would be to provide physical facilities (workshop, warehouse, and reception center) and a large pool of elderly persons of four types: workers qualified by their lifetime experience; those able to teach needed skills; managers and office personnel; and unskilled elders who would have to be trained. Any or all of the following services could be supplied by these centers:

Repair and maintenance of electrical and mechanical appliances. Carpentry. Plumbing. Gardening. Messengers for public institutions or hospitals. Watchmen. Clerical work for political or charity organizations. Domestic help on a temporary basis to householders who are sick or otherwise incapacitated. We should like to stress that, although all these are personal services, they all, if indirectly, aid in the conservation of resources or supply socially helpful activity so that the worker can take pride in what he is doing. Doubtless in different regions different services would be needed, but this list gives an indication of the extent of the types of trained help that could be used. We noticed in the New York *Daily News* recently that a seventy-eight-year-old man, Myron Surmach, was called from his home in Saddle River, New Jersey, to help the police at the intersection of Avenue M and Ocean Avenue in Brooklyn. The WALK-DON'T WALK traffic signal there had become engulfed by bees that were swarming on it. Judging from the two pages of photographs that accompanied the report, Mr. Surmach's expertise in handling bees was invaluable! Incidentally, if it were found that there were talent to spare in the second category (those needed to teach needed skills), these persons could well be used by hospitals that have occupational therapy programs.

We must realize that in setting up service centers in this way one would have to consider the realities of existing labor practices. These should by no means be an insurmountable obstacle. A somewhat idealistic approach would be to operate them outside the general labor force because of the special conditions that would be necessary to set up for elderly workers. Political facts of life being as they are, however, it would probably be more practical to visualize incorporating them in some way into a new branch of existing unions.

One could foresee opposition by organized labor to such a plan, in the fear of competition for its members. It would have to be made clear and emphasized again and again that there would be no competition, since these centers would undertake only those services that are not readily available. It should especially be understood that the "new" workers would be paid at prevailing rates. They should be considered an addition to the labor force that would accept an obligation not to undertake any tasks that might displace other workers.

All the older people participating in such an enterprise would work strictly on a part-time basis, according to the amount of time they desired to be occupied or felt capable of sustaining. But whether they decided to work for three hours or four or five at a time, they should be required to come in regularly at their allotted time both for their own sakes and for that of the enterprise. To facilitate this and to encourage cooperation, the center should have a social hall as an integral part of its organization, which members could use in their off-duty time if they wished to do so, as well as if their services were not needed on some days or at some hours.

In talking over our ideas for valuable occupations for elders, it is for this one—the employment of manual skills—that we have found the most resistance on the basis of practicality. It appears that it is far more difficult to find continuing activity for the older members of the labor force than for the white collar or professional retired, and this is the area that probably needs the most attention and ingenuity. It should be a prime field for the efforts of our proposed research council.

We feel that the centers we are suggesting have a precedent in the work that is being done very successfully for and with the blind. Schools for the blind assemble classes of this disadvantaged group for training and for work in many crafts. Their products are marketed in New York through the Lighthouse organization, which arranges for their display and sale and also for the employment of the blind who are able to offer special services, like piano tuning. So far as we know, organized labor has made no objection to this endeavor, although of course it is on a much smaller scale than the effective centers we propose would have to be. Perhaps when both the officers and the rank-and-file members of labor groups come to see that they themselves will sooner or later become part of the group of retired elders we are endeavoring to help, they will be convinced that it is in their own interest to cooperate and even to help work out practical details for such plans.

That the setting up of a network of centers is within the realm of possibility is shown beyond the shadow of a doubt by the existence of multipurpose senior centers that served some 509,000 people in 1969. The centers were located in both rural and urban districts, using available facilities such as housing projects, churches, and public and private buildings. They provided recreation, counseling, referral and information service, and opportunities for volunteer activities. In Maryland surplus school buses were purchased to provide transportation to and from the senior centers at a nominal cost. The Nashville Senior Citizens group operates a multipurpose senior center with twelve neighborhood satellite centers also in operation under the direction of trained older persons. Thus it is possible for the programs to be varied and tailored to the interests of each neighborhood group. Many health services, such as screening, are also offered through these centers, with many of them provided by the older people themselves.

A report of the Special Committee on Aging published in March, 1971, contains the following statement on page 101:

> For most elderly participants, community service is more than just a job or a means of providing badly needed income. It can also mean a most satisfying experience serving people in their localities; a place for association; and a means to engage in purposeful activity.
>
> For many older people, inactivity is the greatest enemy. But employment can overcome this problem.
>
> The enthusiastic acceptance of existing community service pilot programs strongly suggests that there are many low income older persons in virtually every community who are ready, willing and able to perform services. Greater utilization of their skills, experience and wisdom would benefit not only the elderly job seeker but the public as well. The Committee recommends early enactment of legislation—similar to the Older American Community Service Employment Act—to establish a national service program for older Americans.

Coming back to our own suggested service centers, we believe it to be very important that they be made attractive, so that it would be a pleasure for older people to go to them and a source of pride to be associated with them. The rooms should be bright and cheerful, the walls and furnishings in light, bright colors. Window boxes could be kept planted with flowers, and shrubs and flower beds planted around the building where possible. The maintenance of all this could be allocated to the elderly members themselves so that the center would become like a club to them and they would have a feeling of participation in it.

These large centers could also be used to train small groups from nearby areas that might be too small to maintain a facility of the type we have described. In these smaller areas one attractive room or small store could serve local needs. These could stay in contact with the larger parent center as a source of supplies or reinforcement where necessary.

Once in operation, the services of these centers could find new directions, for new applications for them would surely occur to those involved. For example, those elderly members who in their working lives had been craftsmen might be called upon to teach their special skills in craft courses at local schools. The trend in our societies to large-scale manufacturing has led to a condition in which we all have become dependent on machines to fill our needs. When the machine fails us or its product is defective, there is no one left who can substitute for its function. We are not able to help ourselves anymore, and fewer and fewer of us are being trained in the most elementary skills. In assisting schools to provide such courses the elderly would offer society at least as great a benefit as they would be receiving from it.

In industrialized and urbanized societies, moreover, a gap has opened up between the consumer and the producer of his requirements. Between them stands only the salesman, who is not directly connected with the working of a product but is only there to aid in its distribution. The public feels a mounting sense of frustration with the situation, which is being expressed in a great deal of criticism of manufactured products of all kinds. At the moment only the very largest corporations, like those in the automobile industry, are able to afford a wide net of service stations, and even here there are limitations. In these circumstances it would surely be to the long-range advantage especially of the middle- and smaller-sized manufacturers to use the very large source of manpower that is available in the elderly to build bridges back to the public by providing maintenance services in cooperation with each other at regional and local centers.

A charitable effort is seldom as valuable as self-help. In a situation where the manufacturer considers himself a patron providing a "make-work" occupation for older citizens, neither the benefactor nor the beneficiary is ultimately rewarded, for no beneficiary likes to feel grateful and no benefactor likes to be unappreciated. An overly paternalistic attitude fosters resentment and anxiety because of the dependency it breeds. But in a situation where each party has an advantage in the part played by the other, real progress can be made, and this would be the case in this type of effort. The old person would have an occupation that would sustain his place in his community. The manufacturer would have a stepping stone back to the goodwill of the public far more valuable than anything he could gain from any kind of advertising, no matter how much he invested in it.

To end this chapter with a practical example of what can be achieved by a single individual with a little imagination and a great deal of organization, the potential of providing the public with a service it needs is shown by the record of Colonel Harland Sanders.

By the time he had reached the age of sixty-five Colonel Sanders had been a farmhand, a railroad worker, an insurance salesman, a service station operator, and a Chamber of Commerce officer. He had studied law by correspondence courses and had run a restaurant. But a series of business setbacks in his middle sixties gave him the incentive to use his first $105 social security check to make still another start. He felt that in today's servantless society there is an almost limitless need for the substitution of individual domestic service by other means, and that since cooking is one of the most time-consuming domestic chores, any satisfactory assistance in this area had to find success. That his idea was right and that sixty-five is not a too advanced age to start in a new field, he has amply demonstrated. Now eighty-one years old and known as the Kentucky Fried Chicken King, he has franchises dotting the entire country, and when he sold them, they made him a very rich man. Not long ago he was called by a Congressional subcommittee that was studying the problems of aging, and in the course of his testimony he gave the following advice to the nation's older citizens:

One should not plan his retirement in the spirit of being deprived of something, but in the spirit of having something added to his life.

Don't be against things as much as for things.

Even if one can afford it, don't rely on loafing. Life doesn't have to be easy to be wonderful.

Get up every morning wanting to do something.

Seek variety, develop original ideas, go with your whole heart, don't let the minutes rust away.

"In these eighty-odd years of mine," he said, "I've had my share of ups and downs. But every time you go down, get up again. You'll be stronger than ever." And he added, "For God's sake don't think about retiring. There are so many things to do."

Colonel Sanders is surely a living exemplar of the truth of Goethe's statement that we borrowed as a motto for this chapter.

CHAPTER SEVENTEEN

The Higher-Ranking and Professional Elderly

The challenge is to remain a person of worth to society and to one's self to the very end.   —E. S. SMITH

". . . and it now gives me great pleasure to present to our beloved colleague this token of our affection and esteem." For those in the audience of a testimonial presentation such words may evoke a warm glow. They see themselves, at a later date, in the place of honor, with all their virtues finally acknowledged and rewarded. They feel a twinge of envy for the leisure that old so-and-so will have to pursue his hobbies, for his freedom from departmental pressures and maneuverings, for his comfortable pension. But what about the recipient of the engraved gold watch or the silver salver? After the first few weeks of delight in the unwonted rest and free time, how will he feel when he wakes up morning after morning with no pressing task ahead of him, no problem teasing his mind?

Were the talents that brought this man to the position he held suddenly switched off on the day of his retirement? Is it not just one more aspect of our incredible wastefulness of our resources that no use is found for the lifetime experiences of such leaders from the moment their retirement consigns them to oblivion? Is it not possible to find a means to retain their knowledge at the service of their organizations in a way that would not disrupt the promotion and incentives of those still rising in their careers?

To our own knowledge several large business organizations have recently adopted some plans to ease the retirement of their executives. One large company progressively prolongs the vacations of a retiree over a period of about five years so that he has time to get used to his freedom gently. Another prepares the way by part-time employment, reducing the working time over a period of years until it is phased out. A third has a plan whereby its candidates for retirement work first four, then three, then only a couple of days a week in stages from their sixtieth year to their sixty-fifth. Doubtless other corporations have other schemes along these lines. It seems to us that, laudable as they all are in their efforts to ease the pain of retirement for their older executives, they are based on an entirely faulty premise. Such plans are designed to ease *out* the retiring person. We have not heard of any plan designed to *retain* his interest in the welfare of the company he helped lead.

In the spirit that the conservation of our resources, as well as the well-being of our older citizens, should be a consideration, we should like to suggest to such organizations a way in which these ends could be achieved simultaneously.

It occurs to us that it would be entirely feasible to establish an emeritus status for the retired administrators of an organization, as is already in existence in the scholastic world. These honored retirees could then have the option of joining a panel that would have no executive function but would continue to serve the organization in a consultative or advisory capacity. In such a position the value of their experience would be retained by their companies, which would not be under obligation to follow their advice but would surely find it valuable to have the benefit of it. Neither would it be costly for the company, since in almost all cases these retirees are paid a pension anyway. As a kind of senate of senior statesmen remaining at the service of their organization, the retired personnel also would reap benefit by being able to remain involved in their community and in life.

We have a perfect example of such a system in England, in the political world. There the House of Lords no longer has legislative or executive powers (although it does have power to delay legislation), but it acts as a disinterested forum for the discussion of matters of national importance, and the conclusions it arrives at carry considerable weight. Because their positions are not subject to the whims of an electorate, its members are able to express honestly their opinions, and they may bring before their colleagues and initiate debate on matters that they believe should be brought into the open, without fear of losing a voter or contravening party discipline. It is an assembly that a politically active man or woman may retire to, or be retired to, with great honor, and in which he may continue to engage in his political interests as much or as little as he pleases or is able. It would serve as an admirable model for the kind of advisory panel of retired executives we have in mind as a valuable adjunct to large organizations.

Besides the executive staff, large organizations employ scientists and researchers who in due course will be retiring. Persons in these categories, too, would make extremely useful members of an advisory panel, and their usefulness would probably be multiplied if a way could be found for them to continue to use their companies' laboratories for their own research projects, even after their retirement. In many cases it would present no problems at all to permit them to continue to use the company's facilities. We happen to know a retired biochemist who has been enabled to continue her research on this basis at Columbia University. In other instances use of the facilities would perhaps be limited to before or after working hours or to certain sections of the laboratories, but it would surely be rewarding for all concerned to find a way of making room for this type of "free research," not tied to the companies' immediate requirements.

This leads us to professional people in other categories, who mostly work independently of organizations. Many physicians, technicians, or scientific consultants in a wide range of fields have at the back of their minds ideas and projects that they would like to carry out but never had time for in their busy professional lives. The same is true for many teachers, writers, or other scholars in specialized fields. If every university were to establish a small residential academy for those who retire from such occupations, what a wealth of creative work might be accomplished:

Small residential academies for retired scholars and professional men and women would not be difficult to arrange within the framework of universities. In these institutions laboratories and libraries already exist that would be ample for their needs. They would not be a burden on the host academic centers, for they would largely have pensions, insurance benefits, or their own retirement funds at their disposal to maintain themselves. Any initial expenses involved in setting up these small academies for elderly professionals and scholars would probably meet with sympathetic consideration, if not by government agencies, then by private endowments. In such places these trained and mature people could find in their years of retirement the time and opportunity to carry out investigations and work out ideas that otherwise would remain only dreams in their minds.

Although it does not offer residential facilities, there is an institution that has made a valuable beginning along these lines. The New School for Social Research, in New York, has an Institute for Retired Professionals among its departments. The president of the New School, John R. Everett, said he had always hoped to encourage retired professionals to remain productive, and he stated, "Today we find some actual, physical, tangible book evidence that something has been done." He made these remarks on the occasion of a "book-warming" for a seventy-three-year-old author, Ida Cowen, a retired schoolteacher, who had just published her first book. Ida Cowen is a "graduate" of the Institute for Retired Professionals. She had always enjoyed traveling, but as she put it, "I can't think of anything more horrible than just looking and looking and going on." Instead, on her travels, she sought out people who could throw light on her special interest and interviewed them. Incidentally, in line with the spirit of the institute, in which she enrolled to polish her writing skills, one of her teachers was Viola Paradise, who, at the time of this writing, is eighty-five and is still conducting the weekly writing workshop there.

Besides the value of such work in itself and its added value in the enrichment of the later years of the seniors performing it, there would be an inestimable social benefit. The very presence of a group of elderly scholars on every campus might reawaken in the rest of the university community, students and professors alike, the same kind of veneration that was evoked by the wise old people in many primitive tribes. Respect for the work and persons of the elders in universities, which are the training grounds of a society's leaders, might then be carried into the wider world and do much to raise the status of the elderly at large.

There is another section of our population that is overlooked by all when it comes to consideration of the problems of aging. This is the comparatively small group of the rich and the very rich. Most people think that because they have the means to satisfy their own requirements they have no problems. But this is far from being the case. The rich understand just as little of their true needs in old age as any other segment of the population. Just as large a proportion of them suffer boredom, with its consequent mental and physical ailments, as any other. They form a large part of the contingent frequenting health spas, doctors' offices, and clinics and of those who travel aimlessly. Having the means, they are more inclined to chase the will-o'-the-wisp of eternal youth than others. They subject themselves to costly and not so harmless cosmetic operations. Some of them feel driven to make a full-time occupation of the care of their health.

To such of our readers as may come into this category we heartily recommend the example of Mrs. "Baba" Fallas, whose acquaintance we recently made. She is eighty-two years old and recently made the very wise remark, "Nobody wants to visit an old lady for her own sake. I make sure the conversation in my house is interesting, and I employ a first-rate cook."

Mrs. Fallas began her present "career" at the age of about sixty, when she began seriously adding to and filling out her collection of French seventeenth- and eighteenth-century furniture and objets d'art. She occupied herself at that time in supervising the building of a home in Cross River, New York, which is a near replica of the Petit Trianon, to house the collection. She had acquired a vast store of knowledge of the social history of the period, as any collector does in the course of making acquisitions, and she added greatly to it with the reseach involved in the planning of her house—as her library testifies. Her knowledge became so extensive that her services as an expert have been sought by the Metropolitan Museum of Art. She acknowledges her social obligations from time to time by opening her home to students of this period and by acting as a consultant for the museum.

Besides this, Mrs. Fallas is an active member of a kennel club. She breeds Pekingese dogs, several of which have won prizes, and at times she sells one at no mean price. Some twenty-five of them live with her on her beautiful property, along with several fierce and well-trained Alsatian guard dogs. She has made herself as knowledgeable in canine lore as she is in that of seventeenth- and eighteenth-century France.

Nor is this all. Because she likes to hear the birds singing when she awakens in the morning, she has assembled a collection of songbirds from all over the world and houses them in a specially built aviary adjoining her bathroom. Since she feeds them personally, they invariably start singing whenever they hear her footsteps. Needless to say, she is a fount of knowledge also on the subject of exotic songbirds.

Constantly learning in the fields that interest her, constantly passing on her knowledge to those who seek it, how much more satisfying an existence is hers than an endless trailing from doctor's office to spa and from spa to doctor's office.

Lest it be thought that age eighty-two is an ultimate limit for such intense involvement in life, we should also like to mention the mother of one of our close friends. This lady is ninety-one years old. Although wealthy, she runs her country home and garden and her city apartment largely without help, partly because no maid has been able to satisfy her exacting standards, but also partly because she enjoys and takes pride in doing so. On her ninetieth birthday she invited all her children, their husbands and wives, and all her grandchildren with theirs to a party for which she herself cooked the meal, personally cut and arranged the flowers, decorated the house, and attended to all the details of the festivity. She makes it a point to keep up with her social work (special teaching projects for blind children), and since we have not mentioned her name, we may add that she enjoys the constant companionship of a distinguished-looking retired doctor, who is extremely appreciative of her cooking skills as well as admiring of her dauntless personality.

To cap even this example of vigorous advanced old age, on December 29, 1971, two of the world's leading string musicians, Pablo Casals, the cellist, and Lionel Tertis, the violist, celebrated their ninety-fifth birthdays (which happen to fall on the same day) and their warm friendship and forty years of playing chamber music together by toasting each other with champagne from opposite sides of the Atlantic. Asked how he felt at ninety-five, the violist quipped, "I'm feeling as fit as a fiddle."

CHAPTER EIGHTEEN

Distinctive Clothing

Grow old along with me!
The best is yet to be,
The last of life, for which the first was made.
—ROBERT BROWNING

Apart from the face and the head as a whole, the outer clothing is the first thing about a person that one notices, and therefore when two people meet for the first time, their immediate impression of each other is formed by these visible features. Probably for this reason clothing has at all times been felt to have an importance greater than its presumed function of protection.

We have speculated in another work that the chief purpose of clothing may indeed have been the assertion of its wearer's rank and role rather than the utilitarian one of protection and warmth. But be this as it may, it is indisputable that throughout the ages men and women have used their clothing as a whole, or certain items of it, to proclaim their membership in certain groups to the world at large.

Scholars have donned cap and gown to identify their calling; the solid burghers who sat for their portraits to be painted by such artists as Frans Hals put on their best silks and laces to assert their economic standing; Englishmen wear blazers or ties to associate themselves throughout their lives with the schools of their youth; military men, clerics, judges, sports teams, diplomats, and Swiss chimney sweeps all wear special clothing that announces their identity and their pride in it.

Besides the apparel that identifies a calling or an allegiance, special clothing has also customarily marked the stages of life. The dress of infancy is different from that of the child, the child's from the adolescent's, and the adolescent's from the mature person's. In most periods before the present time there was a further category of clothing that was worn by older adults who no longer wished to be identified with their virile or nubile juniors, but who wished to identify themselves as worthy of the respect due to their age and experience.

The acceptance of a new role—which means the relinquishing of a role with which one is identified and probably enjoys—is no mean task. Yet such transitions were made to perfection by almost all the great ladies who were the mistresses of the classic salons of the seventeenth and eighteenth centuries and by those who led their many offshoots both in Paris and in the provinces. Through their salons, gifted and intelligent ladies as they became older played an influential role in literature, providing a congenial atmosphere and a proving ground for talent. The whole intellectual world of their times awaited the verdicts of these gatherings. Mme. de Lambert's reception indeed was considered a way station to the Académie. Mme. de Sévigné and Mme. de Maintenon wielded vast influence. One of the earliest and greatest of these ladies was Ninon de Lenclos. She was born into a family of good position. In the first part of her life she was a member of the gayest and most licentious circles of Paris, but as she became older, she changed her role deliberately rather than allow herself to be edged out of it without grace. In her later years she then became the arbiter of fashion and a patron of the gifted. Voltaire was presented to her when he was but a young and promising boy, and he received encouragement and tangible help from her. Later he delighted in the company of Mme. du Châtelet for many years and subsequently in that of Mme. Denis. One of the greatest salons of all, perhaps, was Mme. de Tencin's. Mme. Doublet's had a more political character, as had those of Mme. du Deffand, Mme. Geoffrin, and Mlle. de Lespinasse.

Some of these great women and also the lesser ones who followed their style found purpose in their old age in lives of piety, some in political intrigue and the quest of power, but many others as they reached their fifties consciously said farewell to love and gallantry and cultivated friendship. With their worldly experience, wit, tact, and good taste, they found new lives that blended tradition with tolerance and dignity without prudishness. They led fashion and set the pace for their societies. One of the ways in which they made an unspoken declaration to the world that they themselves considered their role changed and that they wished to be recognized on a different level was by means of a change in their style of dress. They adapted themselves to their years and indicated their mental attitude by means of their clothes.

In our own time the poet Edith Sitwell understood very well the agelessness and drama of a very distinctive style of dressing. She did not follow the fashion. She, too, created her own aura partly by means of her clothes. Recently, as the scramble for perpetual youth has accelerated, this last category of clothing has fallen into disrepute and disuse. Older people have not wished to announce their seniority; they have not demanded respect; they have not the least desire to identify their caste membership; and they have clung pathetically to the self-delusion that they still look young, feel young, and identify with the young.

The chief reasons for this attitude are the ones we have been detailing in this book: the loss of function and loss of status of the elderly, which cause those who are able to reject old age, to attempt to postpone it, and to avoid acknowledging its arrival. Their own poor image of old age has caused our elders to refuse to identify with it and almost to go overboard in their efforts to remain identified with younger stages. In some cases this is being done to a degree that can only reinforce the poor image currently associated with being old, for it is incongruous and creates an impression of age as pathetic rather than as wise.

We deeply believe that if our older people were to accept their age in a positive way, assert their prerogatives, demand respect, and clothe themselves in a way that calls for these responses, they would surely remain younger in spirit, and probably in appearance, than by following the current pursuit of the mask of youth that is so unbecoming.

This attitude has been self-feeding, for manufacturers, discouraged from producing styles designed for the elderly by a lack of demand for them, have fallen back on offering clothing that can be described only as dowdy, unattractive, or old-fashioned as an alternative.

The campaign we suggested, to be directed to the elderly for the purpose of improving their self-image and increasing their pride in themselves, should most definitely include urging them to demand clothing that is suitable for their years and attractive and dignified. Clothes designed for the older person should deemphasize sexiness and emphasize stateliness and individuality. Flowing rather than fitted lines; rich colors rather than fussy ornament; flesh concealed and not revealed—these ennoble the appearance of an older woman. For older men a certain formality that remains consistent with comfort (the velvet smoking jacket was a good example) is becoming. Doubtless our gifted designers could find many versions of the theme. Apparel of this type could provide a distinctive caste mark aiding in self-esteem and not destroying it as does much of what is offered to the old today. Why should the older person be recognizable to us only by his aging skin? Why not by a magnificent robe?

What We Can Do About It

In the introduction to this part of our book we acknowledged that some of the ideas we would present might not seem feasible, and even naïve, given the realities of the situation. We have to admit that our belief in the usefulness of fostering a pride in self-identification through distinctive clothing appears to be one of these. We have talked to many people connected with the design and production of clothing for older women and find a very great resistance to an idea of any distinguishing type of garments.

A good example of this attitude was expressed by the head of the Fashion Department of Parsons School of Design in New York. She told us that her own seventy-five-year-old mother took great pride in being able to wear any designer clothes that she herself could wear and that by far the greater number of women of her age would feel the same way. All the manufacturers we spoke to confirmed that the dresses made for seniors differed from what their daughters or even granddaughters are offered only by being of modified size and perhaps sleeved instead of sleeveless, or provided with a jacket.

Of course we are aware of this strong feeling. It is the feeling itself that we should like to see changed. Whenever any group of people feel that they are at a disadvantage because of what they are, large numbers of them will attempt to deny their identity and will seek to blend in with the dominant group and be as indistinguishable from it as possible. In this respect there are many parallels between the outlook of old people today and that of the American black less than thirty years ago. Then, most of their women and many of their men, too, spent a great deal of time and money having their hair straightened in imitation of the majority group, they dressed like their white compatriots, and they put high social value on a light skin. Any suggestion at that time that they might find pride in an appearance that would identify them as what they are, black, and not attempt to pass themselves off for what they are not, white, would have been deeply resented and felt to be rank discrimination.

What our elders are doing today is precisely this. They are attempting to deny what they are, postmature, and cling to an appearance of being what they are not, middle-aged or even young. The reasons for this are not to be found in superficial matters of taste. They lie in something much deeper. It is the same as the feeling of a persecuted minority that desires by all means to avoid the penalties of being what it is. They feel the pressure of the low value that is put on them by their society. They come to share the same attitudes toward themselves that their society holds. They fear being old and being considered old—being old for the ideas of ill health and decrepitude they associate with the condition, and being considered old for the social disadvantages that ensue. Therefore they passionately desire to remain young or, since this is impossible, at least to find safety in a camouflage of youthfulness.

The last fifty years have seen rapid changes and innovations in all walks of life, and inevitably tastes and fashions have changed rapidly in pace with them. Efficient manufacturers have found it necessary to have a feel for these changes when they are incipient and to be prepared for them in advance, so they can offer the public what it seeks when the demand arises. They take the risk that their intuition is correct. They prepare for the trend that they foresee at a time when it is not yet present. Some then go a step further. They foment the demand and prepare the public mind to receive what they have to offer. Their timing has to be on target, but should their foresight prove to have been correct, their rewards are great.

We feel that clothing manufacturers could well perform a service of great public importance as well as of private profit if they placed themselves in the forefront of a campaign to promote the idea that old age can be desirable and attractive.

So far, attempts by some individual manufacturers to cater to the senior market have been unsuccessful because, largely for the reasons we have cited, the time was "out of joint." But with today's growing awareness that something has to be done for the elderly and with interest stirred by numerous national commissions and international conferences, the time would now seem to be more appropriate than ever before.

An initiative in this direction by the clothing industry could well be an opening wedge in making the elderly segment of the population a separate consumer entity with its own needs and tastes catered to. Later other consumer industries could be brought into the picture.

A great deal can be done by leadership in setting style and taste, and much can be done by what is apparently superficial, like clothing, in reinforcing a feeling. One of the best examples of this is the assertion of identity and pride shown today by the black population of the United States by wearing their hair in a style consistent with its own texture rather than by having it straightened into an imitation of the hair of the dominant group. The self-confidence fostered by this assertion of identity is so positive that in these days there is imitation in reverse, for some young people who are not black are seen sporting hairstyles in imitation of theirs. Clothing has also played a part in this transformed attitude. Costumes of Africa are much in favor, even though the people wearing them would probably be at a loss to name the tribe of their origin. It is not even important that they should, for their costume is not meant to say: "I am a member of this or that tribe." What it is intended to say and what it announces loudly and clearly is: "I am black. I am different from you. Respect me for what I am."

This change in attitude toward their personal appearance would not have been possible without the great efforts in indoctrination that were undertaken by black leaders and the feelings of self-worth they were able to inspire. It also needed the cooperation of designers and manufacturers who understood the meaning of that current of feeling and who had the imagination to produce styles that would express it.

An older person needs to be able to go into a store and find there clothes that will announce to the world just as clearly: "I am seventy years old. I have no desire to appear to be forty. My person is the embodiment of a lifetime's experience. I have much to offer you. Respect me for what I am."

CHAPTER NINETEEN

Enrichment of Life for the Very Young: A Role for Grandparents in Nursery Schools

'Tis not too late to seek a newer world. —TENNYSON

One of the recommendations offered by the Administration on Aging was that legislation be enacted to continue the work of the retired senior volunteer program (the RSVP we mentioned in Chapter Five). In fact, legislation has been enacted—albeit the program has not been funded—to "provide new opportunities for community service for senior citizens who would serve their communities without compensation except for reimbursement for transportation, meals, and out-of-pocket expenses. . . . RSVP would provide a new national resource to allow communities to benefit from the skills and experience of senior citizens, including counselling and tutoring of schoolchildren; assisting schools as lunchroom supervisors, playground monitors, and teacher aides. . . ."

As a matter of fact, it is in this type of endeavor, involving the very old with the very young, that one of the most successful officially sponsored schemes has emerged. This is the Foster Grandparents plan, which originally was set up to make the lives of children confined to institutions happier.

This plan immediately proved to be richly rewarding, so it was extended to mental health clinics, hospitals, correctional institutions, Head Start classrooms, day centers, and classes for exceptional children—in fact, wherever deprived children might be found.

National authorities on child care have commented on the excellence of the Foster Grandparent program. Typical of this appraisal were the statements of Dr. Maria Piers, dean of the Erikson Institute for Early Education, who said, "As a preventive program, Foster Grandparents is the best thing known to combat the pernicious influence of neglect. Children who are ignored, cut off from adult contact and love, can face a total deterioration of the intellect with lifelong crippling effects. Foster Grandparents give the children the warm, loving contact with adults that is so necessary to their growth and development. We have seen the positive results of this program. Every institution or agency caring for children could benefit from the work of a foster grandparent in every child care unit."

Institutions and agencies caring for children have actively responded to the program. Literally hundreds of requests for federal help to start new projects are turned down each year for lack of funds.

Foster grandparents serve four hours a day, five days a week, and receive a stipend of $1.60 an hour; they are reimbursed for transportation costs and, where possible, provided with a nutritious meal daily. "Beyond this, the Foster Grandparent program offers to the older persons all that makes us most human—communication, self-awareness, sympathy, conscience; it gives the older person an opportunity to serve and be served, to love and be loved, to achieve happiness in striving to meet moral responsibilities in relation to and in interaction with other human beings."

Comments gathered both from the staffs of institutions employing them and from foster grandparents themselves are equally enthusiastic about the scheme in actual practice. Some of the statements submitted to the Administration on Aging by the staffs of various institutions were:

"Kids are walking. Kids are talking. Kids who used to have to be tranquilized aren't being tranquilized anymore. Kids who couldn't go to school, go to school now. It just makes all the difference in the world. For the first time in a child's life, he's got someone who is all his."

"As a result of foster grandparents' calming influence upon our emotionally disturbed and hyperactive children, we frequently receive unit clinical team recommendations that a foster grandparent be assigned to a particular child. . . . These recommendations [are] based upon our psychiatrist's evaluations, and supported by the social service, psychological, and medical clinical team members."

As for the grandparents themselves, in the following we hear a repetition of the theme we find everywhere the elderly are involved:

"I have something to look forward to."

"I have a reason to get up in the morning."

"It's good to be needed again."

It is especially interesting to note that the attendance records of the grandparents are as good as, and sometimes better than, those of the regular employees.

We feel that it is not at all surprising that the Foster Grandparent plans are proving so exceptionally successful, for we think that they touch on the very relationship (between the very old and the very young) that is the essence of the function that perpetuated old people among us. Foster Grandparents probably has the greatest potential of any of the programs for the elderly. We wholeheartedly agree with Dr. Piers in her conviction that every institution that takes care of children ought to have a roster of foster grandparents.

A pediatric hospital, for instance, or a center for neglected children could allot funds in its budget to procure the services of a certain number of older persons to serve as foster grandparents. On a very modest scale this has already been done in some states. Illinois, Iowa, and Delaware funded 81, 60, and 84 Foster Grandparent positions, respectively. Pennsylvania appraised the need for such grandparents at about 5,000 and has funded 61 positions. The Administration on Aging states that it knows of a total of more than 600 positions similar to Foster Grandparents that are not funded by the federal government, and that there are reasons to believe that other communities have developed similar opportunities that have not been brought to its attention.

For a country the size of the United States the numbers involved are pitifully small when one thinks of the great value of the service to all concerned. So far, the Foster Grandparent program, to quote the report of the Senate committee, "has provided many insights into the potential utilization of the elderly in community settings. It has not only provided low income older persons with a drastically improved standard of living but has demonstrated to communities that older persons have the talent, skill, experience, ability, and desire to serve their communities by meeting some of the unmet human needs. . . . Thus far the benefits resulting from the foster grandparents program extend far beyond the direct gains to the children and foster grandparents who have participated."

In a service of this type, where many people of many different backgrounds are involved in relationships that involve their feelings, it is inevitable, and even desirable, that the services will be varied in different regions in accordance with the personalities of the old people and the needs of the children concerned. In a Foster Grandparent group in Westchester, New York, for example, the old people enrolled take young children recommended to them by their schools on outings on a one-to-one basis—that is, not in group excursions, but one "grandparent" to one child. They take them for visits to a zoo, a museum, or a park, as their own grand-parents might have done if it were not that they were too poor, too sick, or not there, and so unable to do so, and we think that theirs is an example that could well be emulated.

Since the whole concept has proved so popular and is limited only by funding and lack of initiative, we think it a pity that private groups or even individuals do not take it up where the government agencies have shown the way.

We ourselves had several ideas that coincide in part with RSVP and the Foster Grandparents programs, and we think that private initiative could very well find ways to include these in an even greater enrichment of the lives of young and old alike.

Visits

As we have discovered, the art of printing and the wide dissemination of the printed word had an effect on our elders very similar to the effect of the invention of the internal combustion engine on the horse: The erstwhile primary function in society of each was rendered obsolete. The spread of written information was slower than the adoption of the motor, and so it was more difficult to connect cause and effect in the first case than in the second, and we do not see the association so clearly. In the case of the elder there is the added factor of the rapid obsolescence of knowledge in modern times, rendering his position as a fount of information assailable, as it was not in the times when entire social groups depended on the storehouse in his head. But there are very many areas where the services of the horse are still irre-placeable, and many more where they enrich our lives, and the same is true of the kind of knowledge in the minds of our grandparent generation.

What the grandparents know is different from what the parents know. Their memories go back before the parents were born, and they can bring the period and place of their youth alive to their grandchildren as no textbook can. This was beautifully illustrated recently in an issue of a widely circulated magazine which featured a series of photographs and vignettes of great-grandparents with their very young great-grandchildren. In these cases the elders had emigrated from the lands of their birth, and so the tales of their youth were particularly fascinating to their American great-grand-children. But in a country where immigration is not so usual, the grandparent not infrequently grew up in a different part of it, and his knowledge of that place is just as exotic and interesting to the very young as a faraway land.

The series of photographs we are referring to appeared in a pre-Christmas issue of *Life*. Significantly, the headline read, THE OLD PEOPLE HAND ALONG TO THE YOUNG THE LEGA-CIES OF OTHER PLACES AND TIMES, and the brief text stated, "In their toys and books and schools, the youngsters live in a fully American world. But through the language and the memories of the old people—and often in the atmosphere of their homes—these young Americans share in the flavor of other lands and other cultures, listening to the ancient tales of youth long ago in the mountains of Greece or the islands of the Caribbean or the farmlands of Ireland, and sharing in the misty nostalgia of alien rituals of childhood."

All the great-grandparents' pictures had brief cameos of their early lives included in the captions. Typical was a state-ment by an eighty-six-year-old from Poland: "Ours was a little town, just a halfway point between wherever you were coming from and Warsaw. Sometimes our teacher would hire a wagon and take us to the railway station, a big room with seats, to watch the train to Warsaw, which passed twice a day."

An eighty-five-year-old from the Dominican Republic said, "I had eleven brothers and sisters, and in the house we also had two horses, a burro, goats, dogs and cats. They all ran loose in the patio. There was no school, so we girls could spend the day washing, ironing and cooking. On holidays everyone gave parties. After a big dinner we little ones would sit around on the floor playing while the older people danced. We'd decorate our burros with flowers, place wreaths around their necks, and race them."

And an eighty-one-year-old from Sweden was quoted as saying, "Most of our childhood games centered round snow and ice. We would skate with a big sheet between us and the wind would catch the sheet and pull us along."

But the heart of everything we should like to convey in this chapter was summed up by the great-granddaughter of a seventy-five-year-old Chinese who said, "I love visiting great-grandfather. He doesn't exactly play with us. He talks, and that's lots of fun."

We personally had similar benefits in our own situation, for our children were born in the United States, whereas our origins were in Europe. As a result they had no trouble with their geography lessons when they were in the primary classes at school, while many other children had difficulty in comprehending that there were other places in the world where people lived not too differently from themselves. The other children asked questions like: Where is it? Where does it begin and where does it end? How do you get to it? What is the place like in between? Our children were able to grasp the idea of "other places" because it had been made familiar by their grandmother's visits to them. They knew that she lived in a big city like their own and that she had to go in a car or train to reach the ocean, as they often went in a car to the beach on this side of the ocean, and that she then had to sail or fly across it before she could see them. Their concept of the world was heightened by her answers to their questions about her journey. Their idea of "other places" was made even more real by her stories of their parents' (our) youth, of which they never tired, and of all kinds 6f information about their relatives in another country. Such stories, of course, are just as delightful to children whose grandparents live around the corner, but in our case the world was a bigger, fuller, richer place for our children than for those who could see it only as bounded by their own limited horizons.

We found that children who had had the opportunity to listen to their grandparents' tales of other times or other places had a better understanding of differences of opinion, different standards, and different ways of doing things. They were shocked to learn that boys in English schools were caned for minor infractions in their uncles' boyhood, and they considered themselves lucky when they heard of the restrictions that were placed on children and young people there at that time.

There could have been no substitute for the actual presence of their grandmother to convey the reality of these other worlds to them. The fact that she herself had lived in those times and places made an impact on them that was quite different from that of the information they gleaned from books, no matter how greatly this interested them and although they were early and avid readers. Her visits to them and theirs to her amounted to an enriched liberal education for them. No school courses could have conveyed the degree of comprehension that they absorbed without being aware of it.

One of the more successful plans involving the very old and the very young is the government-sponsored Foster Grandparent program in Michigan, in which senior citizens become "grandparents" for institutionalized children without families.

We believe that there should be a place for visits by elderly persons in the schedules of all nursery schools and kindergarten classes. There should also be informal visits, in which the children could feel free to ask questions about anything, particularly about the older person's youth, as they would ask of their own grandparents. The answers should be the plain facts of the elder's experience, unvarnished by current social philosophies. The experience would be of the most precious kind for the children. Slowly they would build up in their minds, by the most natural means in the world, an authentic background into which they could arrange in good order much of the knowledge they learn later by more academic means. For the older person these sessions could provide a lifeline back to usefulness and involvement of the most basic kind.

This suggestion arises out of our personal experience at a nursery school attended by two of our own children when they were small. The influence of the one white-haired, grandmotherly teacher there was out of all proportion greater than that of her young colleagues on the three-to-five-year-old pupils. All the children behaved better in her presence. They were more attentive, and they must have been more impressed by what she told them, because she was the only teacher whose stories and musical games they ever remembered sufficiently to tell us about after school.

The Telling of Fairy Tales

The nursery schools and kindergarten classes of which we have personal knowledge are almost entirely preoccupied with providing occupations through which their children can express themselves. They provide material and encourage the child to build with blocks, to draw with crayons, to daub paint, to model clay, to cut out paper; they encourage acceptable social behavior by organizing group activities such as games, dances, songs, and races. Some allow them to work off a little energy by providing apparatus. All these pursuits are pleasurable and useful for the small child, but in the interest of providing all these means of self-expression those who arrange the curricula are apt to overlook the great educational value of having children sit quietly for a little while and listen while an older person reads them a fairy story.

Fairy tales put the fantasies of mankind into a form a young child can digest. They are organic in that they repeat the thinking patterns of primitive man. The ideas of good and evil spirits, of ghosts and witches, of fairies and monsters express the realities of the child's imagination as did the animistic beliefs of tribal man. That trees, or frogs, or pumpkins can be transformed into maidens, princes, or chariots seems as perfectly natural to the one as to the other. A child can live in those tales. More importantly, he can grow out of them, as primitive man grew out of his beliefs as his comprehension of the world around him became more sophisticated.

Today the period at which a child is receptive to traditional fairy stories is compressed into a very short time. The modern world crowds around him via his exposure to television; he no longer lives separated from adults by nursemaids or separate rooms, and so ill-understood snatches of the conversations of his elders and inklings of their concerns early invade the world of his imagination. Moreover, few adults take the time to sit down with their children as a regular part of their day, as was usually done in the past, especially in the hour before the child's bedtime. It is easier for today's parent to say to the child: "You may watch television now until it is time to go to bed."

As a result the early fantasies of many a modern child do not have a harmless outlet that can easily be left behind at a later stage. A child needs a period for fantasies as a part of his emotional maturing, but these are now focused on the real world around him, since he does not yet have the emotional development and understanding to see it impartially. Unfortunately, when fantasies are tied into experiences of the real world, it is harder to leave them behind and grow out of them than when they are solely concerned with the make-believe world of fairy tales. Often the fantasies focused in this way persist into adult life and cloud the grown person's understanding of the real world.

A return to the telling of "old-fashioned" fairy stories would do much to prevent this from happening, and since parents today are often too busy or unwilling to undertake this task, it would be an ideal solution to assign it as an additional service by the elderly. A time set aside in a nursery school curriculum, perhaps following the informal visit or on alternate days, when an old lady or man might come into the schoolroom and say simply, "Children, I am going to tell you a story," and do just that, would vastly enrich the children's experiences there.

The stories read or told by the elderly visitor should be the old tried-and-true yarns enjoyed by many generations of children or the myths and legends of ancient peoples. They should not read to the children those new stories with a social slant that are so much in evidence on nursery school shelves, for many others will do that, and those stories do not have the same effect on a child's emotional and mental growth. Many of the stories favored by modern writers of children's books do little for their imaginations; they are closer to being disguised sermons. They take as themes idealized situations in which a white child and a black child, by loving each other or by overcoming difficulties to help each other, wipe away the prejudices of their neighborhood; or one in which a child, by being thoughtful or kind, saves an animal or redeems a hardhearted villain. These stories are myths, too, and of a kind that the child will hear many more later on. Well intentioned as they are, they are far more dangerous than the most frightening ogre of a fairy tale because the child grows up believing that the world can be changed by these simple means—and this is a fantasy that it is hard to grow out of.

There are many modern educators who believe that the

261

stories told to children should be brought up to date and therefore changed in each generation to adapt the child to the changing world. But it doesn't work this way. A child's body progresses through certain stages in every generation, and each stage has its own needs. A child's mind does the same. At each stage those needs must be met to create a sound foundation for his optimum development in the next. Demanding "relevance" to modern life in the mental sustenance of the earliest years is equivalent to suggesting that mother's milk is out of date!

What every child needs, for a short period in his early life, is an opportunity to indulge in the pure fantasy of the type the fairy tales provide, for this can easily be recognized for what it is. When he has outgrown this need, he then has no difficulty in leaving it behind, and he can go on from there unhindered by false ideas and oversimplifications.

It would not be the same if the regular teacher, usually a young person, undertook this task. The arrival of a special old person to read the children a story would lend the occasion a special attraction, like the occasional visit of a grandparent, and would make a greater impression—an impression of the kind that was made by the "presence" of the Viennese anatomy professor on his students in our own experience.

Unlike several of the other suggestions we have made for bringing older people back into our lives, this one would be easy to organize. We do not have to wait for every school to undertake such a program before some can make a start. A little individual initiative by those concerned or by those with suitable connections would go a long way toward bringing a great deal of joy into the lives of the very young and the very old together by these means.

CHAPTER TWENTY

Continued Learning as a Factor in Longevity

Never ceasing to learn, I still march onward in age.
—SOLON

It may be stating the obvious that experience increases knowledge, but until now it has not been shown that gains in experience and knowledge improve or increase the substance of the brain. We know from observation that exercise improves the capacities of the muscles, and we need no further proof of this than when we look at the physique and the performance of an athlete. We feel that the more we learn, the more we are able to learn, but so far, in man, we have not proved that there is an increase in brain substance with the use of the brain that is an equivalent of the athlete's bulging muscles that are a result of his use of them.

In the last decade a great deal of work has been done on animals to try to find out whether, when they are offered opportunities to increase their learning vastly, this has any bearing on the size of their brains.

Interestingly, this question was posed as far back as the latter half of the eighteenth century by the Italian anatomist Michele Gaetano Malacarne. He worked with pairs of dogs from the same litters and pairs of parrots, goldfinches, and blackbirds from the same clutches of eggs. In each case he trained one of the pair extensively and not the other. Upon dissection he found that the surfaces of the small brain of the trained individual of the pair had more folds than the untrained one. Although he recorded this result and it was acknowledged by some of his contemporaries, no application was found for the information and it lay unused and largely unknown.

Today scientists are working in many universities on this important finding. At the University of California at Berkeley, for example, a group is at work with rats. The rats were put into separate cages, some of which were bare and others of which were filled with all kinds of toys, ladders, tunnels, and other devices to stimulate their curiosity and thus their learning to use them. The devices were changed frequently to encourage ever new learning to deal with the environment.

After ten weeks the animals were dissected and their brains compared. It was found that the animals that had lived in the enriched environment, and that had therefore had more opportunities for learning, had a greater weight and a greater thickness of cerebral cortex and a considerable increase of the supporting tissue, which is called the glia. (The main function of the glia is to carry nourishment to the neurons.) In further experiments another set of rats was placed in an environment that was a natural one for them. It was a huge sandbox. which permitted burrowing, the building of nests, food storage and all the rest of the rats' normal activities. After a suitable time the brain sizes of these rats were compared with those that had lived in the enriched artificial environment, and an even greater increase was noted. It was apparent that the stimulations of a normal life in a natural environment produced the greatest positive effect on the size of the rats' brains.

In other experiments it was found that rats from an enriched environment had 50 percent larger synaptic junctions and that these were also thicker. The synaptic junctions facilitate the transmission of information along the pathways of the nerves. If they are bigger, then, presumably, more information can be transmitted more readily. While it cannot be taken for granted that these findings on rodents also apply to human beings, they give a pertinent indication of probability, since all mammalian brain tissues have much in common.

It is a fact that the human brain is capable of growth until the fourth decade of life. This is based on the fact that the sutures of the skull remain open until that time. We do not know for certain that further growth occurs later than this, but there is no reason why it should not, since growth of the brain can involve its complexity as much as its volume. Available evidence indicates that the maximum *number* of cells in the brain (neurons) is reached in the first year after birth. We must assume then that any increase in size after that time is due to the increased size of individual cells, their number of fibers, and the thickening of the synaptic plates. In view of this it seems to us that the effect of the enriched experiences on the brain cells of rats is very significant.

The experiments show conclusively that in rats greater use of the brain promotes its greater growth. The growth, in turn, facilitates greater activity. There is a circular effect. In man we have evidence in reverse that supports similar conclusions. The elderly in the nonstimulating environments of old peoples' homes show less initiative and spontaneity, less inventiveness, and less reactivity to novel situations than their contemporaries who remain in the more stimulating environments outside them. Inactivity at any age promotes atrophy of tissue. Any bedridden person, no matter how vigorous in mind and body at the beginning of the enforced inactivity, after a short time shows a wasting of muscles, loss of calcium from the bones, a weakening of the respiratory and cardiovascular systems, and a lessening of the flow of digestive juices; there is hardly a system that is not affected.

A human brain that is not stimulated by an enriched environment is obviously less active and therefore promotes fewer responses from the body, resulting in effects approaching those seen in bedridden patients. Again, there is a circular effect, each round making the next stage worse.

Indirect evidence that the brain has the capacity of retarding the aging process is all around us. G. Brandes, a zoologist, drew attention to his observations that training seemed to him to delay the onset of senility in chimpanzees. There is no question that in animals, on the whole, the rate of aging is uniform for the brain and the rest of the body. But in man, where there was a premium on the use of the brain to ensure the survival of the species, selective pressures favored its continued growth and a longer life for the body that housed it. If we were to personify this process, it is as if the brain were to muse: "The only way I can fulfill my task is to keep this body going. I cannot let it wither away when it has completed its procreative function, for the longer I have to fill my memory banks, the more useful I shall be."

This may sound overly whimsical, but the fact remains that activity in the brain promotes the activity of other bodily organs and is therefore a factor in keeping them in good working order.

The chief means the brain has to keep the body working is the drive to satisfy curiosity, and this drive is a powerful one. In many experiments on animals it has been shown to supersede other vital drives, even hunger.

Therefore if we stimulate our brain, we automatically, if indirectly, stimulate the rest of our body. This goes a long way toward explaining the remarkable fact that so many of the great intellectual creations of man were achievements of old age. Especially in art and scientific research, both highly cerebral occupations, astonishing heights have been reached very late in life, when the body could have been senescent.

266

How then can we explain the apathy that is seen in many of our elders and the appearance of what is commonly referred to as senility in them? Unless brain damage is present, we have to assume that curiosity has been gradually diminished by the lack of environmental stimulation. But curiosity is such an intrinsic force that it never disappears entirely. It can be smothered, but not beyond the possibility of being reawakened. Even brain-damaged elderly persons, when their interest is sufficiently provoked, can often be reactivated to a point where they are capable of useful function. Thus if we keep this thought in mind, even the apathetic old people filling the wards in homes and state institutions are redeemable.

It is their uselessness to themselves and to society that leads them into this vegetablelike condition, merely waiting for merciful death to overtake them. This need not be so. It is only a question of the extent to which society can supply the means for the stimulation and reawakening of their deadened curiosity and interest that results could be attained, ranging from their ability to maintain their own environments as a minimum, all the way to reactivating old skills or even finding new ones.

For the hardheaded, budget-minded legislator who is less moved by humanitarian than by practical considerations, this effort should be appealing. In the long run it can only lead to a material saving of public funds. To any protest that might be raised that a shortage of qualified help would curtail any such program, we can only reply that a very large pool of healthy older persons is available and awaits being tapped for such a task.

Besides the gift of experiencing the gratification of a useful and interesting life in the wake of greater cerebral development, there is the inestimable bonus in doing so of fulfilling the apparent evolutionary goal of keeping old age viable. The brain has the power to activate life processes. To keep the brain stimulated, we must use it, and the use of the brain implies constant seeking, constant curiosity, and constant learning. If we can keep our brains supplied with these essential elements of its sustenance, we shall surely improve our health in old age, and we may actually prolong our lives.

CHAPTER TWENTY-ONE

Emptying the Rocking Chairs

Old age hath yet his honour and his toil.
—TENNYSON

Whenever we speak about large categories of human beings, we have to be constantly aware that no generalization is
completely valid. We can no more state that *all* the elderly
feel a certain way or suffer certain disabilities than we can
assert that all women are poor mathematicians or that men
are stronger than women. These statements are plainly false.
The utmost we can say with any accuracy is that many or
most women do not show great interest in mathematics and
that many or most men are stronger than many or most
women. Any suggestions based on these statements would
then have to take into account the minority of women who
are excellent mathematicians and another minority who are
stronger than many men.

The same type of awareness must be present when we
make suggestions for the elderly. In this book we have been
stressing the importance of *not* retiring from active work; of
not giving up a home; of *not* moving away from one's own
community; and of taking up new work if forced out of old.
But we know that there are some older people for whom
none of these recommendations is possible. There are a large
number who are forced to give up their work either by the
retirement policies of their employers or unions or by a phys-

ical inability to continue it. There are those who are not able to keep up their homes for reasons either of finance or of health. And there are those who are not able to take up new activity for the same reasons. These older people, if they are then not able to find homes with their grown children or if they have no grown children, are often obliged by the necessities of their circumstances to seek the shelter of institutions, boardinghouses, or other types of homes for the aged.

Again, it is not possible to write of "homes for the aged" in general terms. There are many kinds of institutions or commercial enterprises that exist to serve the residence needs of old persons, and these are run according to the various philosophies of their many different directors. However there are unfortunately a large number, especially those in the public domain (run by states or cities), where the guiding philosophy seems to be that they exist only to provide a way station between retirement and death. The attitudes are negative. The services provided are purely custodial, a matter of providing food, shelter, and minimal health care for as long as the inmate lives.

The tremendous waste of all these lives—those of the old people themselves and those of the staffs that tend them—is horrifying. There is not one inmate, no matter how disabled or unskilled he may seem, who could not be given something to do that would justify his existence to himself and to society. As a very minimum, the assignment of duties to each old person has been shown to have an enormous positive effect on health and spirits wherever it has been tried. Several homes have been reported as showing gratifying results when the inmates were responsible for making their own beds, keeping their own rooms clean, assisting in kitchens and maintenance, and helping one another perform such tasks.

A telling experiment somewhat along these lines is in operation at Winter Park, Florida. A group of old people there live together in a "commune" arrangement in the home of a middle-aged couple and their eight children and

270

three grandchildren. The father of the family, Jim Gillies, acts as manager for the group, which is called Share-a-Home Association. "According to the articles, the members share a common ownership of the home and of all the facilities of the home. They have the right to hire or fire a manager and assistant manager, whose duties include providing food, lodging and other needed services for the members of the association. The manager, who must post a $10,000 bond for himself, also takes care of the finances of the home. Additionally, he is responsible for providing transportation, laundry services and medical attention to the members, and three regular meals a day for members and their guests.

"Members must provide a power of attorney to a person of their choice to act on their behalf if they become incapacitated. They must be ambulatory—able to move about with or without mechanical devices. New members are chosen by the manager and have a thirty-day trial period before becoming full members of the association. During this time any of the full members may bring up any objection they might have about the proposed member. The articles also provide for all new members to receive equity in the association, and for members who withdraw to be reimbursed for any payments made and not used."

At one time legal proceedings were instigated against this association, asserting violation of the zoning laws regarding family dwellings, but after a personal visit to the group Judge Claude Edwards ruled in its favor. "In court I was afraid that it might be a paper operation," he said, "but then I went out and saw they were living as a family and as a single housekeeping unit. I was delighted to see that it was a happy, well-run family. There are so many lonely, alienated old people who lead restricted, unhappy, unproductive lives alone because they would rather die than go into an institution. I think this is an answer to this type of problem. It is a superb idea."

The arrangement has worked out so well that a group of

Winter Park citizens has formed Share-a-Home of America, Inc., a nonprofit corporation collecting money to subsidize memberships in other homes that it hopes will be founded on the Gillies plan. Three other homes are already in the planning stage, and another, in Orange County, Florida, will soon open its doors, if it has not already done so.

We could go even further than this. We note that in Basel, Switzerland, they had an excellent experience when they located an old people's home in a municipal hospital complex. The members of this home could then take an active part in auxiliary work in the clinics and dispensary. They came to think of themselves as part of the hospital community and as useful members of a living concern. They were stimulated by the new acquaintances and friends they made; the new possibilities for most of them in fresh fields; the comradeship of shared work and duties; and the new horizons that opened up for them there. In these circumstances their transplantation provided sufficient compensation to overcome the distresses of the rift from their former lives. In reference to this home, Dr. A. L. Vischer, who reported the experience, stated: "When old folks are offered the opportunity of serving their fellows, with their experience, their maturity, their patience and silence, much psychic energy is harnessed and controlled which would otherwise run amok in pathological symptoms, whims and crotchets, senile maliciousness, and the longing for death."

We think the lessons of this example are extremely important. How infinitely more desirable it is to create an atmosphere of busy activity in a valuable joint enterprise, the hospital, than simply to wash, feed, and house the old people and then leave them to their own devices, to while away their remaining time in rocking chairs on porches or balconies, and to succumb to the desperate and finally apathetic boredom of a vegetablelike existence.

We would urgently recommend to all individuals or

committees concerned with the running of old people's homes that they consider this possibility of including them in hospital complexes where such participation in the general work of the community could be offered to the elderly. No part of hospital work is routine. The acquisition of skills for new tasks and the seeking of solutions to unforeseen problems create and maintain a resurgence of mental function and also promote improvement in physical capacity.

Where it is not possible for these homes to be an integral part of the hospital complex, it might be possible nevertheless to foster a close working relationship between a home and a hospital not too far away, in such a way that all the inmates of the home could identify with the hospital and its work. They could be given badges or uniforms as auxiliary workers, and their feeling of importance could be bolstered by this means.

A dramatic example of what it is possible for old people to accomplish in this field is a volunteer group of elderly people who live in Staten Island, New York, in the vicinity of a large state school for retarded children. Between sixty and seventy of these old people are enrolled in an organization called SERVE (Serve and Enrich Retirement by Volunteer Experience). The state school in their neighborhood has recently been the target of widespread adverse criticism on account of its alleged neglect of some of its more seriously retarded children. The school has countered that it does the best that is possible in view of its staff limitations imposed by the necessity of keeping its budget within the bounds of available funds. Since they became aware of the needs of this state school, the elderly people enrolled in SERVE have taken on the following tasks there:

Three days a week, on Mondays, Wednesdays and Fridays, they visit the school and do everything in their power to brighten the lives of the mentally retarded children with a lot of kindness and help.

An eighty-year-old widower works in the baby ward, feeding the inert children there.

A fifty-seven-year-old widow, herself a victim of Parkinson's disease and whose speech and steps have been slowed by it, wheels a young patient around in his wheelchair to give him a change of scene before his mealtime, and she then spoon-feeds him his liquefied lunch.

Four women, aged seventy-four, sixty-nine, sixty-five, and sixty-two, the last herself troubled by an ear ailment, give midmorning carriage rides to other children and then help give them their lunch.

A seventy-three-year-old retired nurse, who suffers from arthritis, and nineteen other elderly women sort bags and boxes of donated clothes and number them for shipment to buildings housing male, female, and infant patients.

In the school's carpentry shop, six retired men, all over sixty, repair chairs and replace worn handles on baby strollers with sanded pieces of old broomsticks.

In the machine shop a seventy-two-year-old retired machinist grinds square floor tiles on a lathe to be used as disks for the bottoms of bags for the patients' toiletry items.

A group of about half a dozen elders help in the occupational therapy section in another building, where they assist the children with making greeting cards, pot holders, pillow covers, and even with weaving or looping rugs.

Besides their volunteer activities at the state school, these old people assist in a Public Health Service hospital on Staten Island and at a state hospital in Manhattan. Some of them also prepare bloodmobile kits for the Red Cross and others mailing lists for the American Cancer Society. They restore books for distribution to needy children, assist parochial schoolteachers with pupils who have reading problems, make regular telephone calls for companionship to homebound invalids, and work in gift shops to raise the funds needed to carry out their work.

SERVE was started in 1967 under the sponsorship of a nonprofit, nonsectarian social agency that recognized that people over sixty have a tremendous amount of skills and interests that could usefully be put to work. They wanted "to do away with the whole attitude that people are through at sixty-five."

They serve as a model on which the state hopes to base similar groups in other counties, and the federal government's Retired Senior Volunteer Program also intends to organize such groups in other states.

This group demonstrates through its volunteer activities that operations like the Basel old people's home, closely connected with a hospital community, are eminently workable and could be equally rewarding in other countries.

Such a constructive approach, which is essentially hard-headed, economically advantageous to all concerned, non-wasteful of life and resources, and not motivated by sentimental preoccupations alone, in the long run and in the highest sense is the most humanitarian of all.

CHAPTER TWENTY-TWO

To Set Wheels in Motion

What we must build in this country—among all our people—is a new attitude toward old age; an attitude which insists that there can be no retirement from living, no retirement from responsibility, and no retirement from citizenship.

—PRESIDENT NIXON, June 25, 1971

Several great countries in the English-speaking world, perhaps because of their colonial past, have long regarded themselves as nations of young people, and they pride themselves on getting ever younger as material wealth has spread to larger segments of their populations and drawn their youth into the mainstream of their economic lives. In North America and in Australia too, politicians and industry alike address their appeals to the populace as though it were forever young and have geared much of their attention to those actually young out of proportion to their numbers and importance.

Now even the United States, where the youth cult has reached a zenith, is awakening to the startling realization that the nation's youthfulness is a myth. As a matter of fact, the average age not only in the United States but in all technologically advanced countries is increasing, and this trend will continue. All around us we see that improved medical care allows more people to live longer while at the same time fewer children are born, weighting the population toward the higher age groups. The ranks of the retired are swelling as mechanization reduces the need for a large labor force. In spite of this, government social policies continue to put much greater weight on their efforts to serve youth than the aged. Until the present time this was understandable, since education and training are primary necessities in any industrial society. But the changes now taking place in the structure of the population call for a reevaluation of priorities.

The advertising profession, always sensitive to public mood, provides a touchstone by which we can gauge changing demands, and even in this field of dedicated caterers to youth we now hear voices raised expressing a glimmer of doubt as to the value of this direction. A vice-president of an advertising agency recently gave voice to this groundswell of opinion among business leaders in the following words: "As I watch television and read magazines and attend movies these days, I sometimes wonder if anybody besides myself is over thirty. There seems to be a conscious denial of middle age—and certainly of old age. TV ads continue to feature shaggy-haired surfers and long-limbed golden blonds swigging Pepsi or dashing around in Detroit's latest scat-abouts. Seldom does an older face show up, except in those stultifying ads for laxatives and denture adhesives."

Such a statement gives evidence that the realization that older people exist as an important element in our society is slowly reaching the business world as it has already begun to reach political circles.

It is a paradox that in a country with a government service equipped with computerized information on every level and geared to planning for every contingency, no effective overall plans have been formulated for 20,000,000 citizens who are sixty-five years old and over.

It is apparent that new thinking on the part of our policy makers must be stimulated to take into account what is not so slowly becoming the largest minority group and also potentially the most powerful.

A great deal can be accomplished by concerned individuals by their attitudes and actions, and even more by concerned individuals banded together in a common purpose; but for any remedial action to have its greatest effect, sooner or later it must obtain support and leadership from an agency of the government.

Formulating the Idea

Before any government agency can be expected to take up and promote any new idea in whatever field, that idea must be clearly formulated.

In the case of the aged, governments in the Western countries are prepared to meet new concepts halfway, for many starts have already been made, and the wish and intention to meet the need is present. We believe, however, that what has been initiated so far lacks a fundamental and comprehensive philosophy. If any general policy is present at all, it seems to be based on philanthropic principles—to give help. We believe the whole idea of "giving help" is counterproductive. To be the recipient of help is an abasing circumstance for anyone at any age, and for the old it is deathly. We strongly believe that a far more rewarding basic philosophy would be "keep them busy." By this, as we have already made clear, we do not necessarily mean keeping the elderly on in the jobs of their lifetimes as long as they live, but keeping them mentally and actively engaged in occupations suited to their age and status at all times. No human being should ever wake up in the morning totally without objectives for that day. Once this operational philosophy, "keep them busy," is substituted for the philosophy, "help them," and the principle becomes clear in everybody's mind, then the directives that will result from this changed viewpoint will automatically reflect it.

What We Can Do About It

It is inevitable that directives from any high office in any government become watered down as they are adapted to special circumstances by officials in the middle and lower echelons in the course of their practical application; but if one and all fully understand the principle, then the adaptations and modifications of directives that they are obliged to make to render them usable will be guided along those lines.

In this particular case the basic idea comes naturally to our style of thought and is easy to grasp, so it should find ready acceptance.

Often biologically based principles are incorporated into codes of ethics. This is understandable, since ethics that were not biologically sound would threaten the existence of the group practicing them. The Biblical injunction "In the sweat of thy face shalt thou eat bread" converted a biological necessity into an ethical principle that is the basis of the prevailing cultural assumption of Western society—that work is one of the significant experiences of a person's life. But the course of human history, influenced by rapidly developing technology, has separated the biological from the ethical elements of this principle. We no longer see it as a crystal-clear necessity that we should work unduly, since it is now possible to earn sufficient bread with far less effort than was formerly the case. The gaining of leisure seems to be on the way to becoming an ethical principle that many feel to be more appropriate than the ancient Biblical work ethic. But as any impartial observer can see, the human body was not formed through the eons of the past for a life of leisure. Every part of its physical and mental structure and function has been honed by untold ages of adaptation to suit it to self-reliant, self-sustaining work. Only in purposeful activity does it retain its best performance. Perhaps in the far distant future the shape the human body will take will show adaptation to the increasing possibility for leisure, but such modifications will take thousands of years. At the present time the bodies we are endowed with require use, and any return to the direction of the work ethic will serve to restore a unity between our ideals and our biological needs. Philosophically, whether work is desirable is open to discussion. But that physical organs, not excepting the brain, must be used in order to remain at optimal functioning is not.

It should be possible to convey this idea to all the echelons of government agencies concerned with attempting to find solutions to or ameliorations of the problems of the aged. And once the basic idea of the necessity of some form of work or useful activity is firmly entrenched in all minds, the other needs for dignity, respect, and self-respect will fall into place, for in large part they arise from the primary necessity.

"Consciousness Raising"

Concomitant with this effort to realign the basis of official thinking should be an attempt to change the thinking of the public at large. We outlined a plan for this in the first chapter of this part when we discussed the need for using the strategies of a public relations campaign. A great deal of education is necessary to bring to the awareness of the public the importance of the aged person to society and to impart an understanding that his needs lie in the direction of being useful to it and not of being eased out of it. It is a sad commentary on how far our attitudes have deviated from the biologically based that old people themselves would also have to be included in this reorientation effort.

Presenting the Idea

Any new idea, no matter how sound or self-evident, is bound to disturb well-entrenched programs and therefore to meet resistance at every level of organizational operation.

Every large organization, once it is well established, proceeds to a very great extent by the power of its own momentum. It takes an effort four- or fivefold as great to alter the direction of an existing program as it does to start one from scratch. The personnel in all organizations are identified with and have built their careers around certain principles which, right or wrong, function in some way. Because of this we are sometimes faced even with whole departments continuing a program long after the need for it has passed and it has become obsolete or inappropriate. The jobs connected with the program are established and the persons engaged to perform them will go on doing so, and they will resist new directives. Their unspoken thought will be: Why upset the applecart? They will feel that what they had been doing worked well enough. Their reactions at the verbal level will be to find the flaws in any new idea presented—and, of course, since perfection eludes us, it is always possible to find flaws. Since their criticisms may well have some validity, they can then put the valuable contents of the new idea also into disrepute, and so the great positive values of many innovative plans are discarded without trial as a result of this type of departmental conservatism.

Parliamentary institutions follow entrenched routines. New directives, initiated at the top, gradually filter down all the way to the worker in the field, even if we succeed in convincing departmental heads of a new approach, unless the field worker accepts the spirit of it, it will be subverted in practice. In order to achieve any good results with a new idea, one has to pierce the monolithic structure of traditional procedures that in turn are supported by the comfortable state of semiautomatic routine so characteristic of old habit.

To be able to achieve any new approach to the problems of the elderly, it is therefore necessary to imbue all echelons with its new spirit. One of many examples of the progressively widening differences between the formulation of policies at the top and the execution of them at the operational

281

level is found in the Welfare Department. It is often very difficult to recognize the spirit of the directives in the day-to-day operations of the field worker with his clients. Ultimately all directives become human interactions as they filter through the values and beliefs of the social worker.

We are stressing this point because programs for the elderly, especially the elderly poor, have been in operation for the better part of this century, and for that reason a tradition has been built up in dealing with them. But the spirit has been similar to that in the old-age homes: make their lives easier until they die. The social worker who has been dealing with an elderly person on this basis would have to be thoroughly indoctrinated to see in him any potential for useful activity. It would come to him as a surprise to see people who had been considered human wrecks actively performing services of social worth and regaining some vigor in the process. Such demonstrations in the field would obviously be of very great importance in obtaining cooperation to carry out this program—at least as important as policies initiated at the top of the departmental ladder.

Finding a Focal Point to Centralize the Effort

The aura surrounding the treatment of the elderly is heavily overlaid with conflicting emotions. Whenever a situation exists that evokes the kind of personal discomfort that we refer to as a feeling of guilt, we try to do our utmost to free ourselves of the burden. The first reaction, which is the most useless one, is usually to shift the blame onto someone else. Because aiding the sick, the weak, and the elderly is felt to be a duty, not coming to the rescue of a person in need is felt to be sinful and becomes a matter for one's conscience. This feeling is supported by religious belief and also forms the bedrock of secular laws. There is hardly a religion that does not stress an obligation to honor one's parents. What is more, in the case of action or lack of action related to the elderly such feelings are further intensified by our identification of all elderly persons with our own parents.

In such a highly charged emotional sphere it is inevitable that reactions will vary greatly and that they will fall into patterns governed by each individual's relations with his or her own parents. A person who had a good relationship with his own parents will be inclined to be solicitous, sometimes to the point of being sentimental, in his attitudes toward the aged, whereas one who had a trying relationship with his own parents will tend to shift responsibility for the care of the old onto others. In view of the increasing stresses between the generations in today's world, the number of those with negative feelings toward their parents is increasing, and it is this sector that will develop a sense of guilt.

This guilt will manifest itself as a nagging thought, "Maybe I *should* be doing something about . . ." and if this admonition is not heeded, an internal voice will insist, "You are bad (sinful)." The fear of not being loved or respected because of being bad then leads to an internal correction, "It is not I who is bad (sinful). It was not my fault. It is he who is to blame," and we then feel compelled to point a finger at a convenient scapegoat.

There are as many attitudes toward the elderly as there are shades of differences in feeling between the young and their parents, and this may well be a contributing reason for the lack of a unified philosophy at every level of attempts to help the aged. The piecemeal approaches to the problem are certainly largely due to bureaucratic procedures, but we must not forget the strong element of personal feelings that contributes to them.

In this atmosphere feelings of gratitude and affection will be greatly interlarded with feelings of guilt that will point accusing fingers at any scapegoat available. In the United States culprits are nominated in something like these terms:

The Republicans don't want to spend enough money—they hold the purse tight; the Democrats are too wasteful—there is never enough money where it is needed; the unions balk at jobs for the elderly—they want to protect their own; capitalism exploits the worker—when he is no longer useful, he is discarded; Socialists and liberals make the elderly too dependent on the government; and so on. In other countries equivalent scapegoats are available.

There is hardly a political party, political philosophy, or special interest that has not been blamed. Although there may be some validity in some of the accusations, none of them is very fair. Almost without exception political parties and organized groups of all kinds, as well as most individuals, would like to help the elderly effectively if only they knew how, if only for two very compelling reasons. The first is that the elderly are voters, and the second that everyone will be old someday and so identifies himself with this problem.

Faultfinding is an empty exercise that does nothing to further the interests of the elderly, nor does it promote any advantage in the long run either to the accuser or to the accused. The important thing to be done is not to engage in a verbal battle to fix *who* is to blame, but to find *what* is the cause for the state of affairs and *what* we can do about it. Of course we feel more comfortable if we redirect the voice of our conscience to another human being or organization. There is also satisfaction in blaming an impersonal institution in about the same fashion as one would reproach an absent parent for failing to give needed love and care. But we should like to state emphatically that no one individual or institution can be singled out as a culprit. We are dealing with a problem that has an evolutionary background and that has acquired social overtones. Its correction requires the cooperation and skills of scientist, politician, and layman alike. Placing blame on any individual or on any single entity creates the delusion that a simple correction is all that is necessary and that somebody else will see to it that this is done. By emphasizing the *what* rather than the *who*, effort is channeled to where it can be useful. The problem lies in our social attitudes, and nothing but a revision of these will correct it.

It is a familiar fact that there are more old people in our societies today than ever before. Less familiar is the fact that the span of man's life has not changed very greatly in the past several thousand years. Many of the ancient Greeks whose names are household words to us lived well into their eighties, and the Bible records the span of life as seventy years or more. A person of fifty-five in the Greece of Socrates had about the same life expectancy as a person of fifty-five living today. What has changed is that recent advances in medical science permit more babies to live and to reach the age of fifty-five. This does not change the potential length of our lives, but it enables more individuals to fulfill that potential.

It is for this reason that the nature of the problems of the elderly has changed and also become more acute, for the elderly person no longer belongs to any single social category but exists in every one of them. We cannot say, as could many earlier generations, that an old person is either well to do, in which case he can look after himself, or poor, in which case society must take care of him. Today the older person's difficulties are as varied and different as are those of all the sectors within a complex society. No single or simple solution can deal with them all equally. Therefore a multiplicity of effort is essential, for the needs of the retired executive are different from those of the retired locomotive driver, as are those of the retired teacher from the retired laborer's. Certain general principles, which we have outlined, underlie the needs of all of them, but the specific solutions are everywhere different.

Of its nature, then, the work in this field must necessarily be diffused into many areas and diversified in many projects. This will require a vast effort that must be used to best advantage so that undertakings do not overlap but reach all who need them and so that basic principles are understood by everyone concerned. To do this, we urgently need a single center as a focus for all the varied work that is necessary both in education and in practical projects.

We believe that just as the government contains a Department of Education, primarily for the needs of the young, it should also contain a Department of the Aged to educate and to initiate and promote all the enterprises that are needed to serve the elderly.

CHAPTER TWENTY-THREE

Political Strength and Political Action

Let us pray that we may long retain the old men
whom we still have in this chamber. . . . In the course
of their long journey all the sanctuaries of the human
mind have been opened to them, and in them they
have learned the science of the useful truths, the
science which sets a just valuation on both the resistance of habit and the enterprises of the imagination.

—TALLEYRAND

When we walk into the offices of any large industrial organization, what meets our eyes? A shiny new building, a
modern decor, and a sea of youthful faces. Should we pass
through the main office and be ushered into the private
offices beyond it, we catch glimpses of middle-aged managers,
each individually enthroned behind a palace guard of youthful assistants. But an old person is nowhere to be seen.

Markedly in industry and commerce, and to a lesser degree
in science and the arts, old people are conspicuous by their
absence. If we want to meet them in any larger numbers, we
must seek them out in the few preserves left to them in our
society among the Senators or the judges; otherwise we must
look for them in resort hotels. As self-employed artists, musi-

cians, medical men, or scholars may remain active to a ripe age and prove by their performances what it is possible for old age to achieve, but these individuals are isolated and not part of the general scene.

Many, if not most, large enterprises today subject applicants for employment to numerous tests, including rigid physical requirements, that effectively exclude older people. Large industry, of course, is not the only realm of life, but it sets a pace that is followed by a great number of others. Together they create a hostile atmosphere for any person seeking employment who is past the middle years, and since gainful employment is the rock upon which our society is based, this attitude has its effects also in the social and cultural domains of our lives.

This attitude is in many ways contradictory, for industry in Western countries is past its own youthful stage of rapid growth and limitless expansion. It is well into a mature phase of consolidation, but reflecting its image of itself as still in a youthful stage, it continues to seek the services of the young in the idea that with them it will continue to reach and conquer new horizons. This view that industry takes of itself is somewhat askew. It lags behind the present realities. The major industries in the Western world have reached a stage where the steep rise of early growth is slowly flattening. True, new industries still arise and expand quickly, but they expand into an arena that is already filled with mature giants, and after a short while they take their place with them. In such circumstances industrial and commercial leaders would do well to reassess their ideas about the type of personnel that could best help them achieve new goals. These new goals, which must include conservation of resources, improvement of the quality of goods and services, and better industry-consumer relations, could use the stable qualities of older people, who fit supremely into this pattern. The older employee is usually conservative, feels a greater loyalty to his work and company, and is less inclined to indulge in job hopping. These traits are essential to the maintenance of quality and service.

G. Rosenberg, a professor of sociology at Case Western Reserve University, stated that older workers could be a "gold mine" for many companies. "They are just as committed as young people. Their absentee rates are lower. They are steady workers and are serious and conscientious." A president of an old-age job placement company in California noted that he had placed at least three thousand older men and women in jobs and helped them back into the mainstream of life. He mentioned that one woman had told him that he had saved her from suicide.

The entrenched idea that older people are not adaptable to new circumstances is given the lie by many examples of retired management personnel who have started new businesses with their savings, especially since many of them have abandoned their earlier vocations and have turned to completely new fields. H. J. Friedsam, director of the Center for Studies in Aging at North Texas State University, said that it is not really a question of whether the old person can work or not, but that we have never really faced the issue of what kind of work older people can perform and of how to absorb them into the labor market. "We need to take a hard look at this," he said.

A representative of one electronics firm that has led the way in hiring retired executives as consultants, particularly in technical matters, stated, "We are in a know-how industry, and we see no reason to let this know-how go simply because a man has passed sixty-five."

Hastings College of Law, a part of the University of California, has uniquely demonstrated the usefulness of the experience of the elderly. All of its twenty-two full-time teachers are over sixty-five, and all were victims of the compulsory retirement policies of other colleges.

A major stumbling block to the fuller employment of older people is the greater expense of insurance policies and pension funds to cover them, and this is something that has to be worked out by political action. It should not be an insurmountable hurdle. Industry has to awaken to the facts of longer life expectancy of the population as a whole and the improved health of the elderly. By itself it is not going to do this. It will take concerted action by dedicated political workers to force it to their attention. And this is only one of the very many battlefields that call for devoted political activity, for the elderly person faces barriers in all walks of life.

One start in this direction has been made. Ralph Nader, the crusader for the consumer, recently formed a Retired Professionals Action Group that will seek "constructive social changes." They intend "to grapple with such problems as housing, taxes, medical care, consumer fraud, nursing homes and pensions." The first office has been established in Washington under the direction of Charles E. Adkins, former president of Briarcliff College. At a news conference Mr. Nader almost echoed the practical points we have brought up in this part of our book. He said that "one solution to the personal problem faced by many older people of continuing to live useful, challenging lives is to provide them with opportunities to help solve society's problems." Their involvement will also help deal with one of the central tragedies of old age: the underutilization or total neglect of their "rich resources." He added, "Retired professionals generally have not only valuable experience, but sufficient leisure time, community contacts, few family obligations and a potential for free thinking unhampered by career ambitions or institutional restrictions. These combined assets hold a promise that such groups can have considerable impact." Earlier retirement, combined with the "educational stretch-out" of the young going for more advanced degrees, leaves only about three to four decades for productive contributions to society. Mr. Nader said he hoped that formation of the Retired Professionals Action Group would provide a "turning point in changing society's attitudes toward the old in a country obsessed by youth and give expression to thousands of people who are tired of playing shuffleboard."

It is a simple fact of life that, on the whole, people do not go too far out of their way to help others. If the persons concerned do not take steps to help themselves, no one else will do it so effectively for them. The elderly will have to take up their own cudgels, organize into politically active groups, utilize the power of their numbers, their importance as consumers, and their rights as citizens, make demands, and see to it that these are met.

It is some indication of how far in our thoughts we have dismissed the elderly from active life that the idea of old people banding together for political purposes should strike us as strange. And yet throughout history, there have been countless societies in which older people either held the reins or played a leading part, and there is no reason why they should not become politically effective again.

Many tribes of Australian bushmen are ruled by an oligarchy of elders and not by a single chieftain or king. They all treat their aged with great respect. In West Africa, too, among the Krumen, it is the ancients who wield political power. In Sparta, by the constitution of Lycurgus, the authority to govern was allotted to three powers: the Lacedaemonian kings; five ephors, or overseers; and the council of gerontes, or elders. This was a council of twenty-eight men over sixty years of age who had proved their worth and who were elected by popular acclamation. In ancient Athens men of fifty were called upon to speak first in public conferences, and although in the Roman Empire younger rulers emerged, the very name "senate" indicates that an assembly of elders was the earliest tradition of Rome. The Papacy, too, has been, with a few exceptions in the early history of the church, a decided gerontocracy. The selection of Popes exclusively from the College of Cardinals has ensured the character of the Papacy as essentially a council of elders.

Another decided gerontocracy was the Venetian Republic, where the doges were by preference old and experienced men, especially in times of crisis. For example, when Venice was threatened in 1192 by the Emperor Henry VI, the octogenarian and half-blind Enrico Dandolo was chosen by the unanimous vote of the electoral college to lead the defense of the state, and he proved to be as ruthless, as desirous of fame, and no less shrewd or less able than his youthful adversary. At the age of ninety-three Dandolo himself triumphantly led the assault on Byzantium, and again in 1205 he battled in its defense against the Bulgars. He died in that year from the aftermath of a serious wound. The Doge Marino Falieri was elected in 1354 at the age of seventy-six because the republic was in a difficult position and he was considered the shrewdest and most capable man to lead it. Giovanni Gradenigo, who was also seventy-six, followed him. Later Marco Cornaro, an octogenarian, sat on the ducal throne, and Venice was liberated from the danger of conquest by Genoa by his successor, Andrea Contarini, also an aged man.

Venice affords us impressive evidence of the capacity of the aged for rigorous work and political activity, and these few examples could be multiplied many times in other countries. Bismarck was in his sixties at the height of his power, his Chief of General Staff, Helmuth von Moltke, was seventy-five, and his War Minister, Albrecht von Roon, was seventy-two.

We do not even have to delve into history to confirm the political potential of the aged and their ability to assume leadership and guide societies for the benefit of all. In our own times Winston Churchill and Konrad Adenauer provided archetypes of the breed; Charles de Gaulle in his late years resurrected his country from defeat to new life and dignity; and neither Gandhi, Jinnah, nor Ben-Gurion were young when they presided over the liberation and independence of their respective nations.

Political life is a natural amphitheater for the activities of the elderly, so why should they not be able to take leadership and guide public opinion in their own cause? Only the thorough brainwashing we have subjected ourselves to could have induced us all, including the elderly themselves, to believe that they are not strong enough or politically interested enough to organize and to take up the challenges.

Political Power

Historically, relatively few persons in our society reached what we should today call old age, and of those only some, through the force of their individualities and through their knowledge and the respect they commanded, wielded power. Today the picture is different. The new factor is that very many more people of all kinds reach old age, and that even if they are no longer the sole repositories of knowledge, by their very numbers they have a potential for wielding great political power.

The last census dramatized this new political fact of life with the information that the portion of the population over the age of sixty-five is increasing at twice the rate of the portion below that age. To give some hard numbers, in the United States in 1970 the over-sixty-five group numbered 20,000,000 and constituted 10 percent of the population. An even more telling fact is that they represent 17 percent of the voting population, and one should be particularly aware of the fact that they have a higher sense of civic duty, for they vote in much higher proportion (70 percent) than younger voters.

It literally cries for organization and leadership when we see that, in spite of their numerical strength, one-quarter of them are consigned to a standard of living below the poverty level; nearly two-thirds of those living alone or not with relatives are merely "getting by" at a bare subsistence level, and their fixed incomes cannot keep pace with the rising rate of inflation. If these 20,000,000 individuals had been an ethnic minority, a hue and cry would have been set up long ago to relieve their situation.

Perhaps one reason why things have come to this pass is that the elderly are not inclined to take to the streets and demonstrate for action. On the contrary, most of them are by their nature a stabilizing force. On the whole, they prefer to make the best of existing conditions and to adapt themselves rather than to make attempts to change the conditions. Their very sense of personal dignity prevents them from advocating and taking part in violent measures. It is for these very reasons that they are a factor for good order in our societies, for which we should support and cherish them. Idealists of the political left see the plight of the elderly as arising out of the present social order, and therefore one more motive for turning our societies over from top to bottom. But what the elderly need is not a turning over of society for their benefit, but to find their way back into the established order and to play their part in maintaining it.

Nevertheless, their situation has deteriorated to such a low point that the absolute need to protect their own interests has begun to light sparks in several places. Here and there the sparks are bursting into small flames that cannot be ignored. In Boston, Philadelphia, Chicago, and Sacramento they are demanding partial tax exemptions. In Philadelphia and San Francisco they are clamoring for better housing. In New York, Cleveland, and Milwaukee they are seeking special transportation privileges. In various smaller cities they are making claims for better job opportunities, discounts in stores and places of entertainment, and more generous benefits.

Here and there older citizens have already banded together on election issues that were relevant to their lives and were able to be decisive factors in the final vote. These issues included, on the one hand, property taxes and school bonds, which tax them unfairly, and on the other, social security, medicare, and other benefits, which they felt were too low to meet their needs.

Elderly citizens have a very good case. If they were only to organize effectively, they would find considerable support from the general population. This was expressed by Herman B. Brotman, chief statistician for the Administration on Aging. "Since time immemorial," he said, "we've wanted to live longer. Now that we've achieved this, our society and technology have pushed older people out of all the roles that gave them status and function in our society. In an agrarian society, the older person represented a wealth of advice and knowledge. Today, all of the roles have disappeared."

Under the pressure of the circumstances a new breed of militant elder is emerging here and there. An example is Henry A. Sherman, a seventy-four-year-old retired Army colonel who was a delegate to the five-day White House Conference on Aging in 1971—the second such conference in ten years. He organized an old-age political action group in Houston and succeeded in obtaining the promise of a fare reduction for senior citizens on city transportation. He told reporters, "When we get the fare reduction, then comes the gas, telephone, and lighting companies, and then the stores. We will take one group at a time and get them to give a special rate for senior citizens." When reporters questioned him as to whether he was using political pressure, he escaped from making the obvious response with a remark conveying typical political innuendo, "The pressure that we have is that we represent one hundred and thirty-three thousand people in the county, sixty-two and above, who will be very disappointed if they don't get any help. And the politicians know that these one hundred and thirty-three thousand are all eligible to vote."

Such straws in the wind should not be lost upon the national leadership either in Washington or in any other capital, subject to democratic processes or not. As a matter of fact, a growing number of Senators have shown themselves to be sensitive to the voices of the old when they are raised.

Nevertheless, isolated actions of this type, while they may bring local ameliorations, will not produce the total reversal of public attitudes that is necessary. Not until they coalesce into a national movement with centralized and regional leadership will they be able to exercise the full punch of their potential power.

Given the fact that elderly persons stem from backgrounds as diverse as the life of the nation, initial organization will naturally consolidate around special interests. In fact, the beginnings of such an effort toward centralization have already made their appearance. Three organizations are headquartered in Washington. One is the National Council of Senior Citizens. Its three thousand members are largely derived from former unionized labor. The other, the American Association of Retired Persons, and its sister group, the National Retired Teachers Association, have a slightly higher membership total and rally retired white-collar workers. It is foreseeable that other organizations of seniors may follow in their steps.

But valuable as these movements are in working for the special interests of the groups that form them, it will take the full force of their united power, together with the latent force of all the elderly people not yet organized, to spark a really effective nationwide change of attitude. The tasks are first to convince the old of the strength of their own position and then to use this strength to change the public image of the old as an ineffective part of society that merely utilizes space and resources and has no further function. On the contrary, the senior group must be seen as the largest unexploited human resource available to society, a resource which, properly utilized, has the potential to contribute a wealth of values and to restore balance and stability to groups.

Consumer Power

To turn from ideology to the realities of everyday life, older people have two basic weapons for remedying their situation. The first, which we have just discussed, is the political power of their numbers, and the second is the economic power they can wield through their impact as consumers.

In this respect we have a valuable peephole into the future in the state of Florida. Because of its agreeable climate, Florida has attracted large numbers of retired persons, and people over sixty-five form 14½ percent of its total population. In the rest of the nation and in other Western countries the proportion of elders to the general population will come to approximate what we now see in Florida as a result of the natural course of events arising from present population trends, and so this state provides us with a model for the society based on a larger proportion of older individuals that is in the near future for all of us.

Twenty years ago, when several enterprising land companies sought to sell property to retired persons from all over the country, they offered undeveloped land. It was easier for them, and their profits were more substantial. However they discovered that, on the whole, elderly people with their limited means were not inclined to commit themselves to speculation. Before they put down their money, they wanted to have an actual view of the home it was proposed that they should buy to make the land useful to them. The land companies found that they could not make sufficient sales unless they met this requirement. Today a retired person thinking of moving to Florida has the possibility there to choose from every imaginable kind of home, already built, many of them already furnished and equipped and ready for occupation. He has many choices in means of financing his purchase, with many companies competing to please him, and he may often look around at their expense until he finds exactly what he wants.

The lesson to be drawn from this is that where large numbers of people make their requirements plain and do not settle for what is available, the business community will find it to be in its best interest to cater to those needs. And what happened in the case of providing housing to suit the retired in Florida can happen in any branch of service or supply that they need if they make their demands known. The very power of their numbers would eventually ensure this, but the process can be speeded up when the elderly are organized into political and economic action.

International Organization

The organization of elders for political and economic action to improve their lot in their own communities could have a very important extension in the wider field of international life.

We have acknowledged the place of the elder as a cohesive and steadying force in the family, and therefore in national life. We should like to suggest that these qualities be used on the international scene.

The elderly have many advantages not available to the prime-of-life population. They have time at their disposal, and their basic financial needs are covered by retirement income. Not unnaturally, many of them like to use these advantages for more extensive travel than was possible for them in their younger years. To what better use could they put this advantages and inclinations than by directing their time and travel toward the founding and fostering of international groups devoted, first of all, to the promotion of the welfare of the aged in all countries and, secondly, to exerting their influence on behalf of more stable relations between countries as a whole? They could also lend their support to already existing organizations devoted to relief in disaster areas, to the preservation of cultural monuments and art treasures wherever they are threatened, to the creation and preservation of national parks and wildlife in underdeveloped lands, and to health programs. Instead of traveling aimlessly, then, and eventually finding boredom at the end of the voyage, their journeys would have a purpose consistent with the status of the old, give a meaning to the later part of their lives, and prove stimulating.

Influence in the field of international life could be more readily attained by organized groups of elders than by any other. Among the statesmen and leaders of all nations are many who are themselves in the same category or approaching it, and they would surely be willing to receive them and likely to find a kinship of ideas with them.

There is a large reservoir of retired diplomatic personnel, legislators, and senior businessmen with international experience from among whom leaders could be recruited.

Meetings could be held frequently, perhaps as often as once a month, and each time in a different place. If they were held in underdeveloped countries, as a by-product of their activity the old people's groups would serve as pioneers in opening up tourist facilities in those regions and perhaps thus help them on their way to economic solvency.

The reason for holding frequent meetings would be to enable all members to participate in some of them, and the programs could be arranged with it in mind that all individuals or groups would not be represented every time.

The practical organization involved in such a large program would also provide considerable employment for the old people themselves. Time not being a great factor, as it is for younger travelers, boats could be chartered, and meetings and associations fostered en route. In connection with the groups of elders responsible for these travel arrangements, local centers to train people to perform these functions could also be initiated.

There is a precedent for this type of organization. The international youth movements attempted something of this sort but, on the whole, were not too successful for very obvious reasons. Youth is a passing phase, and the interests of the young change after a very short time. Any association or forum for youth loses its leaders as soon as they mature. This is not the case with the elderly. At the age of sixty-five most of them these days have a full twenty years of potentially active life ahead of them—enough time for a whole new generation to appear on the scene.

Wherever we look, we see possibilities for older people to consolidate their political strength by associations of all kinds and to promote political action in their own interest and in the interests of human beings everywhere in both national and international arenas.

Means sometimes seem to be in conflict with the ends they are intended to achieve. In this case, in an almost unique degree, means and ends serve and reinforce each other. The goals of such groups would be valuable and worthy, but the means to achieve them would produce valuable results of themselves. The direction and purpose given to the lives of such large numbers of older people by political and politically oriented activities would revivify their day-to-day existences, with immense benefit to their mood, health, and perhaps longevity, for they would absorb their interest in precisely the area in which they are best fitted by nature to be involved.

CHAPTER TWENTY-FOUR

Path to Fulfillment

> Whenever a process of life communicates an eagerness
> to him who lives it, there the life has become genu-
> inely significant. Sometimes, the eagerness is more knit
> up with motor activities, sometimes with perceptions,
> sometimes with imagination, sometimes with reflective
> thought. But wherever it is found, there is the zest, the
> tingle, the excitement of reality: and there *is* impor-
> tance in the only real and positive sense in which
> importance ever anywhere can be. —WILLIAM JAMES

At the beginning of this book we asked a question: Does
the extension and preservation of youth that we see around
us on all sides form a part of some basic trend that would
account for it?

Indeed man's trend to the prolongation of youthfulness is
a natural development. It is bound up with his evolutionary
course, for he was formed by the continuous extension of his
young phases until they came to last for the greater part of
his life. Along with the extended youthfulness of his body
goes an equally long period of youthfulness of mind and
spirit. Man never tires of learning nor loses his desire to play
and to explore. His youthful curiosity remains with him all
his life. In the young of all higher animals, learning is facilitated by a reward system. The satisfaction of curiosity or

the achievement of a skill gives a sense of well-being, promoted by the pleasure centers of the brain. This reward system, too, is extended in man, and the satisfaction of his desires to learn, to explore, and to know why is a source of pleasure for him all his life. But this quality of the preservation of what in other animals is an early stage only—in fact their equivalent of childhood—has meaning only when comparisons are made between the behavior of man and that of other species.

In other animals with only a few exceptions (and these, interestingly enough, are the species that have developed a high degree of intelligence) this type of behavior falls away when sexual maturity is reached. The mature animal then settles down to the business of its life, which is the preservation and perpetuation of its species.

In man these qualities do not fall away with sexual maturity. They remain with him from the time he is born until the time he dies. Nevertheless, and in spite of the presence of characteristics that are features only of the immature phases of other animals, each phase of man's life has, over and above these, its own specific expressions that then very clearly distinguish in him what is childhood, maturity, and old age. These differences are plain to us all. We take them for granted and have no need to spell them out. Thus we must recognize that, while in every age man retains many qualities that are in essence youthful, at the same time, and equally plainly, each of man's stages has its own necessities.

Inasmuch as curiosity, exploration, and learning in man are as much a part of his old age as of any other phase of his life, any relinquishing of them has serious consequences for him, no matter what his age. However, the intellectual and physical skills that an elder has built up over a lifetime are intimately bound up with his or her place, dignity, status, and sense of purposefulness. If any of these factors is eliminated, then the acquired skills find no satisfactory outlet. As a consequence, the elderly person then falls back on using them as a child does. The attributes of dignity, status, and the sense of place and purpose are not yet present in a child; they are in the process of being developed. The child's main motivations are the pleasure of performance for its own sake, which is play, and the desire to please its parents and teachers. When the older person is deprived of the prerogatives of his senior rank, his utilization of his skills will be in no way different from a child's. Since he no longer has parents and teachers to please, they will be expended in hobbies, games, or play all *for their own sake and without relevance to social purposes*, ending, as we have described, in feelings of emptiness.

The removal of function therefore equals a kind of death. It is not a physical death, but it causes a feeling of nonexistence so far as the life of the group is concerned, and this is painful. The only way we can remedy this situation is by restoring elements to older people's lives that sustain their status, dignity, sense of purpose, and feeling of self-worth. In simple words, we must bring back to their lives the possibility for purposeful activity, which, incidentally, should never have been taken away.

It needs to be emphasized, however, that in spite of the general decline in the role and function of the elderly that began with the invention of printing and has continued with increasing speed since the spread of literacy, there has always been a sizable number of old people who manage to find a fulfilled and satisfying old age by carving out niches for themselves in their societies. These have always included not only the geniuses, the famous, and the particularly gifted in the special fields of the arts and sciences and in political life, but also many among the ranks of farmers, craftsmen, country squires, and the learned professions, whether rich and influential or unknown to the world at large.

Throughout this book we have been speaking of those old

people who come into this category. We have mentioned only briefly that there have obviously been others who for various reasons, ranging from extreme poverty and sickness to personal character deficiencies, did not manage to achieve the status of a revered elder, no matter what their social standing.

In the literature of many languages these unfortunate or maladjusted old people have frequently been used as metaphors to illustrate the vanities of the world and the fleetingness of life—so frequently, in fact, that an objective overall view could be blurred by all the examples one could find of destitute, miserly, foolish, vain, greedy, and cruel old people of many writers' invention. These literary creations that served as mirrors for all the misfortunes, vices, and vanities of man undoubtedly had their counterparts in the real world. One could perhaps compare them to the less well-adapted animals of other species that are weeded out in generation after generation of selection, while the well-adapted few carry forward the evolutionary future of their kind.

One of the most instructive questions we could ask ourselves would be wherein lies the differences between these two kinds of elders. What is it that makes one farmer a loved and respected paterfamilias while his neighbor is nothing but a grudgingly tolerated impediment to his heirs; or one highly placed social or political leader esteemed and followed while another of his own time and rank is ridiculed or feared?

Those who are exposed to the exemplary elder are, so to speak, on the receiving end of an impression that emanates from him. There is something in his personality that flows from him and makes an impact on those around him. What the particular qualities of his character are or what his status in life is usually immaterial. What is felt in his presence is that he has confidence in himself, his knowledge, his skill, his ability to sustain himself and others; that he retains an interest in his own and his friends' activities; and that he is able to impart his knowledge, skill, and interest to others so that they, too, partake of his enthusiasms and sense of life. Out of this quality to inspire confidence in his ability and to involve others in his interests comes the gift of leadership. This can be exercised within the confines of a family, in a community, or even on a national scale. The circumstances of education, opportunity, personal inclinations, and the degree of the quality he possesses will determine the extent to which his influence is felt. But in essence these are the qualities that enable a man or woman to make a positive impact on others and gain their esteem.

For every one of us there are names that immediately spring into our minds as exemplifying these qualities. Every country, every town and village, every family has its share of such individuals. There are personalities who are known nationally and internationally, like an Adenauer, a Baruch, or a Mrs. Roosevelt, as well as those known only to their professional colleagues. Among our own good friends is a psychiatrist who at seventy-six years of age is still practicing, still guiding students as a lecturer and teacher at a school of medicine, and still infecting everyone who comes into his orbit with his own enthusiasm for all kinds of knowledge, his lively wit, and his obvious joy in living. Another good friend of about the same age is a renowned dermatologist. He also is still practicing and lecturing. Moreover, since he faced a mandatory retirement situation at the institution with which he was connected, he has set up his own laboratory, where he continues to conduct his research on fungus diseases. He is a linguist of unusual range, still able to speak Chinese fluently as well as many European languages, and his charm and simplicity, belying his vast knowledge, still win him new friends wherever he goes. Then there are the skilled craftsmen (for the self-confidence based on manual skills imparts itself as well as qualities of the mind) who are well known, such as the famous eighteenth-century furniture makers, or known only in their circles, like our local carpenter. This man, in his seventies and in spite of having had his larynx removed and replaced by a tube, continues to work skillfully and conscientiously, so everyone in the neighborhood who obtains his services considers himself fortunate.

Obviously there is no completely simple answer to our question, for a character is molded by many forces over a lifetime, but there is one quality that seems to be common to all individuals who retain their status in old age. This is the quality that is at the heart of the evolutionary origins of the development of the elderly caste: the ability to impart knowledge of the most basic kind. The senior couple of a household retain the respect of its members as long as they are considered founts of wisdom, skill, and know-how, each in his or her sphere. This implies that to retain respect in old age a person must have acquired knowledge or skills over a lifetime and an ability to pass these on. A person who has not acquired skills or knowledge during his life will not be respected in old age. His advice will not be sought, and if given, it will not be followed. He may, if he is lucky, receive loving attention, doled out as if to a child. If he is not lucky, he may be considered an old fool or a nuisance.

To bring us back to current actuality, we have found among the older people in retirement colonies and other segregated groups many who possess this invaluable quality, but who have in those places no forum for its expression. Surely these men and women would be in a far better frame of mind had they remained in their own communities and found new activity there commensurate with their abilities. Even now, if they could be brought to realize that the root of their boredom lies in the purposelessness of their activities, they could be helped to improve their lot by redirecting their energies into socially useful channels. This, of course, applies also to those elders who have not joined retirement groups of any kind but who have nevertheless felt insulated from their societies by their retired status.

John and Martha Newman never got to make a home of the house they had bought against the time of their retirement. One thing after another caught up with them.

Some four years before his retirement John had joined with a group of friends to buy the property of an adult summer camp that was going out of operation. The property was in lovely, hilly, forested country in Connecticut, and it bordered three-quarters of the shoreline of a large lake. John and his friends had bought it as an investment with the idea of eventually reselling it to a housing developer. However, they had made their purchase shortly before a downswing in the economy, and this had made it impossible for them to sell it without taking a sizable loss. Then they had decided to hold on to the property and wait for better days. In the meantime the partners had gone there on weekends from time to time and made use of it. They had used the abandoned cabins for lodging, enjoyed the lake, and taken walks and picnicked in the unspoiled country surrounding it.

It didn't take long after the day of his retirement before John Newman began to feel bored and restless. Martha found that the job of winding up their town household took longer than she had expected, and John found the days very tedious. He had caught up on his reading, and the few occupations he found did not fill the time of this habitually busy man satisfactorily. He began to go up to the campsite more frequently, usually taking Martha with him.

On one occasion, while they were walking around the property, they fell into a discussion as to whether, since they had been unable to sell it, they could restore and develop it themselves. The idea had come to Martha in her concern about both his restlessness and the increasingly rapid deterioration of the neglected cabins. At first he pooh-poohed it.

What We Can Do About It

"What do we know about these things?" he asked. "We'd need plumbers, electricians, builders—and even if we did it all, what do we know about management?"

"Well, we have all the time in the world now," she answered. "Couldn't we take a few courses and learn how to do it? Between us, we should be able to tackle it."

He then sat down and made a preliminary plan. He spent the next few weeks consulting with people in the field, while Martha, freed from having to cater to a chafing husband around the house, found out about available courses.

With their whole scheme backed up by practical propositions, they then went to their partners, who, almost verbatim, spelled out the objections John himself had initially voiced. But they presented the facts and figures they had collected and eventually convinced them.

Now, after a year of working and studying, with courses in hotel management and the rudiments of building maintenance behind them, as well as much reading and consultation with local experts, they are well on the way to the conversion of their property into a year-round adult camp with facilities for both summer and winter sports. Of course they have had all the usual difficulties and hindrances that such an undertaking implies, but it is taking shape under their hands, and each day involves them totally in its immediate concerns. When we went up to visit them once, we were so impressed with all their activity that we asked them, "When are you going to retire from all this retirement?"

They no longer wonder about what they will be doing this time next year. As a matter of fact, they have given their "retirement home" to their married children as a vacation place for them and their very young families.

CHAPTER TWENTY-FIVE

Young till We Die

For him in vain the envious seasons roll
Who bears eternal summer in his soul.
—OLIVER WENDELL HOLMES

How the dream of eternal youth has haunted modern man! The yearning never to grow old, never to die, is woven into many myths, and the search for the fount of an everlasting springtime of life has occupied the energies of as many men, from Ponce de León to James Barrie to Dr. Serge Voronoff, as has the search for limitless wealth, from King Midas to the medieval alchemists to the modern billionaires. Always to be young and always to have limitless means at his disposal are man's dreams of glory.

Is this passionate desire to avoid old age nothing but a dread of death? We think not, because a fear of death would indicate a love of life, and if we loved life so well, we would live it fully in all its stages, which most of us do not do. We fritter it away piecemeal and then wake up one day to find that much of it has gone—passed us by; we have not lived it and would like to have it back to try again.

In most minds youth is associated with vigor, purpose, and living life to the full, but our middle years and our old age, too, can have their own kinds of vigor and purpose and their own deep involvements and satisfactions. These we shall never achieve if we spend those years, the greater part of our life, seeking to recapture and hold on to our evanescent youth. The very search for it forces it to elude us. No young person seeks youth. Pale imitations of the appearance and occupations of youth serve only to emphasize that it has passed, and so the time we spend and the means we use to recapture it defeat the hoped-for end.

Each phase of life has a place in our existence. Youth is a time of preparation. Were some genie miraculously to arrest our development at that stage, we would spend all eternity preparing for life and never living it—never fulfilling our dreams, never achieving our fullest powers. We would end by cursing our fate as profoundly as Midas did his and by searching endlessly for a means to maturity, age, and surcease.

And as each phase of life has a place in our individual existences, so it has one in the existences of groups. All groups, whether of deer or walruses or man, need the perpetual challenges of generation after generation of youth. Through youth's challenges the whole society is invigorated and kept on its toes. Its leaders are goaded to their peaks of performance and are toppled from their eminences if they fail. The status quo is questioned, concessions are enforced; new paths are explored, and a foot tentatively set upon them sometimes journeys the whole way into new directions. In man's societies as well as in those of other animals, adaptations to change are made in this way.

Young people serve their societies in their drive for innovation. In response to the fillip of their spurs, staleness of thought and monotony of procedure are disturbed and not given easy sway. The presence of youth prevents conservatism from becoming ridigity and societies from becoming fossilized because of failure to adapt to the new.

But age plays an equally important part in the viability of groups. While the prodding of youth's radicalism stirs their circulation and keeps them alert, this radicalism must find a check, or our societies would exist in a state of perpetual turmoil—if it were possible for them to continue to exist at all. The presence of an effective group of elders is an absolute essential to the good order of human societies. It is of as equally great importance for the old to perform their separate and distinct obligation to steady and to conserve as it is for the young to challenge and disturb, and for the middle group to hold the balance while they carry on their business of generating and sustaining new life.

It is not without significance that the present turbulence of Western societies coincides with a sharp decline in the influence of the old and the undue influence of youth, accompanied by an excessive concern on all sides with the retention of youthful characteristics for as long as possible. Viewed impartially, even biologically, the one is an expression of the other. The young are fulfilling their function. It is the old who have abdicated from theirs.

In writing this book our aims have been to make a contribution to finding an explanation for the decline of the position of the elders in our societies, to show the consequences of this decline to their personal well-being, and to make suggestions for action that would ease or remedy their lot. But we must not overlook the fact that the old also have a duty, to themselves and to their societies. They must not permit the young to relegate them to the category of interesting, even charming, fossils. They must take up the challenges, not only for their own sakes, but also for the sake of their entire societies, including the young. Without the balance of the experienced life to curb the excesses of the inexperienced, how is the middle group to survive at all in any kind of ambience conducive to renewing life and sustaining it?

In carrying out their own function the old will find many rewards. They will feel invigorated and therefore far "younger" in spirit than they could possibly be by vain attempts to play the role that is not theirs. It is not in human nature to feel esteem for those who sail under false colors. The person who denies himself must not be surprised if others deny him. Older people will find that by gracefully relinquishing youth as it passes and then embracing the duties of a new role as it evolves, they will regain the esteem that had been withheld from them, and the vigor of their youth will be refreshed and renewed in striving for the new objectives of maturity.

Nor will strength of spirit be their only reward. They will be able to experience their own careers whole. They will enjoy the fruits of their own achievement. They will feel not that they have lived and worked merely to establish and pass on a place for their heirs, but that they can win their own laurels in their own lifetimes and savor the honor of their own efforts. To live to an old age while continuing to be involved in life, and to the accompaniment of the respect of one's fellows, is to taste a sip of one's own immortality.

Senescent old age is not an inevitable pattern in nature. On the lower levels of life animals live their brief spans and die in the full powers of their prime. Our medical knowledge and skills are helping us toward the same goal: a healthy and full life until the last moment of it. But even if we should never fully attain that goal and discover that some disabilities are the lot of man, we still have the means always to be young, if not forever, at least for as long as life lasts. The means reside in the vast resources of a vigorous spirit. Old age, as it has been pictured, is not a state of being; it is a state of mind. If youth means strength, it is within the power of all of us, by our mental attitudes, to remain young until we die. In truth, if we do not wish to be pushed aside from the lives of our communities when our own time comes, we have to find ways to live our lives vigorously and fully until the very end.

Bibliography

Boas, Franz, *General Anthropology*. New York, D. C. Heath, 1938.

Burgess, E. W., ed., *Aging in Western Societies*. University of Chicago Press, 1960.

Business Week, "The Power of the Aging in the Market Place." Special report, November 20, 1971.

Carter, Betty W., "Salmon." *Smithsonian*, Vol. 2, No. 7 (October, 1971).

Fabre, J. H., *Social Life in the Insect World*. London, Pelican Books, 1937.

Hanley, Robert, "Aged Volunteers at Willowbrook." New York *Times*, February 12, 1972.

Howard, John, "The Theory of Buyer Behavior," as quoted in *Business Week* (November 20,1971).

Kluckhohn, Clyde, and Murray, Henry A., *Personality in Nature, Society & Culture*. New York, Knopf, 1953.

Krombein, Karl and Dorothy, "Cicadas." *Smithsonian*, Vol. 2, No. 2 (May, 1971).

Jacobs, G., "Neuronal Numeration & Function." *JAMA* (*Journal of the American Medical Association*), Vol. 213, No. 7 (August 17, 1970).

James, Marlise, "A Commune for Old Folks." *Life*, May 12, 1972.

Jones, F. L., "Five Letters To Harvey." *Medical Opinion* (March, 1972).

Lawler, Nan, "Black Widow." *Smithsonian*, Vol. 2, No. 5 (August, 1971).

Lévy-Bruhl, Lucien, *The "Soul" of the Primitive*. London, Allen & Unwin, 1928.

MENGIS, C. L., "Medical Machines." *Medical Opinion*, Vol. 8, No. 1 (January, 1972).

MOORE, W. E., "The Aged in Industrial Societies," in *Industrial Relations & the Social Order.* New York, Macmillan, 1951.

MORETON, ANN, "Spiders." *Smithsonian*, Vol. 2, No. 5 (August, 1971).

ROSENZWEIG, M. R., BENNETT, E. L., and DIAMOND, MARIAN, "Brain Changes in Response to Experience." *Scientific American*, Vol. 226, No. 2 (February, 1972).

SALTZ, R., "Foster Grandparents & Institutionalized Young Children." Mimeo., Merrill Palmer Institute, Detroit.

SCHILLMANN, F., *Venedig*, 1933, as quoted by A. L. Vischer (see below).

SMITH, ELIZABETH S., *The Dynamics of Aging.* New York, W. W. Norton, 1956.

STREIB, GORDON F., and SCHNEIDER, CLEMENT J., S.J., *Retirement in American Society.* Ithaca, New York, Cornell University Press, 1971.

THOMAS, WILLIAM I., *Source Book for Social Origins.* University of Chicago Press, 1909.

U.S. Congress, Senate Special Committee on Aging report, "Developments in Aging," 1969. Washington, U.S. Government Printing Office, 1970.

VISCHER, A. L., *Old Age.* London, Allen & Unwin, 1947.

WYNNE-EDWARDS, V. C., *Animal Dispersion in Relation to Social Behaviour.* Edinburgh, Oliver & Boyd, 1962.

Several interviews quoted in the text were derived from the New York *Times.*

DATE DUE

APR 27 '78			
DEC 3 1976			